WOMEN'S STUDIES
AND BUSINESS ETHICS

THE
RUFFIN SERIES IN BUSINESS ETHICS
R. Edward Freeman, *Editor*

Women's Studies and Business Ethics

Toward a New Conversation

edited by

Andrea Larson and

R. Edward Freeman

New York   *Oxford*

OXFORD UNIVERSITY PRESS 1997

LIBRARY
UNIVERSITY OF ST. FRANCIS
JOLIET, ILLINOIS

Oxford University Press

Oxford   New York

Athens   Auckland   Bangkok   Bogota   Bombay   Buenos Aires
Calcutta   Cape Town   Dar es Salaam   Delhi   Florence   Hong Kong
Istanbul   Karachi   Kuala Lumpur   Madras   Madrid   Melbourne
Mexico City   Nairobi   Paris   Singapore   Taipei   Tokyo   Toronto   Warsaw

and associated companies in
Berlin   Ibadan

Copyright © 1997 by Oxford University Press, Inc.

Published by Oxford University Press, Inc.
198 Madison Avenue, New York, New York 10016

Oxford is a registered trademark of Oxford University Press

All rights reserved. No part of this publication may be reproduced,
stored in a retrieval system, or transmitted, in any form or by any means,
electronic, mechanical, photocopying, recording, or otherwise,
without the prior permission of Oxford University Press.

Library of Congress Cataloging–in–Publication Data
Women's studies and business ethics : toward a new conversation /
edited by Andrea Larson and R. Edward Freeman.
p.   cm.—(Ruffin series in business ethics)
Includes bibliographical references and index.
ISBN 0–19–510758–6;   ISBN 0–19–510759–4 (pbk.)
1. Business ethics. 2. Feminist theory. I. Larson, Andrea.
II. Freeman, R. Edward. 1951– . III. Series.
HF5387.W66   1997
174'.4'082—dc21   96–45166

1 3 5 7 9 8 6 4 2

Printed in the United States of America
on acid-free paper

BE
174.4
L334

$40.00

Baker & Taylor

9-20-99

To
Eleanor G. May
and
Patricia H. Werhane
for their leadership

Foreword

The essays in this volume join the field of business ethics to a broader conversation about the roles of women and men in our society. It is especially important for those who want to see business as a full participant in the moral realm to subject business and business ethics to the same kind of critical analysis that has been leveled at other institutions in society.

The conference at which the first four papers in this book were presented had the feeling of an important event. Scholars from women's studies who had had little contact with business or business ethicists, together with business ethicists and organization theorists, created some common ground and, more important, began a conversation that is still quite alive.

Gender plays a pervasive role in society. It cuts so deeply that we still do not understand all of its implications, nor perhaps can we. The remarkable achievements of scholars in women's studies can no longer be ignored by those who wish to redescribe business in more human terms. No set of essays could be more suitable for this series.

The purpose of the Ruffin Series in Business Ethics is to publish the best thinking about the role of ethics in business. In a world in which there are daily reports of questionable business practices, from financial scandals to environmental disasters, we need to step back from the fray and understand the large issues of how business and ethics are and ought to be connected. The books in this series are aimed at three audiences: management scholars, ethicists, and business executives. There is a growing consensus among these groups that business and ethics must be integrated as a vital part of the teaching and practice of management.

The thinkers whose work is in this volume have greatly advanced the progress of business ethics. By engaging in this multidisciplinary conversation they have made each of the disciplines more interesting, and they have challenged each of us to think more deeply about the role of gender in society.

Charlottesville, Virginia   R. Edward Freeman

Acknowledgments

Over the past several years in which the essays in this book have been completed a number of people have contributed to this volume. First and foremost, Karen Musselman has been responsible for all that the Olsson Center does, especially producing the Ruffin Lectures and the resulting volumes. Recently Kristi Severance has done far more work than anyone could ask in getting the book through a complicated production process. Herb Addison and all of the unnamed staff at Oxford University Press have shown patience and always offered their excellent help and advice. Finally, this volume, indeed the entire series, would not be possible without the vision shown by John Rosenblum, former dean of The Darden School. Rosenblum engaged in the conversation around gender with the scholars who came to Darden and has spent a great deal of his professional life trying to make a difference. As always, Sture Olsson and the Olsson family's support of the Olsson Center for Applied Ethics, and the support of the Ruffin Foundation in particular, have been important for our work. Associate Deans Robert Harris and Jim Freeland have encouraged us and sped us along. Thanks to everyone.

Contents

III NEW DIRECTIONS FOR BUSINESS ETHICS

Contributors

George G. Brenkert is professor of philosophy and department head at the University of Tennessee, Knoxville. He specializes in the areas of business ethics, social and political philosophy, and ethics. He is the author of *Political Freedom*.

Marta B. Calás is associate professor of organization studies at the School of Management, University of Massachusetts at Amherst. She teaches courses in management in other cultures and international management and is the author of *Critical Perspectives on Organization and Management Theory* (with L. Smircich).

Robbin Derry is a senior fellow in the legal studies department at the Wharton School, University of Pennsylvania. Her research focuses on issues in which individual and organizational values collide, including sexual harassment in the workplace and the role of feminist ethical theory in organizational theory. She has taught ethics and professional responsibilities since 1985.

Thomas J. Donaldson is the Mark O. Winkelman Professor of Business Ethics at the Wharton School, University of Pennsylvania. He is the editor of *Ethical Issues in Business: A Philosophical Approach* (with P. Werhane).

Dawn R. Elm is associate professor in the department of management at the University of St. Thomas, Division of Business. She is the author of *Influences on the Moral Reasoning of Managers*.

Kathy E. Ferguson is professor of political science and women's studies and chair of the political science department at the University of Hawaii at Manoa. Her works include *The Feminist Case Against Bureaucracy* and *The Man Question: Visions of Subjectivity in Feminist Theory*.

Edwin M. Hartman is professor in the faculty of management and the department of philosophy at Rutgers University. He is author of *Substance, Body, and Soul: Aristotelian Investigations, Conceptual Foundations of Organizational Theory*, and *Organizational Ethics and the Good Life*.

Kathleen Knopoff is a Ph.D. candidate at the Graduate School of Business, Stanford University. Her research interests include managerial bias and its effect on employee empowerment and the effects of well-presented but misleading data.

Joanne Martin is Fred H. Merrill Professor of Organizational Behavior at the Graduate School of Business and, by courtesy, in the department of sociology, Stanford University. Her current research interests include organizational culture, with emphasis on subcultural identities and ambiguities, as well as diversity in organizations, particularly subtle barriers to acceptance and advancement. Her most recent books are *Reframing Organizational Culture* (with P. Frost, L. Moore, M. Louis, and C. Lundberg) and *Cultures in Organizations*.

Daniel R. Ortiz is professor of law and Harrison Foundation Research Professor at the University of Virginia. Before teaching, Professor Ortiz worked as a judicial clerk to Judge Stephen Breyer on the U.S. Court of Appeals in Boston and to Justice Lewis F. Powell, Jr., on the U.S. Supreme Court.

Linda Smircich is professor of organization studies at the School of Management, University of Massachusetts at Amherst. Her research interests include exploring connections among culture, feminism, postmodernism, and organization and management theory. With Reba Keele and Marta Calás she received a grant from the National Science Foundation for the project, "Questioning the Ethics and Values of Organizational Science from Feminist Perspectives." She is the author of *Critical Perspectives on Organization and Management Theory* (with M. Calás).

Robert C. Solomon is Quincy Lee Centennial Professor of Philosophy at the University of Texas at Austin. He is the author of *Above the Bottom Line, Ethics and Excellence,* and *New World of Business.* He is also author of *The Passions, In the Spirit of Hegel, About Love,* and *A Passion for Justice.*

Jesse Taylor is associate professor of philosophy at Appalachian State University. His research interests include the metaphysics of racism and developing new arguments for affirmative action. He is the author of "Toward a Philosophy of Recovery: A Prolegomenon to Any Future African-American Ethic," published in the *American Philosophical Association Newsletter,* Fall 1992.

WOMEN'S STUDIES
AND BUSINESS ETHICS

Introduction

Andrea Larson and R. Edward Freeman

Business ethics is at a crossroads. As earlier volumes in this series have demonstrated, a role for ethics in business is now widely accepted. It is no longer necessary for academics or managers to explain or justify linkages between the world of business and the realm of ethical reasoning.

On the business front, a group of entrepreneurs led by Ben Cohen of Ben and Jerry's and Anita Roddick of the Body Shop are demonstrating that business and ethics go together in the real world. They are engaged in commercial projects that are at once financially successful and socially beneficial. These entrepreneurs have been visible figures in the creation of two new national associations, the Social Venture Network (SVN) and Business for Social Responsibility (BSR). SVN was formed in 1987 and by early 1994 reported close to 500 members. The organization is comprised of entrepreneurs and investors committed to business practices that integrate ethical, social, and environmental principles. Founded in 1992, BSR is a national organization of companies formed as an alternative to the Chamber of Commerce. In January 1994, BSR membership stood at more than 700 affiliates, with fifteen new corporate members joining every month. Closely aligned with these organizations is the newly formed Students for Responsible Business, a national organization of MBA students, whose agenda includes reform of business school curricula. Concrete and practical efforts by these groups yield an emerging model of business that integrates an ethic of social and environmental responsibility with successful business economics.

On the academic front, most major business schools offer a curriculum of ethics in business, and a few have made major commitments to lead the production of scholarly and pedagogical materials for wide distribution to others. There are now no shortages of outlets for new ideas in business ethics. From the managerially oriented *Harvard Business Review* to this Ruffin Series published by Oxford University Press, there are many opportunities to publish ideas about the connection between business and ethics.

And yet, the very legitimacy that the discourse of business ethics has obtained is under an ominous cloud. As this discourse becomes more refined and more technical, it threatens to lose its critical edge—the very lifeblood of its success. Business ethicists have insisted for some time that the dominant mode of thinking about business needs to be opened up and enlarged. "Stockholders" must be replaced with "stakeholders," "profits" with "multiple objectives," "managerial control" with "social contracts," "simple economizers" with "complex psychological beings," and so on.

The problem now is how to ensure that there is some degree of enlargement and openness in the discourse of business ethics. With these issues in mind we convened an unusual group of scholars at the Darden School for the third Ruffin Lectures. We invited scholars who had not participated in the discourse of business ethics—their primary work having been in what we broadly call women's studies—and leading scholars in business ethics. The resulting conversation was rich and lively and the topics hotly debated.

During the years since the conference, a number of these scholars developed the themes of these conversations into the essays that comprise this volume. These essays call for a thoroughgoing revision and reinvention of the ways we think about both business and ethics.

We believe that the expansion of women's studies research to the understanding of business institutions and the critical discourse of business ethics offers a significant new intellectual opportunity. This growing body of writing, diverse in its approaches and content, opens our eyes to new understandings about the role of business in society, the nature of management, and direction for change.

The four main chapters in this volume are stimulating in their challenges to the field of business ethics and in their criticism of the theories, ideologies, and epistemology of management theory underlying corporate structure and activity. The value of these central chapters lies in their critique of business ethics, and by extension, business organizations and management.

Four themes emerge. The first emphasizes the socially constructed nature of business. Corporations are presented as socially constructed organizations that assume, in their practice and ideology, that men are the standard of measurement. The failure to acknowledge this reality blinds management to the deeper implications of business decisions and possibilities for change. Pointing to the cognitive and gendered biases that are integral parts of the social construction of business organizations, these chapters question the foundation of knowledge that girds business institutions. They demand nothing less than a reconstruction of our corporate institutions under a very different set of epistemological considerations.

A second theme is the power of feminist critiques to bring gender into sharp focus as a central organizing principle of economic life. Gender, along with skin color and social class, is a primary fault line within societies. Yet, for most people, gender—as a division within society with significant implications for action and knowledge—remains invisible. The topic is a difficult one to discuss because it is embedded in both language and ideology.

A third central theme is the existence of a "frame." Each of the four essays describes it variously as theory, ideology, or paradigm and posits that unexamined frames become habitual and assumed, so that the dominant views are ultimately reified and naturalized (assumed to be present in nature). This relatively invisible and implicit process results in conclusions presented as reality or truth, somehow natural or god given, and therefore not to be challenged and beyond human ability to change. Frames dominate and order our thinking so powerfully and comprehensively that alternative ways of thinking are silenced. The accepted frame is the "center." In order to deconstruct the center to understand its assumptions and inherent values, we must first identify the center. Yet, understanding the center's hold over thoughts and actions requires seeing the periphery, seeing what and who are left out of the center. An important contribution of this volume is to make some of the underlying intellectual and institutional structures of Western business explicit (the center) by examining them from the perspective of the periphery—that is, from the standpoint of women. The authors suggest that unless we can take this perspective we begin to believe that the patterns, everyday routines, and regularities of the business world are "natural," simply "the way things are." Although socially constructed, these patterns are projected outside ourselves as objective realities that govern us, regardless of their fit and usefulness.

The fourth theme is the unorthodox and, for some people, unsettling, view of business ethics. As a field, business ethics is portrayed as feminized in its subordinate position relative to the more central and dominant areas of business management (e.g., finance and accounting). Yet, at the same time business ethics is seen as in collusion with management ideology, the proponents of the field create business ethics arguments that will find acceptance within traditional business school environments.

The feminist criticisms question the role of business ethics within business schools. They argue for business ethics to be more provocative and challenging. To free students to use their creative abilities, business ethics should be encouraging students to understand the socially constructed fragility of knowledge. This is not to say there is no order, nor that theory is useless, nor that the scientific method is a pointless exercise in fantasy. But instead, the criticisms caution us that we can become too enamored of our explanations of the world and of how people behave in economic contexts. Rather, the authors argue that business ethics courses should be on the forefront of encouraging openness to new knowledge, particularly knowledge that comes from those who have not previously participated in knowledge creation.

With this view we are in wholehearted agreement. Indeed, the main point of the second volume of the Ruffin Lectures published in this series was that the dual purpose of professional schools—socialization of students into the profession and development of students' critical abilities to improve the practice of the profession—was in serious danger without an infusion of fresh ideas and methods from the humanities. This volume can thus be read as having a history, one whose goal is to transform the discourse of professional schools of management to fulfill their mission of developing students' abilities to reinvent themselves and their organizations.

The four central chapters and the discussions by the respondents are relevant not only to business ethicists and feminist scholars interested in business management. They provide at times incisive insights into why our business institutions show evidence of maladaptation to the forces within and around them. Business leaders and management school faculty would do well to heed these criticisms. The voices of feminist scholars, while diverse and at times in conflict with one another, offer challenging ideas. As this body of knowledge evolves, it will be increasingly discussed in wider forums and will gain currency as its power and relevance are recognized.

It is important to note that there is no univalent point of view called women's studies or feminist studies. Feminisms are many and varied, and the authors of the four main chapters represent often conflicting and different points of view, even though they are in some agreement about our central themes. Robbin Derry, Joanne Martin, Kathy Knopoff, Marta Calás, Linda Smircich, and Kathy Ferguson illuminate for us, each in distinctive ways, the gendered world that constrains our understanding of business.

Robbin Derry's chapter is a critique at the level of business practices, which argues for acceptance and appreciation of the differences between men and women in corporate contexts. Building on the tradition in women's studies that has come to be called feminist standpoint theory, Derry suggests that it is important for all members of an organization to understand and value the differences between men and women. Working in the tradition of Jean Baker Miller and Carol Gilligan, Derry asks managers to learn to hear a variety of voices in the corporation.

Joanne Martin and Kathy Knopoff examine the gendered theory of Max Weber, whose work on bureaucracies remains an intellectual cornerstone of organization theory taught at every business school across the globe. Working in the postmodern tradition, where the accepted readings of texts is to be questioned, their approach is at the level of ideology and theory. They ask us to read Weber in a very different way. Even though Weber does not claim to be telling us anything about gender and business, Martin and Knopoff's analysis reveals a hidden meaning that shows how bureaucracy is not gender neutral. Thus, our naive assumption that organizations are merit based is open to question.

Marta Calás and Linda Smircich explore the epistemological roots of business ethics as a discipline and its uneasy collusion with traditional management beliefs and methods of knowledge production. Again, working in the postmodern tradition, Calás and Smircich reverse figure and ground. Rather than ask, "Isn't ethics necessary to make business better?" they suggest the question, "Isn't business ethics necessary to prop up our traditional conceptions of organizations?" Reminiscent of the work of sociologist Erving Goffman, business ethics has the effect of "cooling out the mark," where the mark consists of affected stakeholders or those shut out of the capitalist process.

Kathy E. Ferguson's powerful statement on the effects of the collusion of the powerful on the powerless again calls into question our traditional conceptions of organization life. She argues for a deconstruction of gender, a de-gendering of our worldviews in order to assess their usefulness and dangers. Ferguson's work posits the view of business ethics as a tinkering around the edges of a capitalist system whose underlying premises remain implicit, invisible, and therefore unquestioned. She calls for a new framing of the issues so that different questions about business and the economic system can be raised and addressed.

The responses to these essays fall into two categories. The first group consists of those that question the analysis of the four main chapters and that suggest alternative approaches. George G. Brenkert argues that the radical feminism offered by some of the authors is not unique from a moral point of view. Indeed, he suggests that a careful and historical rereading of Kant will produce the same moral result of a revision of capitalism as that propounded by, for instance, Ferguson. Further, he suggests that merely "letting difference be" does not go far enough to combat evil. Thomas J. Donaldson agrees with Brenkert that "letting difference be" is not enough from a moral point of view and that the postmodernist goal that he sees in Ferguson's analysis cannot do "moral work" from nowhere. He suggests that we get the moral assumptions out in the open for debate and clarification. Jesse Taylor beats the Kantian drum one more time, suggesting along with Brenkert and Donaldson that a proper understanding of Kant is all that is necessary. Finally, Edwin Hartman finds the philosophical view that underlies Martin and Knopoff's analysis of Weber unnecessarily outmoded. He claims that something like the liberal pragmatism of Richard Rorty provides a firmer foundation for deconstruction.

The second set of responses point to a more constructive dialogue between scholars working in business ethics and those involved in women's studies. Daniel R. Ortiz claims that the chapters based on deconstruction are not radical enough. He suggests that scholars need to locate the analysis of business and business ethics in the linkage between corporations and sexuality—thus the title "Phallocorporatism," and he makes a number of recommendations for further work along these lines. Dawn R. Elm tries to sidestep the whole issue of whether or not Kant can be "properly" read to be a feminist and suggests that a view of business ethics in which "different" does not mean "unequal" would be interesting to develop. She believes that something along Derry's implicit understanding of difference is worth further exploration. Finally, Robert C. Solomon argues that a concern with care and compassion, his reading of one kind of feminism, is not necessarily the concern of just feminists. He locates care and compassion in David Hume and Adam Smith, suggesting that a rereading of these basic texts around the history of capitalism may well lead to some of the revisions sought by a number of the essays in this book. Thus, Ortiz, Elm, and Solomon point to further work in each of the feminist traditions represented here. In so doing, they seek to weave a new tapestry of business ethics, with threads of difference, gender, compassion, care, and a thoroughgoing critique of business practice.

What we have collected here is a beginning record of a conversation that may well have a lasting impact on the practice and profession of management. As one of the authors, Edwin Hartman, says: "[These essays] in their necessary brevity can only hint at the subtle and complex issues that lie under the surface, at the powerful lessons feminists can teach all of us, and at the enlightening conversation only begun."

The essays challenge conventional thinking, and in so doing they teach us how to learn in new and vitally important ways. They represent a needed warning to avoid self-deceptions about received wisdom and a reminder of the contextual contingency of knowledge. The information they provide is critical to better assess how well suited theories, models, and frameworks of management and business ethics are to the natural and social world around us. In combination with the responses, the perspectives of the participants invite us to remain open to new ideas and to consider alternative constructions of knowledge about business, business ethics, and capitalism.

I

Feminist Theory and Business Ethics

1

Feminism: How Does It Play in the Corporate Theater?

Robbin Derry

This chapter was conceived as an interview study of women in corporate positions. I had decided to research the question of how women and their values are fitting into the corporate world. I thought I would just report what I found. I did not want to articulate new theoretical perspectives, especially in front of my philosophy colleagues. But as I found women's voices emerging in their corporate lives and reflected on the feminist movement that was arguing for change and not just acceptance, I realized that I wanted to express a perspective about business ethics that I have not heard articulated. That perspective is for me what unites feminism and business ethics.

In a world in which business ethics has something useful to say about feminism, feminism and business ethics come together around the concepts of voice and listening. The metaphor of voice represents women expressing themselves (Belenky et al., 1986). The history of the women's movement over the past 200 years can be seen as women's struggle to make their voices heard. Although the movement has focused primarily on the achievement of specific rights, women are now realizing that the expression of their unique voices is the overriding goal. In corporations in which women have been coached to adapt and blend in, the feminist movement is finally asking that women's voices be listened to.

Listening is what ethics should be about, but the concept is not addressed or included in traditional approaches to ethical theory. As women are learning to speak—or "unlearning not to speak," as Marge Piercy (1973) put it—ethicists have not yet figured out that listening is an important part of ethical decision making. Only when we are quiet enough to hear others are we able to comprehend the perspectives of those we must consider. Listening is significantly different from project-

11

ing our own view of how others feel. Listening is *not* doing unto others as we would have them do unto us; it is listening to what others would have us do unto them. It is the voices of others that we must recognize as unique and worth hearing.

Listening face-to-face to the least advantaged member of society is a great deal more effective than trying to imagine oneself as the least advantaged member, particularly while one is shrouded under a veil.

Initially, I will share some experiences that led to my interest in business ethics and in how women and men adapt themselves to the values and norms of organizations. The history of the women's movement offers a view of women's values and voices that have been outside the mainstream values of society. Feminism is considered in this context as representing the ways in which women have expressed their own values and strengths within our male-dominated society and organizations. The ten women I interviewed for this essay offer differing perspectives on what feminism means to them in their own lives and how they express that part of themselves in the work environment. Finally, I will suggest why business ethics as it is currently done does not offer useful insights or solutions to the problems of sexism.

VALUES AND ORGANIZATIONAL FIT

My interest in business ethics is more precisely an interest in how people express their values within organizations. What happens to people when they realize that their values do not fit the organization's norms and expectations? We cannot know all the unwritten expectations when we join an organization. As we become more familiar with the way an organization works, we become aware of fit and whether or not we fit. Perhaps we fit for a period of time, but as we grow and the organization evolves there is gradually less overlap of values than there once was. What happens if we do not fit? People do not hold jobs simply for reasons of value consistency. They hold jobs and hold onto jobs for economic, psychological, emotional, and many other reasons. And since most people do not let go of jobs simply for reasons of misfit, what do they do with their values in an organization that does not share their values?

These questions shaped my graduate study several years after they began to influence my personal life. I was raised in a church that has strong and all-encompassing teachings on the proper way to live life. Throughout high school, college, and well beyond I was actively committed to this church. I did not experience the difficult times others felt during adolescence or the psychological and intellectual questioning during college years. For me, there were ready-made answers to guide me through the guiles of religion courses as well as the dangers of fraternity parties.

Only in my mid-twenties did I open myself up to critical examination of that given worldview. I suddenly had all kinds of questions that didn't match the answers I had carried around for so many years. The process was fundamentally disturbing, but one I knew I had to continue once I was embarked. I could no longer ignore questions about sexuality, medicine, and psychology, and there were urgent issues in my family history that I needed to examine.

I did not find room within my church to ask these kinds of questions. It quickly became apparent that the answers were not to be found among people who were so certain of their authority that they couldn't tolerate my questions. They preferred to reframe my questions and thereby pull me back into their descriptions of reality.

As difficult as it was, the process of challenging old beliefs had its rewards. I noticed that the less I attended my church, the more I began to hear other people. I understood other people's perspectives when I stopped trying to translate them into my vision and just listened. The term "friends" came to mean people who were asking interesting questions about life, not those who had firm answers. I was growing at a rate and in directions I had never imagined. The questioning process became an imperative.

I could not go back to the church. My new values outweighed the importance of staying within an organization that had powerfully shaped the first twenty-five years of my life. For several years I struggled in a very personal way with the question of what a person does when her values and self-definition are not acceptable within the limits of a particular organization. As I learned from this experience, usually it is not the organization that gives way but the individual who either conforms or leaves the organization. Either she forgoes the freedom to express herself or she gives up the significant benefits and associations of that group.

Professionally, I was gaining experience in several other organizations, notably during my brief but brilliant career as a chef. These jobs taught me that the values of the people in decision-making positions determine the physical and psychological environment of the workplace. For example, in one New York City restaurant, the management decision to routinely bribe health-code officials resulted in unsanitary conditions as well as in an organization-wide understanding that business is conducted by deceit. Accordingly, it was assumed that false advertising, mislabeling of ingredients, and employee abuse were consistent with management's values. Five years in the restaurant business were all I could manage.

These experiences combined with the questioning in my religious life to formulate the issues I have since pursued. Can organizations be responsive to individual values and their questioning of the operant norms? In the face of fundamental value conflicts, what can one do besides quit? What action can people inside an organization take when the culture of the organization clearly represses a large segment of its members? How do people survive in jobs in which they are not able to express their deeply felt values or in which they are expected to act contrary to their values?

Feminism is, in part, a set of values that focus on changing the patterns of sexism in society. For many individuals who subscribe to these values, the questions of fit within existing institutions are essential ones. How does one both fit in and call for change? Is it possible to express views critical of the organization? In my questioning of my church these questions ultimately led to issues of faith and belief. In business organizations the issues have to do with job security and power. I was free to make my own choice about staying or leaving the organized church. In the workplace the decision about staying with the job does not rest entirely with the individual, but may be made at any point by one higher up in the bureaucracy who is uncomfortable with questioning.

Women in male-dominated fields, including most professional-level corporate jobs, are rewarded for their ability to assimilate and adopt the male norms (Freeman, 1990; Powell, 1990). Unique skills that draw on women's experiences or strengths are for the most part neither recognized nor welcomed (Joyce, 1990; Gilligan, 1982). In this type of environment how is it possible for women to be themselves?

THE FEMINIST VOICE

We are just now finding our way out of a phase of integrating women into a male work world during which the ultimate goal for women was to be like men. Look like men, talk like them, learn their games, and you will succeed in the male world. Unfortunately, following those rules brought women many unhappy consequences as well: emotional distance, isolation, loss of connection to other women, devaluation of family responsibilities, and the hollowness of pretending to be someone else for a dream of success. Women did not change the workplace by entering it in this way—they merely sacrificed themselves to it. Adrienne Rich (1986) described the situation this way:

> The working mother with briefcase was, herself, a cosmetic touch on a society deeply resistant to fundamental changes. The "public" and "private" spheres were still in disjunction. She had not found herself entering an evolving new society, a society in transformation. She had only been integrated into the same structures which had made liberation movements necessary.

As women and men have begun to recognize the repercussions of women adopting roles that once belonged to men, and playing them as men do, the need for changing the roles and the expectations has become more obvious. For the slow minded, the solution is still to keep women out of "men's jobs." Those who understand the times see that women will gradually reshape the jobs themselves.

In the relatively rare situations in which women head large organizations, they are able to establish new structures and patterns of communication that represent their values. These include organizational webs rather than hierarchies and meetings in which careful listening and information sharing are expected (Helgesen, 1990). The emphasis is on reciprocal communication.

These women see their leadership as effective because they are true to themselves in the process of managing. For some women this means integrating personal and professional responsibilities throughout the day—definitely not an approach taken by executive male leaders (Mintzberg, 1973). Francis Hesselbein, National Executive Director of the Girl Scouts, described her approach to an extremely full schedule: "It's not hard work that wears you out, but the repression of your true personality, and I've found a way of working that does not demand that" (Mintzberg, 1973:229).

The idea that women should be free to structure their day and work environment around their own strengths is not widely accepted (Freeman, 1990; Hochschild, 1989). Several women in my interview study indicated they were accepted most readily on projects when they modeled their behavior and communication on those of male colleagues. However, the same women also recognized that they were generally more comfortable with themselves if they acted in ways consistent with their own values of sharing information, building trust with clients, and drawing co-workers into collaborative dialogue. By these means they were able to express who they are in environments in which such expression is not explicitly recognized or valued.

Men are often unaware of women's feelings that women do not fit into the norms or that their values are not recognized in the organization's patterns. While women may say that they are forced into a rigid mold, men may see nothing out of the ordinary: "The failure to see the different reality of women's lives and to hear the differences in their voices stems in part from the assumption that there is a single mode of social experience and interpretation" (Gilligan, 1982:173).

The inability to hear or recognize this different reality may be ascribed to ineptitude and the wearing of blinders. It may also be attributable to the role of power within social structures, which carefully limits what women can do: "Power refuses to look at any truth which has so far evaded it. . . . Women have been unable either to establish power or invade it" (Heilbrun, 1979).

Women's use of the metaphor of voice to describe their intellectual and moral development was richly presented by Belenky et al. (1986). These researchers found that women frequently talked about "being heard," "speaking out," "being silenced," and "finding no words" and used many other phrases associated with voice and silence to portray their own sense of worth and adequacy, as well as feelings of isolation and connection: "We found that . . . the development of a sense of voice, mind, and self were intricately intertwined" (Belenky et al., 1986:18).

Clearly, women today are becoming conscious of expressing themselves with a confidence that eluded many women in the past. Perhaps the most recent wave of the women's movement is responsible for this development; or perhaps the ongoing changes in the demographics of the workplace have forced a recognition that there are variations in the entrenched patterns.

THE FEMINIST VOICE IN HISTORY

The importance of the woman's voice has been an undercurrent theme in the women's movement for at least 200 years. In March 1776, Abigail Adams wrote her husband, John, from Braintree, Massachusetts, about her concerns that women be taken into account in the formulation of the Declaration of Independence:

> I long to hear that you have declared an independency—and by the way in the new Code of Laws which I suppose it will be necessary for you to make I desire you would Remember the Ladies, and be more generous and favourable to them than your ancestors. Do not put such unlimited power into the hands of the Husbands. Remember all Men would be tyrants if they could. If particular care and attention is not paid to the Ladies we are determined to foment a Rebellion, and will not hold ourselves bound by any Laws in which we have no voice, or Representation. . . . (Rossi, 1973:11)

John Adams's response included the following rebuff:

> As to your extraordinary Code of Laws, I cannot but laugh. We have been told that our Struggle has loosened the bands of Government every where. That Children and Apprentices were disobedient—that schools and Colleges were grown turbulent—that Indians slighted their Guardians and Negroes grew insolent to their Masters. But your letter was the first Intimation that another Tribe more numerous and powerful than all the rest were grown discontented. . . . Depend on it, we know better than to repeal our Masculine systems. . . . (Rossi, 1973:11)

Women's demands have been heard as demands for rights—and indeed much of the energy of the women's movement has focused on securing rights for women equal to those of men. But more than calling for specific rights, women have demanded to be heard. Rights may have been the vehicle to be heard in the political spheres of society, including the home, the economy, the government, and the military.

Women seek participation in these arenas so that they can have a voice. This may seem to be a simple claim. But when the focus of women's demands has been on achieving particular rights, such as the right to vote, the right of access to particular jobs, and the right to political candidacy, the overriding issue, the right to a voice, has often been neglected. The fact that many legal rights for women have not been achieved makes it obvious that the struggle is not merely about rights but about acceptance and recognition of women.

Among the voices of the Enlightenment who argued for women's rights were Harriet Martineau, John Stuart Mill, and Margaret Fuller. These intellectual activists stressed the importance of education as the source of women's freedom, and they maintained that if women could be educated as men were, they would have the same potential for participation and contribution in the social realm. Martineau, often described as the first woman sociologist (Rossi, 1973:124), was an articulate observer and critic of a society that declared freedom and justice for all, but accorded it to only a portion: "If a test of civilization be sought, none can be so sure as the condition of that half of society over which the other half has power . . ." (Rossi, 1973:125).

Whereas Martineau, Fuller, and Mill relied on writing and lecturing to persuade and enlighten, the roots of the movement for social change were established with another group of activists who crusaded, held meetings, called for reforms, and submitted proposals—who, in short, began to organize. For these women, solitary voices were insufficient. For political guidance they made use of the structure of other reform movements that were sweeping the states.

In 1840, Elizabeth Cady and Henry Stanton, a young couple active in the abolition movement, traveled to London to attend the World Anti-Slavery Convention, as did Lucretia Mott, a Quaker minister, and her husband James. Although these women and two others had been chosen as delegates to represent the abolitionist groups in Philadelphia and New York, the delegates in London voted to exclude them from participation in the proceedings. At least some of the American delegates vigorously protested, although Henry Stanton was not among them. This now famous action led to the friendship of Elizabeth Cady Stanton and Mott and ultimately to the Seneca Falls Convention in 1848.

Women who were active in the antislavery movement in the 1830s, 40s, and 50s gradually took up the cause of women's rights when they recognized that their participation in the abolition cause was limited. Among them were Sarah and Angelina Grimke, Elizabeth Cady Stanton, Susan Anthony, and Lucy Stone—women who had sharpened their political sensibilities as well as their organizational skills in the movements for moral reform, temperance, and abolition before they turned to the cause of women.

Although harshly criticized as radical and troublesome, these women activists found support in the egalitarian ideals underlying the French and American revolutions. Women's extension of the theory of equality to themselves in the domestic as well as the political realm did not result in a collegial welcome by men, who cherished such ideals for themselves. Instead, these women were increasingly ostracized and isolated for speaking out.

The issues addressed in the 1848 Seneca Falls Convention Declaration of Sentiments included the right to vote, the right to hold property, equitable divorce laws, access to educational institutions, full participation in the church, and equal opportunity in trades and professions. Of these resolutions only the right to vote was not unanimously passed by the members of the convention. Its opponents feared that the right to vote was such a "radical" demand and had so little hope of being achieved that the other resolutions would be tarnished and seen as absurd in association with it.

Ironically, of these resolutions made 140 years ago, only the right to vote has been fully realized, while the "less radical" demands have proved more problematic. The right to vote has increased the possibility of women's voices being heard in government, but in practice women have not been able to elect candidates to fully represent their voices.

Over the past century and a half a handful of issues have dominated the women's movement. Of these, the issues relating to women in the workplace have been equal pay, equal opportunity, and protective legislation, and none of them has been adequately resolved, despite major legislative initiatives. At stake for both men and women are fundamental attitudes about the right and propriety of women to work.

INTERVIEWS WITH CORPORATE WOMEN

In order to understand the issues feminists in the corporate world face today, I interviewed ten women in five large corporations. These women were not randomly selected: some I met in corporate seminars, and others were friends of the original women or colleagues of friends. Each was chosen because she had thought about women's issues in the workplace and was willing to participate in a study of feminism in the corporation. The women I interviewed admitted to being feminists, but they did not say it loudly, and certainly not at work.

For most of them, the term "feminist" carried a significant liability. Recognizing this, at the outset of the interview I asked each woman to define what feminism meant to her.

While these ten women do not represent all corporate women, their voices are worth hearing for several reasons. First, as academics, business ethicists, and feminist theorists, we do not do enough listening to the people about whom we write. Theories are dry and abstract without the self-descriptions of the daily lives of the people we study.

Second, there is a shortage of women's stories, although there is no lack of salary surveys, demographic studies, and advice on managing diversity, choosing clothing, parenting, and gamesmanship for women. But there is insufficient awareness of what life is like for women on the job. How are they treated? How do they feel? Do their expectations fit their goals? Are they respected? Do colleagues listen to them? Are women well integrated in this age of diminishing political concern for civil rights and affirmative action? I wanted to document these voices and perspectives. The women interviewed here were a first step in that process.

Third, and most important, hearing women's stories is as critical an aspect of morality as listening. I present these stories as practice in the method. Morality as listening doesn't require great philosophical study, but it does require lots of practice.

DO YOU THINK OF YOURSELF AS A FEMINIST?

In preliminary discussions it became apparent that for many women the term "feminism" evoked dissonance and discomfort. So I began with some questions to help define the terms we would be using. Do you think of yourself as a feminist? What does feminism mean to you?

The first question was supposed to be easy—a throwaway question. After all, I had intentionally forgone a random sample of corporate women to ensure that I spent my time listening to women who cared about the issues that interested me. I had selected women whom I had heard speak out in corporate seminars, expressing concern about sexism in the workplace. Others were friends and acquaintances of the initial participants, all sharing concerns about the roles that women are allowed to play in corporations.

In response to the first question, "Do you think of yourself as a feminist?" only half the women responded with an unqualified "yes." Several other women expressed concern about what the term meant to other people, particularly men. They hesitated to adopt the label for fear of incurring a negative image. Anne, a woman in her early forties with a successful career in sales and marketing, responded, "I always disliked that word. I'm very uncomfortable with it because I think a lot of men interpret it as a negative. Here comes a bra burner. That's what they think. Someone who is going to make trouble. These women who want men's jobs. . . ."

Anne went on to describe her childhood, having been raised by an aunt who taught her the value of hard work and who marched on picket lines for equal pay. Her aunt had set a strong example of independence and resourcefulness in supporting an extended family, but she denied any identification with the women's movement. Anne and her sister, Alice, another participant in my study, both (independently of each other) described teasing their aunt about her unspoken feminism. Anne described herself and her aunt as survivors. After reflecting more on the meaning of feminism, Anne concluded, "I guess I am a feminist."

Linda, an attorney, described her experiences over the past twenty years since law school. She had spent many of those years struggling for acceptance in a man's world and refusing to be identified with other women lest she be seen as less competent or less professional than her male colleagues. But Linda had come to realize a strong commitment to supporting other women at all levels in the company. Her candid response to the first question was: "Yes, today I think of myself as a feminist. . . . Today and henceforth . . . but it's not something that I've always felt comfortable saying, in a mixed crowd particularly, that I'm a feminist."

Although Linda had been active in law school on some women's issues, when she joined a corporate legal department she learned that fitting in was easier than standing out:

> The reality of the workplace was . . . there existed a nonhealthy view of women in general, and then I heard and experienced many derogatory comments about women. . . . And so, what I got was a sense of that was not something to be valued, and I drifted more toward being as much one of the boys as I could. . . . I didn't fully appreciate what that was doing to me personally for a long time. There were things like sexist jokes and the *Playboy* magazines and that kind of thing around, which I would go along with, and I knew it went against my grain to do that. But I also felt a need to be accepted and to show that I could be just like one of them and laugh at their jokes and actually behave in a way that would indicate I didn't value other women as well. . . . I tried to set myself apart as being okay. . . . I would isolate myself from other women. . . . What wasn't conscious was just what that was doing to me in terms of denying a large part of me. . . . There were things, values and outlooks, that I did not even recognize I had in me because I would work so hard at being something else.

A few other women in the study begrudgingly claimed the term "feminist" for themselves, quickly defining it in terms they were comfortable with. They viewed themselves as somewhat outside the women's movement:

> I've never thought of myself as an aggressive player in the feminist movement. [Ruth]

> It's not a word I would pick to describe myself. . . . I'm not personally someone that does a lot of demonstrating. That's not my style to take an extreme approach. . . . I have seen women who have a lot of anger, and they see everything as a feminist issue even when it's not. . . . I've never been a crusader in that sense. [Emily]

In her interview, each of these women described conscious actions they took in their jobs to express their own strongly feminist values within organizations that actively squelched such behavior. To me, they appeared to be strong individual feminists, hesitant to adopt a whole movement to explain or justify their actions, but committed to principles of supporting women and women's rights.

While the first question was not meant to be an interesting one, the responses were instructive. On the corporate scene, identifying oneself as a feminist is done only with caveats and clarifications, and probably not in public. The women who had responded affirmatively just as quickly pointed out, as Diane did, "You don't talk about being a feminist in the workplace—you don't even raise notions of feminism, if you know what's good for you. Because it's just threatening."

HOW DO YOU DEFINE FEMINISM FOR YOURSELF?

When I gave each woman the opportunity to define feminism, I wanted her to reflect on the concept and share what it meant in her own life. The women did respond in personal ways, and their voices concurred on several central meanings of feminism. The contrast between their shared definitions and their initial reservations about what the term "feminism" might convey to men was noteworthy. The concerns about being perceived as "a bra burner," "an extremist," "a crusader," "a radical," and "an aggressive player in the women's movement" were offset by equally strong but more gently worded descriptions of feminism. In rejecting the former terms, it was apparent that these women did not think of themselves as militant. It was important for their corporate roles not to be perceived this way.

Beyond image and perception of others, I focused on the issue of personal values and positions. Half the women indicated that they did not carry a banner for feminism. They had some strong feelings about how women should be treated in the workplace, and they expressed those when necessary, but they did not actively look for ways to articulate their values. The other half also had strong views and values and described themselves as taking a more activist stance. What emerges is the reality that all of the participants acted in ways to change the corporate workplace. Some admitted to doing it intentionally with goals they described as feminist. Others worked for changes in hiring practices or encouraged greater collaboration and participation, but did not necessarily see these activities as representing feminism.

Before looking at how the women expressed their feminist outlook at work, let us review how the participants defined feminism. There were two strong convergences of issues. The first was about choice and self-determination:

I want to have control . . . and influence my direction in life . . . not feel constrained just because I'm a woman. . . . I want to have equal footing with men in controlling my destiny. [Ruth]

Knowing that you have some options and wanting to act on those options . . . having a sense of identity . . . that you can do whatever you want to do. [Diane]

Being a true feminist for me . . . is that gender does not pose a particular barrier . . . to anything I would want to do. [Joan]

Feminism for me is the ability and power as a woman to pursue my potential . . . and if I'm lacking . . . to find a way to do it. [Kathy]

These were not the women in their early twenties that a 1990 *Time* magazine special edition called the new generation that wants to have it all. These women had been in the workplace for periods ranging from five to twenty years, with most closer to twenty years. Their words represent their personal challenges at work. Ruth was personnel director struggling against an Equal Employment Opportunity Commission (EEOC) deadline to further integrate her plant. Diane was a corporate labor lawyer looking up at a glass ceiling that remained just above her, despite a recent title change and consistently high performance ratings. Joan, a marketing director, was considering a position in Japan, where she would be the first woman in that organization in a high-level management position. In order to pursue her potential, Kathy was leaving her position in corporate communications to enroll in graduate school. Each woman faced significant questions about how to carry out that which she defined as feminism: "Being anything we want to be" [Anne].

The second convergence of issues was about a sense of self. This theme is interwoven with the issue of choice and control, but here there are some unique facets that involve understanding and appreciating oneself. Here are some of the ways this theme was expressed in response to the question, "How do you define feminism for yourself?"

> For me it is acknowledging womanness, femaleness, style and emotion, manner . . . it's asking that this style that comes out of being a woman be acknowledged. All too often in the corporate world, styles coming out of womanness aren't acknowledged or recognized or celebrated or welcomed. [Nancy]

> . . . believing in or supporting women's rights, women's freedom to be themselves in terms of their style and values. . . . Being able to express themselves in their own way and not having to fit into a male culture. [Emily]

> . . . advocating for women and the values that women bring into the business environment. [Linda]

> For me it means . . . having a sense of self—a sense of worth as a woman. [Diane]

These are the voices of women wanting to be listened to, understood, and acknowledged as unique and capable of making significant contributions.

As feminist concerns and demands have evolved, so have women as individuals. Of course, women and their concerns are inextricably linked—the voice and the chorus. Equality, equity, and access are still issues, but they are not the whole of the women's movement. More than just a foot in the door and rules for rapid assimilation, women want to be welcomed and celebrated for who they are: "Young women do not want to slip unnoticed into a man's world; they want that world to change and benefit from what women bring to it" (*Time*, 1990:12).

Time magazine and I drew similar conclusions from our respective research. Initially, I was miffed about getting preempted by *Time*. But being scooped by a special issue of *Time* is a pretty good indication that everybody's already talking about something and it's old news.

Women's voices are not new voices, but they are voices that have been quiet for a long time. They have finally emerged from the echo chambers of the women's movement, loud enough to be heard by the rest of the world.

EXPRESSIONS AND REACTIONS

Several questions in my interviews addressed how women express their feminism in the work environment and what reactions such expression evokes. Women are choosing to act more consistently with their own values and views, despite men's continuing unwillingness to acknowledge or recognize these actions as significant contributions to the workplace. The participants in this study described the ways in which they express their feminism as support for other women: being honest about their abilities, openly sharing rather than trading information, improving family-oriented policies, paying close attention to the responses of co-workers and clients in conducting meetings, and nurturing a project with careful attention to detail. In these actions, they did not see themselves waging a battle for sexism, but were simply doing their jobs in ways that came naturally from their own experiences and priorities.

Emily described a collaboration with a man, in which her offer of information was entirely unfamiliar to him:

> I was in a rather high-level staff assistant job to the deputy chief, and one of the other staff assistants was a man who . . . very much dealt in the "I'll do you this favor and you'll owe me one." . . . I went in once with some information that I knew he needed and I just said, "Here's something you need, and I wanted to share it with you"; and he said something about, "Oh well, I'll owe you one"; and I said, "No, you don't need to owe me anything. That whole system bothers me. I just can't deal with the way you guys trade chips all the time." He said, "Well, I don't understand, what do women do?" I said, "We just help each other because it's a nice thing to do," and he got this look on his face like that had never occurred to him and he just said, "Oh, people do that? Do you mean you'd help me when you weren't going to get anything back for it?" . . . In that job it was becoming an eye-opener to me to realize how that system operated.

Emily's education and her experience as a consultant in organizational development had prepared her to respond to people's concerns by trying to draw them out and encouraging them to share their concerns within the context of projects. In the past, her approach had been highly successful. In the position she had at the time of the interview, however, her boss, who neither shared nor appreciated her awareness of the dynamics among her fellow workers, did not want to hear about such concerns. His increasing irritation with Emily and others who challenged his impersonal style and autocratic control resulted in the sudden removal of these employees from various projects. In this work environment Emily learned, for the sake of survival, to express her own values and use her own approach less frequently. She is convinced, however, that her approach is a good one, and she planned to look actively for a different job in which she could be herself and thereby work more effectively. To the extent that she was adapting, she saw it as only temporary.

Several women were in positions in which they directly influenced the hiring practices within the organization. They were able to recruit, hire, and promote increasing numbers of women and minorities, as well as establish expectations that their managers would do the same.

Alice was reminded at a reunion of a group of managers that she had always encouraged them to pay attention to the balance of women, men, and blacks in their departments:

> I can remember one manager coming to me and saying she had seven men, and I said, "Why don't you look at not just hiring men all the time? Why don't you look for some talented women? You haven't looked at any black people." . . . I really believe that promoting minorities and women within the work force begins with yourself. You have to make sure that you're setting the right examples, doing a good job, but you also have to be able to help other people. . . . I thought it was very important to do that as a woman. I still do.

While this practice may have made an impression on the managers under her supervision, those above and around Alice took no notice. She felt no positive or negative reactions to her recruiting and hiring practices: "I have never had a problem with [reactions], but I could honestly say that I work for a company that doesn't care one way or another. I mean, they're not into promoting so many women and hiring so many blacks. They're not into that at all. As a matter of fact, they're just the opposite."

Alice was expressing her own commitment to creating opportunities for people who have been excluded from particular jobs. Her views were not endorsed by upper management, nor did she receive any rewards within the organization for such actions. But despite being ignored on this issue, Alice continued to integrate her values into her role as a middle manager. In fact, being ignored on this matter was not all bad, because she could "get away" with actions that she believes in.

On the same issue, hiring and promoting minorities and women, Carol was able to encourage and support these practices as assistant controller of a division. She established the policies and practices for the directors and managers throughout the division. Each time an individual was hired at any level, the person met with her for at least a few minutes. She did not work only to promote women or blacks, stressing repeatedly that anyone who worked hard would be recognized and rewarded.

As a black woman, Carol knew that she had broken new ground in each position. She was always "a first among firsts." Such a role required her to be sensitive and responsive to other people's reactions, ready to talk out any distancing behavior that she felt from co-workers. Essentially, she thought of herself as hard working and fair. These qualities shaped her approach more than any explicitly feminist views. Interestingly, her style echoed that of other women who saw such patterns as reflective of women's strengths:

> I like to share information with people. If I make decisions, I let people know why the decisions are being made, why they were considered, why they were not considered, and I get their feedback on how they're feeling, how they're reacting to that, and this is kind of ongoing. I emphasize training and development for people, and I'm concerned with people's careers moving ahead and getting the right people into the right jobs. People are aware of that . . . because we've done so much of it in the group . . . it becomes visible how we provided growth opportunities for people.

Carol was not a human resources person but a financial manager overseeing a major division. Yet she was responsible for an actively carried out progressive integration. She also initiated sharing rather than trading or hoarding information. In her position of authority, it appeared that her system was working. Not everyone wanted to be promoted, and much of the structure that she had inherited was intact, with female secretaries and male bosses. But she opened doors for those who were interested in moving forward. Carol herself was waiting to see whether there was an invisible barrier between her and the next promotion, which would be to vice president, an executive-level position.

The desire to support and promote women and minorities did not prove to be as easy for Ruth to carry out as it was for Alice and Carol. Ruth was personnel manager for a manufacturing plant. Faced with a very low representation of women and minorities, Ruth negotiated an agreement with an EEOC auditor that would require aggressive hiring over the following two years. The company had been in a unique position to hire and promote as a result of growth and an acquisition. But despite Ruth's efforts to achieve the target representation, by close to the end of the two years there had been only minimal progress. The president and the managers agreed to target jobs and promotional opportunities, but the willingness to follow through seemed nonexistent. All of the women and minorities brought in for interviews were considered not qualified:

> I have never heard "qualified" used in front of males. It is always in front of females and minorities, and I can't find any qualified ones. They just aren't there. Yes, we said we'd do it, and I set a 45-day exclusive search period for a minority or female for those positions that I targeted, and we agreed to all of that. And in 45 days I brought in people and (according to the managers)

LIBRARY
UNIVERSITY OF ST. FRANCIS
JOLIET, ILLINOIS

they are just not qualified. Qualified women and minorities just don't exist. . . . There is a grave inconsistency. Just recently, a manager basically compromised some qualifications on a job to fit a white male. Yet, he tells me that the minority candidates he has in front of him aren't qualified. He deliberately changed the spec to fit an individual. I pointed that out to him. This situation indicates that you are flexible. All I expect of you is to show the same degree of flexibility. . . . I have thought long and hard about this problem. I'm not convinced corporate America is the place to be.

In positions of authority, Carol and Alice were able to hire and promote a broad range of qualified women and men. Carol was also able to establish patterns of communication in which sharing information was valued. However, in positions with less authority and in situations in which the men were clearly threatened by a change in style, Emily and Ruth were blocked from carrying out practices they felt would improve communication and establish a caring work environment.

For Ruth, acting on her values as a woman also meant trying to build and implement family-sensitive policies, such as personal leave and child care. But here, too, there were barriers to her proposals. In the process, Ruth's own competence was questioned by individuals who did not share her goals of changing the workplace. She described herself as

doing some things that are maybe a little beyond the policy or trying to influence the policy . . . so that it is a caring, sensitive policy for those issues that do affect women. . . . We don't do that very well in my organization. I mean, we are generally not viewed as a pioneer in these kinds of issues. . . . When you bring up these issues, you get labeled a do-gooder or a social worker, or this is the real world. . . . And sometimes I get the reaction that we will do what we have to do, but, you know, we are really not doing a lot more than that, and if you expect that then maybe you are not well placed. You're not in the right place.

Two of the women interviewed indicated that they simply could not express their feminist views or values at work. Diane, a labor lawyer in a corporate home office, was categorical:

If you talk about things that are just generally supportive to women without using the label feminist . . . you could only speak so far, and once you just start to get to that threshold where they think, "Here comes something that sounds like this woman's rap," you have to back off fast. . . . They're threatened enough by your presence. . . . If you intensify the fear at all by mentioning notions of feminism—which really means something radical—you're dead. . . . You have to go through clone training every morning as you're coming in on the subway to try not to interject your womanly instincts.

The reactions women evoked when expressing feminist values and goals ranged from being ignored to being openly threatened. In no cases did women describe managerial support for their individual approaches, although there were examples of appreciation from subordinates.

Two observations are worth making here. First, women were expressing their voices despite significant threats and barriers. These women were not shaping their behavior entirely by the corporate reward systems but implementing their own values in the face of strong disincentives and criticism. Their strength and persistence are seen not only in how well they fit into male-dominated worlds but also in how true they were able to be to themselves.

The second observation is a question. Why do women bear the responsibility for change? Dinnerstein defines feminism as "the broad task of restructuring our male-female arrangements: one part of this task is to understand why, in practice, it has for so long been carried out mainly by women" (1976:viii).

Why, indeed, is it so hard to listen to other voices? Heilbrun notes, "Those in power, like those in Dante's Hell, go on doing what they are doing. Without pressures from the outside, they never change. Resistance to genuine dialogue is one of the chief signs of power" (1979:209).

If power is the obstruction, the job of ethicists is to recognize these patterns within our lives and to look around us for answers. It will not do to write about the power of kings, of presidents, or of CEOs because power is an issue in our day-to-day relationships. It is there we will find the solutions when we are ready to admit the problems.

WHY ETHICAL THEORIES DO NOT PROVIDE SOLUTIONS TO SEXISM

At the risk of impaling myself on the philosophical lances of colleagues who have devoted years of their lives to restatements of Kant, Bentham, Mill, Hobbes, Rawls, and the like, I offer a brief criticism of the current state of business ethics. Although I don't have a full-blown alternative theory, I have some ideas about what such a theory should include.

Contemporary business ethics generally draws on the major ethical theories and the use of the case method to apply these theories. Both the ethical theories and the case method as currently used are problematic; that is, there are deficiencies in how business ethics is done as well as in how it is taught.

The major ethical theories that provide the groundwork for business ethics are the utilitarian, deontological, contractarian, and rights theories, with significant overlap of these in actual usage. Despite an emphasis on impartiality and attention to stakeholders in these theories, they do not provide adequate solutions to many ethical dilemmas. None of the major theories results in impartiality, the greatest good for the greatest number, or in universal principles, except in theory.

Business ethics is an application of theories. The criterion for measuring the adequacy of ethical theories in this field is their usefulness. Theories must actually guide students and managers to better moral reasoning and ethical action. Using this measure, we see that the major ethical theories fail to provide guidance in the areas of sexism and racism.

I believe the reason they fail is that when others' views, perspectives, and experiences need to be taken into account, as they always do in ethical decisions, these theories advocate the use of the imagination to divine others' perspectives. But the imagination is limited by experience. We cannot truly imagine what it is like to be people who are quite different from ourselves.

Further, persons in power do not recognize the extent to which the lives of those not in power are different from theirs and cannot hear the unique voices of the people who are not empowered. As a result, individuals in decision-making positions, as well as those who expound the ethical theories, hear only people who are like themselves. The population in consideration is limited in imagination and in truth to those who are most similar.

The following are a few oversimplified versions of the rules for making decisions offered by major ethical theories:

1. Think of all the consequences to all the affected people and add them up. Repeat this process with each alternative course of action. Compare the resulting totals of positive and negative consequences to find the optimal ethical solution.
2. Imagine that you are many different people, and determine how you would decide if you were in their shoes. Don't forget to imagine how you would feel if you were the least advantaged member of society.
3. List all the rights of the people affected by this action. Choose the decision that respects and protects the greatest number of rights.

None of these theories, in practice, encourages recognizing, listening to, or hearing voices other than our own. Theories of rights, justice, and universal principles suggest that it is possible to use one's imagination to understand the ethical dilemma from many different perspectives. But these theories strive for impartiality and universality, which require distance and abstraction. In a cogent critique of this tradition, Seyla Benhabib points out, "the moral self is viewed as a *disembedded* and *disembodied* being" (1987:81).

Benhabib's suggestion is that we include a concept of the "concrete other" to balance the "generalized other" invoked by universalistic theories. In this way we would avoid a system in which "moral impartiality is learning to recognize the claims of the other who is just like oneself" (Benhabib, 1987:85).

The "concrete other" would require greater attention to individual needs, desires, traits, strengths, advantages, and disadvantages rather than eschewing such information in an attempt to achieve blind justice and impartiality. This feminist approach sees morality as increased connectedness and responsiveness rather than greater distance and autonomy.

Benhabib specifies that the "concrete other" be added to theories that rely on the concept of "generalized other":

> My goal is not to prescribe a moral or political theory consonant with the concept of the "concrete other." For, indeed, the recognition of the dignity and worthiness of the generalized other is a necessary, albeit not sufficient, condition to define the moral standpoint in modern societies. In this sense, the concrete other is a critical concept that designates the ideological limits of universalistic discourse. It signifies the unthought, the unseen, and the unheard in such theories. (1987:92)

Benhabib's critique proposes ways of incorporating the previously unseen and unheard perspectives. There is a great deal of work to be done before this occurs. The necessity for it must be recognized, and the willingness to hear must replace unwillingness.

My views of the necessary conjunction of business ethics and feminism are simple in theory and complex in implementation. Feminism in the corporate world is increasingly about women expressing their unique voices to change the way work is done. They no longer want merely to fit in. From their experiences women have strengths and abilities that can contribute to organizational strength once their voices are heard and celebrated. But these voices are still muted, still subject to approval and acceptance by the male hierarchy.

Ethics—particularly business ethics—must address sexism by incorporating the concept of listening. Only by learning to listen will ethical theorists be able to formulate theories that increase understanding and recognition of women. It is enormously more difficult than it sounds: "As we have listened for centuries to the voices of men and the theories of development that their experience informs, so we have come more recently to notice not only the silence of women but the difficulty in hearing what they say when they speak" (Gilligan, 1982:173).

2

The Gendered Implications of Apparently Gender-Neutral Theory: Rereading Max Weber

Joanne Martin and Kathleen Knopoff

The bureaucratic form of organization has proliferated throughout the industrialized world. It is the rare institution that does not evolve some sort of organizational hierarchy and division of labor once it attains a certain size and age. Periodically, it becomes fashionable for organizations to announce the death of bureaucracy. In an attempt to reduce the rigidities of the form, lateral networks among organizational components are developed, teamwork is declared the latest panacea, managerial authority is partially and painfully eschewed, and attempts are pursued to institutionalize flexibility, flux, and decentralization. The core of the classic bureaucratic form, however, remains intact and continues to proliferate.

Academics in the fields of organizational behavior, strategy, and even business ethics sometimes contribute to this proliferation. Rather than challenging the fundamental tenets of the bureaucratic model, most researchers ask, "What can individuals do to succeed within bureaucratic institutions? How can bureaucratic organizations be made more efficient, more profitable, and more ethical?" Those who study women in organizations, the focus of this chapter, often simply address variants of these mainstream questions, asking merely, "What can women do to improve their power, productivity, compensation, and advancement opportunities within bureaucratic organizations?"

In contrast, critical approaches to organizational theory and research have challenged the basic assumptions of bureaucracy (e.g., Alvesson and Berg, 1992; Deetz, 1992; Hassard and Parker, 1993; Mumby, 1988; Perrow, 1986; Reed, 1985). Feminist theory, for example, starts from the assumption that it is not enough to explore ways women can better fit into structures created and controlled by men. It asks instead, "How should bureaucratic practices change if women's capacities are to be more fully developed and valued?" (e.g., Acker, 1990; Barrett, 1985; Billing and Alvesson, 1994; Calás and Smircich, 1990; Collinson, Knights, and Collinson, 1990; Ferguson, 1984; Ferree and Martin, 1995; Hearn and Parkin, 1987; Lugones and Spelman, 1987; Marshall, 1984; Mills, 1988). This chapter draws on feminist theory and research (especially Bologh, 1990, and Ferguson, 1984) to analyze Max Weber's theory of bureaucracy. In order to clarify the purpose and scope of this analysis, and to model how similar analyses of other theories might be framed, several questions need to be examined: Why this text? How can one present a feminist analysis of a text that does not even mention women? What techniques of analysis are best suited to this task?

WHY WEBER?

Weber's theory of bureaucracy describes an ideal type of organization. As an abstract and academic text it bears a complex and attenuated relationship to the bureaucratic practices that it claimed to describe at the time it was written (it was published posthumously in 1922) and that prevail today. Nevertheless, Weber's model is still taught today in sociology departments and business schools throughout the world; arguably, no other organizational theory has enjoyed its pervasive, continuing influence. Although the relation between any organizational theory and business practice is at best tenuous, Weber's ideas have been continually reinterpreted, in terms of both an ideal type and a description—albeit limited—of contemporary business practice. Thus, by dissecting Weber's ideas we gain some indirect insight into what managers are taught and, to some extent, how their organizations actually function. Nevertheless, an important limitation of this essay is its focus on the language of Weber's text rather than on its material context and influence on past or current business practice.

This chapter analyzes passages from the portions of Weber's theory that define the characteristics of a bureaucracy. These passages were selected because they are frequently assigned in introductory courses and are often included in collections of readings carrying such titles as *The Classics of Organizational Theory*.[1] Of course, selected passages cannot represent all of Weber's work. It is essential to examine what Weber thought, what he intended to say, what he actually wrote, how his writing was translated, and how what he wrote might be interpreted in various ways by contemporary audiences.

Weber wrote at a time when the particularistic favoritism of feudal paternalism was giving way to a new organizational structure—the more impersonal, rule-based bureaucracy favored by the new bourgeoisie

(Rosenberg, 1958). Weber's reactions to these developments were ambivalent, subtle, and complex. Students of Weber still disagree about whether he approved of the spread of the "iron cage" of bureaucracy that he predicted was inevitable. The interpretation offered in this chapter cannot, therefore, reflect what Weber intended to say or not say. This interpretation represents one among many possible views—one that might offer, because of its focus, some fresh insights.

This chapter challenges some of the fundamental assumptions Weber used to develop the distinguishing characteristics of bureaucracy. Working within the critical tradition of feminist theory and research, the chapter seeks to unveil the gender implications of Weber's apparently gender-neutral language (see Calás, 1993; Ferguson, 1984; Flax, 1990; P. Martin, 1990; Mumby and Putnam, 1992; Rothschild and Davies, 1994). Elements of Weber's language that are shown to be congruent with the subordination of women are then transformed, to provide leverage points for identifying needed gender-related organizational change and for generating alternatives to classic bureaucratic forms.

It must be noted at the outset that the discussion which follows requires the analysis of gender in Weber's text—in which women are seldom mentioned. Such a task is more difficult than countering arguments that openly demean women. Contemporary social norms of "political correctness" and scientific claims of objectivity work against the open expression of sexism and other forms of prejudice (e.g., Pettigrew, 1988). Apparently gender-neutral assumptions pervade theory and research in organizational behavior, business strategy, and business ethics, as well as actual managerial practice. This chapter uses a method of exploring gender implications of gender-neutral discourses that may be useful to scholars and practitioners in all of these domains.

AN ABSENCE OF WOMEN

At the time that Weber wrote, women were usually not allowed to own property, attend university, or hold most paying jobs. Weber consistently referred to managers (and clerical workers) with words such as "he" and and "his," in accordance with the sex of the bureaucratic employees at the time he was writing (Rosenberg, 1958). At the present time, Weber's theory may be—and often is—interpreted as ostensibly gender neutral because masculine nouns and pronouns can be interpreted as referring to both sexes (e.g., "mankind").

In contrast, a feminist analysis of Weber's text would begin from the observation that although Weber was keenly aware of the workings of power (as evidenced in his careful analysis of class dynamics), he generally refrained from discussing gender issues. Rather than interpreting this silence as neutrality, a feminist analysis would, for example, look for the implications of what is omitted. Such an analysis would show that the theory is constructed in ways that perpetuate men's dominance while facilitating women's subordinance—in a text that does not even mention women. Although many analytic techniques might be applied to this task, recent feminist work that draws on poststructuralist philosophy has found deconstruction to be a powerful way to study the ways language (and its absence, silence) can be used to suppress women and other subordinated groups (e.g., Calás, 1993; Flax, 1990; Ferguson, 1993; J. Martin, 1990a), sometimes without mentioning women directly. Deconstruction is an analytic strategy that exposes multiple ways in which a text may be interpreted. Here deconstruction is used to examine gender-related issues in key passages from Weber.

This analysis of selected Weber passages does not imply that Weber was thinking about women or that he intended particular passages to contain a subtext about women or that he meant to hide the implications for women in his text. An analysis of Weber's theory from a gender perspective does not suggest that Weberian thought has at its core a focus on gender issues. Indeed, many would argue that Weber's views of bureaucracy, and bureaucracies themselves, continue to be problematic, even if sexism were eliminated.[2] Instead, a contemporary reading of Weber's text, focusing on the gender implications of his ideas, illuminates aspects of bureaucratic functioning that are not usually brought to our attention precisely because they apparently were not Weber's central concern. Some of Weber's ideas that seem gender neutral can be reseen as reflecting and supporting, with or without authorial intention, gender inequalities in contemporary organizational life. One way to describe this analytic process is as an exercise in substitution: one bias is removed, not in order to achieve some kind of mythical value neutrality but to replace it with a feminist viewpoint, to see what different kinds of insights into organizational practices might emerge.

Before proceeding to this feminist analysis, for those who are unfamiliar with deconstruction, an introduction may be helpful. Because good texts are available elsewhere,[3] and some readers may be familiar with poststructural thought, this introduction will be brief.

AN INTRODUCTION TO DECONSTRUCTION

Deconstruction is able to reveal ideological assumptions in a way that is particularly sensitive to the suppressed interests of members of disempowered, marginalized groups. Traditional texts often gloss over issues that involve conflicts of interest, denying the existence of points of view that could be disruptive of existing power relationships and creating myths (for example, regarding shared values, rationality, and objectivity) that conceal the opposite. Deconstruction peels away layers of theoretical obscuration and exposes conflicts that have been suppressed; the devalued "other" is made visible. Thus, deconstruction reveals "power operating in structures of thinking and behavior that previously seemed devoid of power relations" (White, 1986:421).

How then does this mysteriously powerful deconstruction do its work? Eagleton's relatively succinct description is as follows:

> It is in the significant silences of a text, in its gaps and absences that the presence of ideology can be most positively felt. It is these silences which the critic must make "speak." The text is, as it were, ideologically forbidden to say certain things; in trying to tell the truth in his [*sic*] own way, for example, the author finds himself forced to reveal the limits of the ideology within which he writes. He is forced to reveal its gaps and silences, what it is unable to articulate. Because a text contains these gaps and silences, it is always incomplete. (1976:34–35)

This chapter relies on just a few deconstructive strategies: a search for significant silences, a focus on claims that a given state of affairs is "natural," and a questioning of dichotomous thinking. Each strategy will be described briefly.

Deconstruction attends to signals that something is not being said. For example, when authors place phrases in quotation marks, they are signaling, without explanation, that these words have problematic status. Other, more subtle signals that a difficulty has been concealed may be found in the margins of a text. For example, a text may relegate a problematic idea to a metaphor, an aside, a footnote, or an example. Analysis of these apparently tangential aspects of a text can reveal concealed contradictions.

Deconstruction also focuses on claims that something is "natural," implying that it could not be any other way. The dogmatism inherent in naturalizing claims signals weakness in an argument. The claim is both essential to the theory and somehow flawed. When deconstruction exposes the supposedly "natural" as unnecessarily limited, previously forbidden ways of thinking can be explored.

A third deconstructive strategy is the dismantling of dichotomies. Theories usually begin with the construction of categories, which are then placed in an oppositional relationship—a dichotomy (which may later be elaborated into a continuum or a more complex classification system). Deconstruction is suspicious of dichotomies, in part because such distinctions exaggerate differences, deny similarities and ambiguities, and omit all that does not fit. Furthermore, one half of a dichotomy is usually devalued. The devalued half is often associated with women, for example, active versus passive, objective versus subjective (e.g., Benhabib and Cornell, 1987; Calás, 1987; Flax, 1990; Keller, 1985; Showalter, 1989). Deconstruction of dichotomies is the theoretical equivalent of a computer's "undo" command: oversimplifications are demolished, often revealing what the text is trying not to say. A deconstruction cannot escape the use of categories; it must "inhabit them while contesting them" (Ferguson,

1990), but it can ask, "What are the effects of constructing this discourse on oppositional grounds? What has been left out?"

This chapter, for example, uses the categories of man and woman; these categories gain meaning when they are in opposition. In this process of opposition each term oversimplifies itself and the other. Different types of women seem more similar when they are placed in opposition to men, a move that in effect denies that the lived experience of what it means to be a woman can be radically different for women of different classes, races, religions, nationalities, and so on. The unfortunate tendency of relatively privileged white feminists to generalize from their own experience to that of all women (a move Spelman, 1988, labeled "essentialism") is a criticism that has generated a decade or more of feminist research focusing on differences among women. Similar observations have been made about the ways the category man masks differences among men, some of whom have suffered subordination, powerlessness, and injustice to a much greater degree than many relatively privileged feminists. The point here is not who has suffered the most or who has least power but rather that language leaves us few alternatives to the use of such categories. In the process of contesting the categories, we must use and thereby reify them. The "essentializing" language of the present chapter offers no escape from this dilemma.

Deconstruction, then, means taking apart a text piece by piece in an attempt to reveal some of the conceptual and linguistic building blocks that were used in its construction. A feminist deconstruction can take this process one step further—beyond destruction to rebuilding a very different kind of edifice.

Before proceeding, one caveat is essential. Deconstruction questions the validity of absolute statements about what is "true," claiming instead that multiple interpretations of what is true or ideologically desirable are always possible. In contrast, ideologies make a truth claim. For example, feminist ideology argues that it is essential to end the subordination of women. Because deconstruction questions the validity of any ideological position, any ideology-based deconstruction can in turn be deconstructed by focusing on the ideology that provides a foundation for its truth claims. In this chapter I have shortcut the endless process of deconstruction by choosing a stopping point that supports a feminist ideology. This chapter, like other ideological deconstructions, could in turn be deconstructed by focusing on the truth claims of the feminism that is its raison d'être.

These aspects of poststructural thinking provoke controversy. Some people say poststructuralism promotes social nihilism by undermining shared commitment to any ameliorative strategy for effecting social change. Others disapprove of poststructuralism's unremitting focus on inescapable uncertainties, which pose a challenge to the scientific search for knowledge. It is understandably difficult for empirically based researchers to see the worth of studying a point of view that challenges the validity of their professional activities. However, it is possible within the constraints of poststructuralism to maintain some comforting verities. For example, although poststructuralism (like some other points of view) argues that there is no neutral, value-free ground from which the "objective truth" of theories can be evaluated, it is still possible to criticize theories as being one-sided, exaggerated, poorly formulated, and otherwise inept. Some accounts are simply more coherent than others. This said, there remains an inescapable antagonism between the endless multiple interpretations of a postmodern view and the empirical certainties of logical positivism and its contemporary variants. For those who prefer empirical certainties, however, deconstruction might offer useful insights even if one disagrees with its premises, much as one might learn from listening to or participating in a conversation with people who hold a different view of the world.

BUREAURCRACY JUSTIFIED AS AN ANTIDOTE TO PRIVILEGE

Most organizational theorists are familiar with at least three of the six characteristics Weber defines as essential to bureaucracy: hierarchy, division of labor, and impersonal rule by rules. The cornerstone of bureaucracy is hierarchy. (Some of the quotations that follow are labeled with a letter to facilitate subsequent references to the text.)

> A: The principles of office hierarchy and of levels of graded authority mean a firmly ordered system of super- and subordination in which there is a supervision of the lower offices by the higher ones. Such a system offers the governed the possibility of appealing the decision of a lower office to its higher authority, in a definitely regulated manner. (9)

Hierarchy, according to Weber, offers the governed two guarantees: the lower levels of the hierarchy will be closely supervised by those at the top; and, should a perceived injustice occur, there will be well-defined paths of appeal upward.

Prevention of official abuse of power is also offered as the justification for the second element of bureaucracy: the stable and explicit division of labor:

> B: The regular activities required for the purposes of the bureaucratically governed structure are distributed in a fixed way as official duties. The authority to give commands required for the discharge of these duties is distributed in a stable way and is strictly delimited by rules concerning the coercive means, physical, sacerdotal, or otherwise, which may be placed at the disposal of officials. (8)

The third characteristic of bureaucracy is rule by impersonal rules:

C: The more complicated and specialized modern culture becomes, the more
    its external supporting apparatus demands the personally detached and
    strictly "objective" expert, in lieu of the master of older social structures,
    who was moved by personal sympathy and favor, by grace and gratitude.
    (20–21)

Impersonality is said to protect those in subordinate roles from the need
to curry favor with officials. This supposedly will circumvent the difficulties associated with relationships to figures of power in older systems,
"like the vassal's or disciple's faith in feudal or in patrimonial relations of
authority" (11).

Weber explains that bureaucracy and democracy "inevitably" occur
together because bureaucracy is a response to demands for equality
before the law:

D: Bureaucracy inevitably accompanies modern mass democracy in contrast
    to the democratic self-government of small homogeneous units. This
    results from the characteristic principle of bureaucracy: the abstract regu-
    larity of the execution of authority, which is a result of the demand for
    "equality before the law" in the personal and functional sense—hence, of
    the horror of "privilege" and the principled rejection of doing business
    "from case to case." (24)

This, then, is a justification of bureaucracy in the egalitarian language of
democracy, as an antidote to the horrors of privilege. Weber's explicit
analysis of the class-based effects of hierarchy, division of labor, and
impersonal rule by rules are reviewed next because they provide a context that reinforces contemporary sex segregation by occupation in
bureaucracies, in which clerical work is the realm of women and the
work of officials is predominantly done by men.

BUREAUCRACY REINTERPRETED AS A
JUSTIFICATION OF PRIVILEGE

The egalitarianism of democracy and the inequalities of bureaucracy
come into conflict over the fourth essential element of bureaucracy, the
need for a long-term vocational commitment and full-time training:

E: Office holding is a "vocation." This is shown, first, in the requirement of a
    firmly prescribed course of training, which demands the entire capacity for
    work for a long period of time. (10)

Because of these prerequisites for official status, bureaucracy and
democracy have quite different approaches to the eradication of privilege. Democracy presses for an alternative to rule by a closed elite, advo-
cating short terms of office and minimal educational background for

rulers. Bureaucracy's insistence on full-time training and a long-term commitment contradict these democratic objectives:

> Democracy inevitably comes into conflict with the bureaucratic tendencies which, by its fight against notable rule, democracy has produced. . . . The most decisive thing here—indeed it is rather exclusively so—is the leveling of the governed in opposition to the ruling and bureaucratically articulated group, which in its turn may occupy a quite autocratic position, both in fact and in form. (25–26)

Although democracy seeks a reduction of inequality between the governed and the rulers, Weber admits that bureaucracy increases this inequality by strengthening the autocratic position of those in power.

If bureaucracy enhances the power of the powerful, egalitarian justifications of hierarchy, division of labor, and impersonal rule merit a more skeptical rereading. In Weber's definition of hierarchy in quotation A, the governed are supposedly given protection against abuses of power by lower levels of the hierarchy. This protection rests on promises of supervision by and appeal to higher levels of the bureaucracy. There are no protections against abuse of power by those with the most power. Furthermore, officials are promised that any appeals by the governed to higher levels will be "definitely regulated," that is, kept under strict control. The right to appeal a perceived injustice does not guarantee, of course, that the injustice will be rectified.

The justification of the division of labor in quotation B also carries promises of comfort to the powerful. The distribution of duties and power is described as stable—not easily threatened. Although coercive use of power is said to be curtailed, no explicit limits are put on other, more subtle uses of power.

Bureaucracy promotes power inequalities by enhancing the status of bureaucratic officials, who are drawn from the wealthiest classes: "The modern official always strives and usually enjoys a distinct social esteem as compared with the governed. His social position is guaranteed by the prescriptive rules of rank order and, for the political official, by special definitions of the criminal code against 'insults of officials' and 'contempt' of state and church authorities." (11)

Bureaucracy should therefore thrive best in a social structure characterized by social and economic inequality:

> The actual social position of the official is normally highest where, as in old civilized countries, the following conditions prevail: a strong demand for administration by trained experts; a strong and stable social differentiation, where the official predominantly derives from socially and economically privileged strata because of the social distribution of power; or where the costliness of the required training and status conventions are binding upon him. (11)

This kind of social and economic inequality creates pressures for consumption by the upper classes, who have excess money to spend:

> The growing demands on culture, in turn, are determined, though to a varying extent, by the growing wealth of the most influential strata in the state. To this extent increasing bureaucratization is a function of the increasing possession of goods used for consumption, and of an increasingly sophisticated technique of fashioning external life—a technique which corresponds to the opportunities provided by such wealth. This reacts upon the standard of living and makes for an increasing subjective indispensability of organized, collective, inter-local, and thus bureaucratic, provision for the most varied wants, which previously were either unknown, or were satisfied locally or by a private economy. (18)

So inequality produces demand from the wealthy for consumer products; bureaucracies are needed to meet these demands; these bureaucracies employ bureaucrats drawn from the wealthier classes, who accrue more status; and so it goes.

Given this self-perpetuating cycle, it is no wonder Weber concludes that bureaucracies are virtually impossible to change: "And where the bureaucratization of administration has been completely carried through, a form of power relation is established that is practically unshatterable" (26). The bureaucratic system as Weber has defined it should be immune to revolution, in the sense of major structural change. When officeholders leave, their roles and duties continue to be fulfilled by replacements. Change therefore means only a change in the individual officeholder; the system stays intact: "this process has substituted coups d'état for revolutions" (27).

Bureaucracy is justified in the egalitarian rhetoric of democracy, yet it perpetuates a class-based system of privilege. In the description of impersonal rule by rules, in quotation D, Weber places "equality before the law" and (the horror of) "privilege" in quotation marks. Weber uses quotation marks to point to the fundamental and inescapable contradictions that lie at the core of bureaucracy. These contradictions suggest leverage points for gender-related change.

BUREAUCRACY AS A RATIONALE FOR GENDER INEQUALITY

Although hierarchy and division of labor are the best-known attributes of bureaucracy, Weber's theory is based on four other essential elements: impersonal rule by rules, written documentation, training, and full-time commitment. This section reexamines these four aspects of bureaucracy. So far, the chapter has focused primarily on issues of class-based inequality. In this section, class remains important, but a hidden dependence on gender inequality is revealed.

Impersonality of Rule by Rules—Revisited

Weber asserts that impersonal rule by rules is a natural attribute of bureaucracy, implying there is no alternative: "The reduction of modern office management to rules is deeply embedded in its very nature (10)."

The defensive absolutism in this naturalizing claim suggests that this element of the theory is a good candidate for deconstruction.

Difficulties appear most obviously when Weber discusses attempts to exclude emotion from the workplace:

> [Bureaucracy's] specific nature, which is welcomed by capitalism, develops the more perfectly the more the bureaucracy is "dehumanized," the more completely it succeeds in eliminating from official business love, hatred, and all purely personal, irrational, and emotional elements which escape calculation. This is the specific nature of bureaucracy and it is appraised as its special virtue. (21)

This passage groups three elements: personal, irrational, and emotional. Such a grouping is misleading because it implies that emotions are always personal (not shared); that emotions are irrational (and therefore not reasonable or justified); and that what is personal is irrational (a proposition that might surprise those fond of assumptions concerning a self-interested, rational economic "man"). The other end of this dichotomy apparently encompasses impersonality, rationality, and an absence of emotion. These characteristics are said to have "special virtue." Problems inherent in this argument become evident when the possibility of dehumanization is analyzed.

Weber places the word "dehumanization" in quotation marks, signaling that this idea is problematic and implying that some emotional/personal/irrational elements will escape suppression. Because a bureaucracy is composed of people, dehumanization can never be achieved. In this context the word itself implies that only the personal, emotional, and irrational are truly human characteristics, making it difficult to conceive of the dehumanized residue.

By placing "dehumanization" in quotation marks, Weber is tacitly admitting that bureaucracy rests on untenable assumptions. For example, if the exclusion of emotions is impossible to attain, impersonal rule by rules is also impossible. Perhaps this is why Weber becomes unusually dogmatic (using such words as "completely," "perfectly," and "eliminate") when he discusses attempts to exclude emotions from bureaucratic life.

Related difficulties emerge in other justifications for impersonal rule. In quotation C, for example, the ideal bureaucrat is described as "objective," personally detached, and expert. The implied alternative is an official who is subjective, personally involved, and nonexpert—that is, with no special training for the duties of officialdom. Putting aside for the moment the question of training, let us consider why the remaining two dichotomies are problematic.

It is impossible to be personally detached because a person's very presence affects what happens in an interaction. Even the most strenuous efforts of scientists to attain purely objective measures of some physical phenomena (such as quarks) have been problematic because the act of measuring itself affects what is being measured (e.g., Heisenberg, 1958; Popper, 1959). These problems are magnified when the object being studied is a subject, with self- and other-consciousness (e.g., Clifford and Marcus, 1986; Geertz, 1988). Furthermore, repressed emotion remains in the unconscious, its power strengthened and less controllable (e.g., Freud, 1965). Weber signals such difficulties by placing the word "objective" in quotation marks.

Quotation C contains another set of implied dichotomies. The old master, whose power is being curtailed by bureaucracy, is likened to the feudal lord or religious leader. Each of these masters is an authoritarian figure who places others in very subservient roles such as vassal and disciple. The range of possibilities considered here is severely constrained. Although the old master is characterized as being moved by grace, sympathy, favor, and gratitude, Weber does not mention the possibility of an egalitarian relationship (friend, partner) or a nurturing relationship (parent, mentor). Weber's examples intensify his abstractions by pointing to the extreme boundaries of his ideas, making it more obvious what has been excluded.

Quotation D advocates a principled rejection of doing business "from case to case." The analysis just given suggests that it may be impossible to avoid doing business on an individualized, subjective, and emotional basis. Furthermore, there are principled ethical justifications for considering, with empathy, the particulars of an individual's situation. These ethical principles stress the importance of emotional commitments to others, caring, and nurturance—precisely the qualities that Weber dismisses with disdain (e.g., Gilligan, 1982).

It could be argued that these implied dichotomies and absences, however problematic, are not crucial. I believe they are important because they point to a hidden, fundamental assumption. For example, the left-hand column of Figure 1 lists the dichotomized concepts that are valued in this description of bureaucracy, whereas the right-hand column enumerates the concepts that have been devalued.

Inspection of the figure reveals the hidden assumption: Weber is valu-

Valued	Devalued
Objective	Subjective
Rational	Irrational
Expert	Untrained
Abstract	Case-by-case
Dehumanized	Humane
Detached	Involved
Impersonal	Personal
Unemotional	Emotional
Authoritarian	Nurturant
Unequal	Egalitarian
Graceless	With grace
Unsympathetic	Sympathetic
Untouched by gratitude	Moved by gratitude

Figure 1.   Implied Dichotomies in Weber's Theory of Bureaucracy

ing some personal attributes (those stereotypically associated with men) and devaluing others (those associated with feminine stereotypes). This is not to say that women are in fact more subjective, irrational, emotional, and so on. It is to say that when Weber's words are applied to contemporary, sex-segregated bureaucracies, the attributes that qualify people for positions of power are those stereotypically associated with men, not with women (Broverman et al., 1972; Smith and Midlarsky, 1985; Spence and Sawin, 1985).

Why does an official need such impermeable, impersonal armor? What would be threatened if an official responded to a feeling of gratitude, exhibited grace, or reacted with sympathy? And who is the potentially sympathetic, graceful, and emotional being whom Weber is working so hard to disqualify for official positions? This who, we believe, is a she. Analysis of Weber's three other defining characteristics of bureaucracy support this contention.

Written Documents

The fifth essential feature of a bureaucracy is the voluminous written record that documents the institution's past actions and inaction: "The management of the modern office is based upon written documents ('the files'), which are preserved in their original or draught form. There is, therefore, a staff of subaltern officials and scribes of all sorts" (9). In this quotation, the word "therefore" stands out as illogical. The existence of written records does not necessitate a staff of subaltern clerical workers. Officials could process, type, and file their own records. However, if a hierarchy is to exist, there must be subordinates for officials to supervise. Because there are fewer positions at the top of a hierarchical structure than at the bottom, large numbers of subalterns are required.

Although Weber devotes most of his attention to officials, the vast majority of bureaucratic workers are subordinates (e.g., Ferguson, 1984). For approximately eight hours a day, five days a week, they process written documents. Their authority to make judgments and their scope of responsibility are rigidly constrained by the division of labor. De-skilled, they are forbidden to make case-by-case deviations from procedures, particularly on humanitarian grounds. They are forced to treat others impersonally, and they are treated impersonally themselves. Their jurisdiction is so limited that to many people their work seems meaningless. Although similar constraints may trouble officials, these problems are more acute (and the pay is less) at the lower levels of a hierarchy.

This is a gender issue because today such jobs are rigidly sex segregated (e.g., Barron and Morris, 1976; Harlan and Weiss, 1982; Hartmann and Reskin, 1986; Ferguson, 1984; Malveaux, 1982). For example, one carefully conducted longitudinal study of a wide range of organizations in California found that before and a decade after affirmative action laws were passed over 94 percent of all jobs were gender segregated (Bielby and Baron, 1986). Jobs at the top of hierarchies tend to be held, with rare exceptions, by men. Jobs in the lower and middle levels of management tend also to be held by men, although entry-level positions may be mixed, and all-women departments—"pink velvet ghettos"—such as personnel, may exist. Jobs at the lowest levels tend to be rigidly gender segregated, with women clustering in clerical positions. To a large extent, the subalterns in charge of processing written records are women, whereas the officials are men.

Records no longer need to be written, however. Executives can scan, process, file, and retrieve records on a network of personal computers. Although the requisite computer technology is available and cost effective, it is not used in this way. Instead, computers have been used for supervisory purposes that reinforce inequalities—for example, tabulating the number of forms a worker processes each day (Zuboff, 1988). Class and gender inequality are left intact.

The Need for Training—Revisited

It might be argued that women are clustered in low-status, low-paying jobs because they lack the skills necessary to perform in higher-status positions. Training requirements do not just serve a skills-development function; they legitimate the status of officials: "The possession of educational certificates—to be discussed elsewhere—are usually linked with qualification for office. Naturally, such certificates or patents enhance the 'status element' in the social position of the official" (11). The claim that such status enhancement is natural suggests the opposite. It implies that training has been artificially constrained in a way that is not being acknowledged. If officials have special skills that justify their positions of power, do they have special abilities that permit them to benefit from some particularly arduous or esoteric training? Apparently not: "The management of the office follows general rules, which are more or less stable, more or less exhaustive, and which can be learned. Knowledge of these rules represents a special technical learning which the officials possess" (10).

If anyone can learn these special skills, then access to training must be somehow restricted. A clue lies in the requirement (in quotation E) of full-time training. This emphasis is not outdated. For example, the Graduate School of Business at Stanford University prohibits students from working during the school year. This policy is disproportionately burdensome for students with limited means who have previous school debts and for those who bear responsibility for child care. In this way, the full-time training requirement helps to restrict access to official positions to those who come from relatively wealthy family backgrounds, who are childless, or who do not take responsibility for the care of their children. This is not the whole explanation, however, because officials are subject to similar requirements after employment.

Full Working Capacity

The sixth and final essential element of bureaucracy is that officials are required to make a more than full-time commitment to their work: "When the office is fully developed, official activity demands the full working capacity of the official, irrespective of the fact that his obligatory time in the bureau may be firmly delimited" (10). Why would an organization require an official to work more than the obligatory hours required at the office? There is no need for such a requirement in order to restrict access to official positions to members of the affluent class because the full-time training requirement already serves this purpose. Weber argues that this requirement binds the official to the organization and dilutes the official's commitment to other, more personal goals.

A hint of why this seems necessary (several explanations may be at work simultaneously here) comes from the attempt to separate the public domain of work from the private domain of the family:

> In principle, the modern organization of the civil service separates the bureau from the private domicile of the official, and, in general, bureaucracy segregates official activity as something distinct from the sphere of private life. . . . In principle, the executive office is separated from the household, business from private correspondence, and business assets from private fortunes. (9)

Feminist analyses have repeatedly explored the ways in which the public versus private dichotomy is a false distinction (e.g., Frug, 1986; Keohane, 1988; Nicholson, 1986; Olsen, 1983). What occurs at work is inextricably intertwined with what happens at home. For example, if a corporation does not provide on-site day care at a reasonable cost, other child-care arrangements must be made. Similarly, what happens at home affects work. For example, an employee who has someone willing to do most (or even half) of the housework and child care can devote more time to work and therefore be more valuable to the organization than co-workers who lack such assistance.

Feminists have focused on dismantling the public/private dichotomy because this is a gendered distinction. Supposedly, the public world of bureaucracies is territory dominated by men, whereas women watch over the private sphere in which children are conceived and family members are nurtured.[4] This gendered characterization of the dichotomy, like the dichotomy itself, is oversimplified:

> [This characterization of the public/private domains] tends to exaggerate the differences and occlude the similarities between them. For example, it directs attention away from the fact that the household, like the paid workplace, is a site of labor, albeit unremunerated and often unrecognized labor. Likewise, it does not make visible the fact that in the paid workplace, as in the household, women are assigned to, indeed ghettoized in, distinctly feminine, service-oriented occupations. Finally, it fails to focalize the fact that in both spheres women are subordinated to men. (Fraser, 1988:37)

When work is conceptualized as separate from family concerns, the conflicts working mothers encounter are viewed as private problems that women must solve individually; the organization is not responsible. This reluctance to assume responsibility becomes untenable when we consider the impact of these organizational policies on families.

For example, the requirement that officials give a more than full-time commitment to their work has a direct impact on family life, placing a disproportionate burden on women, particularly if they have children. Statistics vary by country, class, and (less so) year, but in industrial countries women do an average of 70–85 percent of the housework and child care (e.g., Szalai, 1972; Hochschild, 1989), so that it is very difficult for women to work or attend school full time. A more than full-time commitment is even more difficult to maintain. If evening and weekend work is required, women must do housework late into the night or, for those jobs that can be delegated, hire help (if the money is available). Child care presents a greater difficulty. A child who has been in school or daycare until 5 or 6 in the evening needs parental attention on the weekends and during early evening hours. If a woman does not have a partner, or if the partner is unwilling to take this responsibility (perhaps because of traditional sex role ideology and/or a job that also requires more than full-time responsibility), children may suffer.

It is no wonder, then, that many women who can afford to do so choose not to work outside the home. Many others choose to take a leave or to work part time, even though this makes it very difficult for them to earn equal pay and receive promotions (e.g., Hartmann and Reskin, 1986; Rhode, 1990). For example, even women who earn MBAs from top schools earn less than the men in their classes within a few years of graduation, and this gap widens every year thereafter (e.g., Strober, 1982).[5] Rather than see their families suffer, these women, on average, have chosen lower status and lower pay.

To summarize, the requirement that top officials give a more than full-time commitment to their work makes it extraordinarily difficult for most women to hold these positions. Instead, the majority of women work in clerical or other low-status positions that require only a full- or part-time commitment. In these ways, gender inequality is perpetuated by bureaucratic requirements for subaltern processing of written records, full-time training, and more than full-time work. Weber is correct in his argument that this requirement places the desires of the workplace, for more and more work, in conflict with the needs of the family.

Sometimes a woman (usually a white, childless woman from a relatively privileged background) manages to overcome these obstacles and enter high-level management. Here, however, she is met by the full force of the third essential feature of bureaucracy: impersonal rule by rules. The norms associated with impersonality devalue aspects of life that are central to the feminine stereotype: subjective, humane, emotional, involved, sympathetic, graceful, moved by gratitude, egalitarian, nurtu-

rant, and so on. To the extent that a person wants to embody these supposedly feminine qualities (and many women and some men do), functioning effectively in a high-status bureaucratic position may be difficult.

A woman literally enters a man's world when she attains a high-level
position. Some expect her to conform to a stereotypically feminine
behavior pattern, which is often considered unprofessional. Others
expect her to try to fit a pattern of behavior that has traditionally been
considered masculine. Either way, she is not a he. It is more difficult for
a woman than for the men she works with to find a way of being at work
that is personally comfortable, socially rewarding, and interpersonally
effective.

This feminist analysis has focused on impersonal rule by rules, written
records processed by subalterns, full-time training, and more than full-
time work, revealing how these less familiar elements of bureaucracy
rationalize, legitimate, and perpetuate gender inequality. The next step
is to use this analysis to develop strategies for change.

Evolving Alternatives to Bureaucracy

If these less familiar elements of bureaucracy reinforce gender inequality, then they may provide leverage points for feminist change. Interestingly, all of the strategies for change that emerge from this analysis
should be extended to men as well as women, although women might
initially find the benefits greater.

A crucial priority should be to alter requirements for more than full-
time work. Evening and weekend work should be rare. High- and low-status employees should be permitted flexible hours, part-time work, and
leaves of absence. Training requirements that only enhance status
should be abolished. Hiring and promotion decisions should not be
affected by lack of training that does not provide job-relevant skills, and
part-time training opportunities should be made available. Job-relevant
training should be offered during normal working hours so employees
with household or child-care responsibilities can attend.

These apparently minor changes would necessitate, eventually, alter-
ations in the division of labor. Employees would have to be able to fill in
for each other to accommodate flexible hours, training time, leaves of
absence, and so on. Job rotation and job sharing would become commonplace. There would be more evolving jobs (Miner, 1987) tailored to
fit the needs as well as the skills of particular employees.

Computer technology could be used deliberately to further goals of
gender equality. If executives' jobs were expanded to include tasks for-
merly considered clerical, fewer clerical positions would be necessary.
Clerical workers could be retrained (during working hours) in order to
upgrade their skills, making an increase in responsibility feasible. Each
of these changes in the requirement that written records be processed
by subalterns would alter the division of labor, lessen the degree of

inequality between levels of the hierarchy, and, ultimately, facilitate the erosion of sex segregation by occupation.

The final component of this effort to effect change would focus on the norms associated with impersonality in the workplace. As more women enter new, flexibly structured high-status positions, some would be walking reminders of the inadequacy of gender stereotypes. With more women entering this man's world, it might be possible to change some norms, perhaps first in interactions with other women and then in mixed-gender interactions. In time perhaps both men and women might feel increasingly free to accept and value—at work—the emotional, egalitarian, nurturant, personally involved aspects of themselves and others. More grace, sympathy, and gratitude might improve life in the workplace for everyone.

To continue this optimistic portrait, if these strategies for change were undertaken in a wide variety of organizations, eventually major modifications in the systems of hierarchy and division of labor would become institutionalized, thereby reducing environmental pressures to fail or revert to more traditional bureaucratic structures. In these ways, it might be possible to undermine the ways bureaucracies rationalize, legitimate, and perpetuate gender inequality, creating sustainable alternatives to bureaucracy.

Considerable evidence suggests that even these massive changes in the ways work is organized might not suffice to create lasting alternatives to traditional bureaucratic structures and practices, especially in large organizations that operate—as most public, private, and nonprofit firms do— in a highly competitive economic marketplace. This pessimistic assessment is supported by studies that have focused on just a subset of these strategies for change. For example, some organizations have tried variants of job rotation and job redesign with training, particularly with lower-status jobs. Such programs floundered when increased training, tasks, and responsibilities were not rewarded with financial compensation and promotion opportunities (e.g., Hackman et al., 1975; Walton, 1975). Gender-based inequities in pay and promotion have proven particularly resistant to efforts to implement change, both organizational and legislative (e.g., Bielby and Baron, 1986; Hartmann and Reskin, 1986).

Other researchers have focused on organizations that have adopted many or all of these strategies simultaneously, self-consciously creating alternatives to classic bureaucratic structures. Of these, two approaches have recently generated considerable empirical research: studies of collectivist and feminist organizations. Collectivist organizations do not usually focus on gender issues, but they do deemphasize hierarchy and the division of labor, generally preferring consensual decision making and job rotation with training, with a concomitant demystification of expertise. Leadership is deemphasized and participative, although exceptions exist. There are few reporting channels, employment is based on friendship and shared ideology, rewards are distributed in a relatively egalitarian fashion, cooperation is valued and competition discouraged, and long-term commitment to the collective is expected (e.g., Rothschild-Witt, 1979; Rothschild and Russell, 1986). Internal conflicts can develop between the highly committed individuals who form the core of a collectivist organization and those at the fringes, who are perceived, often fairly, to have contributed less. Unequal contributions and relatively equal rewards can be an unstable combination. Such organizations tend to follow traditional patterns of gender relations, including sex segregation and unequal pay and promotion opportunities. In addition, environmental pressures for organizational isomorphism, especially in competitive marketplaces, have caused most experimental organizations eventually to fail or to revert to more traditional structures (e.g., Hackman, 1984; Kanter, 1972; Mansbridge, 1973; Rothschild-Witt, 1979).

The second type of alternative organization is explicitly feminist. Such organizations generally adopt most of the practices of collectivist organizations just described, other than the traditional patterns of gender relations. In addition, feminist organizations place greater emphasis on the coordination, and sometimes integration, of work and family concerns; expression of both positive and negative emotions at work is expected and valued, and personal self-disclosure is the norm (e.g., Acker, 1990; Ferguson, 1984; Ferree and Martin, 1995; Koen, 1984; Lugones and Spelman, 1987; P. Martin, 1990). Ethnographic studies of feminist organizations provide a richly detailed portrait of work that at its best is deeply and personally rewarding for participants and sufficiently productive that many of these feminist organizations have survived for substantial periods of time (e.g., Brown, 1990; Epstein, Russell, and Silvern, 1988; Leidner, 1991; Pringle and Henry, 1993). In feminist organizations, however, as in collectivist organizations, conflicts between individuals and groups can become intense, given the high value placed on emotional expression and personal self-disclosure (Baker, 1982; Hagen, 1983). In addition, as in collectivist organizations, pressures to remain financially solvent and to conform to normative expectations concerning what an organization should do create pressures to move toward isomorphism (Farrell, 1994; Morgen, 1986; Sealander and Smith, 1986).

A further set of problems raise a warning flag about the application of innovations adopted by collectivist and feminist organizations. Both types of organizations are generally small, usually with less than 100 employees, unless they are members of social movements rather than formal organizations. They tend to be public sector or nonprofit organizations, often founded for ideological rather than financial purposes (e.g., legal clinics, schools, alternative newspapers). Furthermore, feminist organizations tend to be separatist in that they often employ predominantly women (e.g., battered women's shelters, women's health clinics). Often both feminist and collective organizations are unusual in that they tend to be heavily dependent on volunteer participation. These, then, are not the medium-sized and large bureaucracies in the public and for-profit sectors that were the focus of Weber's work and that dominate industrialized countries today. Would these alternatives to bureaucracy survive a transition to larger size and to the demands of a highly competitive marketplace? A few possible exceptions come to mind—the Body Shop International, *Ms.* magazine, NOW—but in each case with the passing of time evidence has emerged to suggest that environmental forces may have led to a reluctant erosion of the commitment to alternative practices.

To summarize, the dynamics of size and the financial pressures of a competitive marketplace create intense pressure on alternative organizational forms either to fail or to abandon their commitments to being different—the "iron cage" of bureaucratic isomorphism that Weber predicted and that institutional theorists have thoroughly documented (e.g., Powell and DiMaggio, 1991: Scott, 1995). Furthermore, the proliferation of the bureaucratic form is based on a support examined by few of us who study and teach organizational behavior, strategy, and business ethics: bureaucracies will continue to rationalize, legitimate, and perpetuate gender inequality—whether they intend to or not—until that time when men carry a full share of home and dependent-care responsibilities. This silence concerning the inseparability of work and family concerns merits deconstruction. Perhaps someday, when a business school student says, "I am interested in learning about family policies," she will not run the risk of being told, "They don't teach that here; try the sociology or psychology department."

3

¿*Predicando la Moral en Calzoncillos?* Feminist Inquiries into Business Ethics

Marta B. Calás and Linda Smircich

Some time ago we, along with Reba Keele of Brigham Young University, wrote a grant proposal to the Ethics and Values Project of the National Science Foundation (NSF) for a conference promoting an analysis of the ethics and values embedded in the written presentation of research by organizational scientists (Smircich, Calás, and Keele, 1988). We observed in our proposal:

> Organizational science research tacitly and explicitly adopts the natural science model of good research. Increasingly textbooks in organizational behavior and organization theory stress the scientific bases of the field. . . . These views go back to Herbert Simon's proclamation in *Administrative Behavior*: "[A]n administrative science, like any science, is concerned purely with factual statements. There is no place for ethical assertions in the body of a science." (Simon, 1947:232)

We also observed:

> Organizational science has proceeded from a position of technical rationality. Research questions considered legitimate are those derived from values ordained as technically relevant to the organization. Thus the organizational science literature focuses on the values, mostly implicit, of rationality, efficiency, and effectiveness of organizational performance. The rhetoric of corporate well-being takes center stage, further fueled by the current meta-rhetoric of loss of world-wide competitiveness, leaving whole areas of social concern unexamined and making it extremely difficult to justify posing critical questions. (Smircich, Calás, and Keele, 1988)

The proposal argued that feminist theory as a form of cultural critique can be applied to an analysis of the epistemological and ethical grounds of organizational science. We hoped to bring into organizational science a form of critical self-reflective discourse that the field lacked.

NSF funded our proposal, and the conference on the relation of feminist theory to ethical and value issues in organization science was held in the fall of 1989. The meetings brought together a group of feminist and management scholars for several days of discussion about how knowledge is constructed. Ed Freeman, who was part of the project, invited us to participate in the Ruffin Lectures. He suggested that we might have some common ground with those of you in the field of business ethics.

But who are we?

We are both professors of organizational studies in a management department of a school of management. We teach courses in organizational behavior and theory at the undergraduate, MBA, and doctoral levels, and one of us (Marta) also teaches courses in behavior in a global economy and in international management. In our teaching and in our scholarship we take a critical and cultural perspective. From this perspective we call attention to the way in which the practices of organizations and their management styles are culturally and historically inherent in certain societies and associated with certain languages. These practices are not logical necessities but represent the outcomes of negotiations and struggles in which the interests of some groups take precedence over those of others, resulting in the social construction of the present. The bilingual title of this chapter signifies part of that cultural struggle for a differential space, which management often pretends does not exist.

In our teaching we avoid following the lead of the majority of texts in management and organizational behavior and theory which show how to manage and organize "better." Rather, we seek to engage students in analysis of the present, part of which involves examining the vocabulary through which management discourse is shaped. For example, instead of discussing motivation theories as approaches to gaining employee compliance with management objectives, we consider how "motivation" came to be a necessary topic to include within a course in organizational behavior in the first place. Is it possible to imagine forms of organizational relationships in which motivation is not a necessary issue?

More recently, our scholarship and teaching have become informed by feminist theories. As a form of cultural analysis, feminist scholarship is concerned with questioning concepts and practices that are taken for granted and with offering alternative ways of seeing/knowing/doing. This approach adds to the general concerns of culture specific considerations of how gender (and its intersections with race, ethnicity, and class) is related to what is valued in a socially constructed reality. At least two distinct issues are at the root of feminist theorizing: male dominance in society (patriarchy) is fully assumed, and a replacement for this form of domination is sought.

Although feminist scholarship subsumes a variety of intellectual positions (e.g., liberal, socialist, radical, poststructuralist), all feminist scholarship focuses on the issue of gender relations. Through gender relations "men" and "women" are created as categories, and their bodies connected to cultural constructs such as organizations. From this perspective, both men and women are "prisoners of gender," although in different ways (Flax, 1987; Scott, 1986).

While feminist theory offers perspectives on such organizational issues as comparable worth, the structuring of organizations on the basis of sex, the glass ceiling, and so on, the feminist critique of epistemology has been most important to us in our cultural perspective on organizations and their management. Feminist discussions of epistemology not only help raise questions about how we think about organizations and their management but they also encourage us to analyze how that thinking is done. Very generally, we would say that feminist theory points to the connections between knowledge and patriarchy.

WHAT KIND OF BUSINESS IS BUSINESS ETHICS?

In order to prepare ourselves for the Ruffin Lecture Series we did some investigating to determine how feminist theory and business ethics might be connected. We spent time reading business ethics textbooks and studying the associated journals. We expected to find "fellow travelers" and to discover in the field of business ethics, not unlike in feminist theories, a discourse of critical force. What we discovered surprised us.

We found that business ethics is "today . . . a mature field" (Hoffman and Moore, 1990) characterized by "an increasingly sophisticated literature" (Beauchamp and Bowie, 1988). The textbooks voice similar aims: to encourage reflection on moral issues in business. They seek to do so by introducing students to ethical concepts and by promoting approaches to moral reasoning. The common textbook model suggests that students first learn the process of moral reasoning and then apply those principles in discussion of case studies from business practice (Furman, 1990; Derry and Green, 1989). The intention appears to be to help students "fashion reasoned arguments and to identify positions in the debate" (Derry and Green, 1989:523).

The books also teach a set of criteria by which moral reasoning can be assessed. For instance, arguments must be logical, the factual evidence must be accurate, relevant, and complete, and moral standards must be consistent (Velasquez, 1988) or involve conceptual clarity, information, rationality, impartiality, coolness, and the use of valid moral principles (Regan's [1984] ideal moral judgment criteria, as cited by Derry and Green, 1989:524). Additionally, another way to assess competing views is to analyze arguments in order to expose the inadequacies of other arguments (Beauchamp, in Beauchamp and Bowie, 1988:15).

We learned that "moral thinking is like other forms of theorizing in

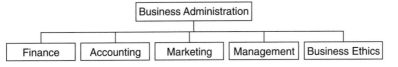

Figure 2a.

that hypotheses must be tested, buried, or modified through experimental thinking" (Beauchamp, in Beauchamp and Bowie, 1988:52). Thus, we found in business ethics a form of scientific method, not unlike that employed in organizational science. Further, we learned that business ethics positions itself alongside other disciplines: "Though moral dilemmas require a balancing of competing claims in untidy circumstances, we can at least be reassured that in the contribution it has to make philosophy is neither inferior nor superior to other forms of reasoning, such as those found in law, economics, and the behavioral sciences" (Beauchamp, in Beauchamp and Bowie, 1988:49).

As with other modern academic disciplines, business ethics claims to offer methods for reasoning that are objective, universal, and gender neutral. The same values held dear by organizational science permeate the enterprise of business ethics. Through these claims we can visualize business ethics positioning in a model such as in Figure 2a.

But as work from feminist theoretical perspectives helps reveal, organizational science, by virtue of the values and procedures it advocates, reproduces a masculine ethos, and so does business ethics. (e.g. Keller, 1985; Gilligan, 1982; Lloyd, 1984). Thus, epistemologically, business ethics, along with organizational science and the other disciplines in the business school curriculum, is patriarchal in orientation and, so far, has excluded what might be called the feminine voice.

On the other hand, within the business school, there is a hierarchy of disciplines, with some areas seen as more important and more powerful than others. Business ethics scholars' claims notwithstanding, in the minds of students these other courses (e.g., accounting, finance) constitute more of the *real* business school. In relation to other areas within the business school, then, business ethics occupies a supplementary or secondary position—subordinated, devalued, and marginalized. Thus, in its institutionalized form, business ethics is feminized. (See Fig. 2b.)

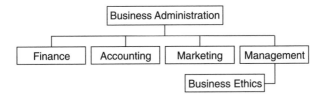

Figure 2b.

These are unsettling observations. Business ethics might be the most important course that business students take, but in its present state business ethics, like organizational studies, is *uni*-vocal and *mono*-logical. The field is based on a conception of philosophy as embodying techniques of clear thinking and, thus, has a tendency to remain uncritical of current or common sense concepts and beliefs (Grimshaw, 1986:33). Business ethics reproduces the standards that are already in place in the business school, but it doesn't do much more.

We believe business ethics could have a different and more important voice as epistemological critique of business disciplines. But first it has to recognize its own patriarchal condition. Feminist analysis can assist in that process by pointing out the ways business ethics is historically and culturally constituted, institutionally based, and limited by its political and rhetorical conventions. Or, said differently, feminist analysis may help business ethics realize, as is suggested in our multivoiced title, that as it stands today it is "*predicando la moral en calzoncillos*"—it is just preaching morality in its underwear*—but that it can do better.

Thus, the question we ask here is, "How can business ethics be remade as more critical discourse under inspirations from feminist theorizing?" To answer this question, our arguments revolve around three feminist epistemological activities: the activities of revising, reflecting, and rewriting. (For a brief discussion of the history of feminist theorizing from which we inferred these three activities, see Calás and Smircich, 1992.) These distinct and complementary activities can provide a strong basis for reexamining any traditional disciplinary body of knowledge, assessing its limitations, and rearticulating its premises with more critical force.

REVISING MORALITY IN ORGANIZATIONS: HOW PATRIARCHY SHOWS UP IN BUSINESS ETHICS

Feminist scholars have been reexamining the production of knowledge in their "home" disciplines. One set of concerns addresses the extent to which the historical underrepresentation of women as scholars skews the choice of research problems and biases theoretical orientations, research designs, and the interpretation of results. Other feminist theorizing examines the problem of "knowing" as an already (male) gendered sphere of action. Thus, historically, feminist theorizing has expressed dual concerns, paraphrasing Sandra Harding (1988), "for the woman question in knowledge" and for "the knowledge question in feminism." The second concern, the knowledge question in feminism, stems

---

*This phrase could be *very loosely* interpreted as "people who live in glass houses should not throw stones."

from the epistemological consequences of the first. Underrepresentation maintains a "silent other" in a network of power relations that defines what is acceptable/unacceptable or voiced/silenced as knowledge. Applying these concerns to the knowledge-making enterprise across disciplinary fields results in a set of tasks for revising disciplinary knowledge (Calás and Smircich, 1992), as follows:

Completing/Correcting the Record.   The first revisionary task implies recovering women's knowledge (or that of other oppressed groups) that has been omitted from dominant theoretical accounts, both as subjects of inquiry and as authors of knowledge. It may imply a reinterpretation or recovery of historical narratives that have been glossed over as time has passed, becoming more exclusionary of the experiences of the silent groups.

Assessing Bias in Current Knowledge.   The second revisionary task implies rereading important ("seminal") works to assess the extent to which misogyny/sexism is part of the mainstream representation of knowledge in the field. It is concerned with assessing the extent to which the concepts with which we produce knowledge are male gendered, and it promotes a reconsideration of the values that guide the interpretation of data.

Making "New" Theorizing.   The third revisionary task implies opening the knowledge narratives of a field to diversity—that is, including different topics of particular concern to women and using different epistemological grounds for judging the adequacy of any theoretical account.

In the next section we will demonstrate how applying these concerns makes the current patriarchal structure of the field of business ethics explicit.

Completing/Correcting the Record in Business Ethics

This section focuses on the impact that recovering omitted knowledge may have on acceptable theoretical accounts within business ethics. As an example we focus on a main theoretical strand of thought that defines moral questioning in this field: teleological theories. Feminist analyses of these theories are extended to include the ways in which these theories have been presented in business ethics.

Utilitarian theory is representative of this strand of thought in most business ethics textbooks. It is discussed as promoting human welfare by "minimizing harms and maximizing benefits against alternative benefits, and harms against alternative harms" (Beauchamp and Bowie, 1988:26). For Beauchamp and Bowie the major criticisms of utilitarian theory are "the problem of quantifying goodness," which is attributed to the original aim of the philosophers who produced the theory, and "the problem of unjust consequences," which stresses, primarily, the harm that is done minorities by the principle that calls for the greatest balance of value for the greatest number.

While we could immediately critique the values embedded in the "neutrality" with which textbooks present the "facts" about utilitarianism, for now we want to show how a feminist completion activity can correct the limits of these traditional accounts. Two commentators serve our purpose: Boralevi (1984; 1987) and Annas (1977). These two authors reexamined documents written by Bentham, Mill, and other utilitarian philosophers, bringing to light less known dimensions of their works. Boralevi's archival search is particularly notable. Having gone back to Bentham's original documents in London, she finds that the philosopher left a very explicit record of his concern for oppressed groups and considered utilitarianism a remedy for the conditions of these groups. In the Foreword to Boralevi's (1984) book, M. W. Cranston writes:

> hitherto his [Bentham's] *Works* have been chiefly known through a notoriously bad collected edition made by a young protégé of his named Bowring—a knight, a general, a Christian . . . but not a utilitarian, not ever a scholar. Moreover, Bowring cut out from what he published anything that might offend Victorian sensibilities akin to his own.
>
> [A] team of scholars is beginning to give us an image of Bentham distinctly unlike that which emerges from what Bowring published. . . . Lea Campos Boralevi's book . . . introduces a Bentham who is not only different from Bowring's Bentham, but different also from the picture of Bentham to be found in the memoirs of John Stuart Mill. . . . Dr. Boralevi demonstrates that this picture is entirely false.
>
> She also shows that some of Bentham's supposedly most vulnerable opinions were not his opinions at all. For example, on the central utilitarian principle of "the greatest happiness of the greatest number," it has been shown that Bentham never believed that the happiness of some could be rightly increased at the expense of the unhappiness of others. The distribution of happiness meant as much to him as the amount of it. . . . A policy which conferred happiness on a million at the expense of conferring suffering on one would not therefore be acceptable to Benthamite utilitarianism. . . . (1984:vii)

Boralevi's investigations, then, present us with a different view of utilitarian philosophy, one that—in Bentham's words—"If there be any difference, it ought to be in favor of the weakest—in favour of the females, who have more wants, fewer means of acquisition, and are less able to make use of the means they have. But the strongest have had all the preference. Why? Because the strongest have made the laws" (cited in Boralevi, 1984:5).

In a later article Boralevi (1987) demonstrates an immediate connection between classical utilitarianism and historical feminism. Not only were the main representatives of each position related to one another (e.g., Mill and Harriet Taylor, William Godwin and Mary Wollstonecraft), they also influenced one another through a contemporary social dialogue that stemmed from Bentham's position. Utilitarians and feminists were wedded in their emphasis on the need for social reform to attain legal, political, and economic justice. Their view of human nature was centered around the notion of human beings as social beings who cannot attain happiness outside mutual interdependence.

A focus of Boralevi's article is utilitarianism's primary concern with legal and political reform. The reform was geared toward accomplishing the utilitarian calculus, but, at the same time, allowed for compensatory discrimination by taking into account existing inequalities. Bentham, for example, was explicit in recognizing that equal consideration for different people or for people in different conditions leads to different treatment because "to treat the 'injured wife and her tyrant' in the same way would only favour the stronger: such an 'apparent equality covers great real inequality'" (Bentham [1838:353] cited in Boralevi, 1987:170).

Now, taking these corrections of the utilitarian record into account, we turn to a business ethics textbook and read:

> Bentham and Mill are hedonists; they believe that only pleasure or happiness . . . can be intrinsically good. . . . Nonetheless, later utilitarian philosophers have argued that other values besides pleasure possess intrinsic worth—for example, friendship, knowledge, courage, health, and beauty. . . . [They] are referred to as pluralistic utilitarians.
>
> In recent philosophy, economics, and psychology, neither the approach of the hedonists nor that of the pluralist has prevailed. Both approaches have seemed relatively useless for purposes of objectively aggregating widely different interests in order to determine maximal value and therefore right action. Another approach is to appeal to individual preferences. . . .
>
> While this preference-based utilitarian approach to value has been viewed by many as superior to its predecessors, it has not proved to be trouble-free as a moral theory. A major theoretical problem arises when individuals have morally unacceptable preferences. For example, a person's strong sexual preference may be to rape young children, or an employment officer may prefer to discriminate against women, yet such preferences are morally intolerable. . . . Utilitarianism based purely on subjective preferences is satisfactory, then, only if a range of acceptable preferences can be formulated. (Beauchamp and Bowie, 1988:27)

Aside from the limitations of using these examples (raping children, discriminating against women) as merely moral dilemmas—since in both cases the behaviors in question are, prima facie, *illegal*—one may notice that any individualistic-based orientation toward utilitarianism violates the premises of classical utilitarianism, whose interest was *social* reform. A different way to understand utilitarianism using the same examples might be to praise its legacy. One might say that due to classical utilitarianism certain activities such as the rape of children and discrimination against women become illegal. As part of our modern intellectual legacy, utilitarianism promoted a generalized moral repugnancy toward such behaviors and led to their eventual regulation because it promoted a view of humans as interdependent social beings whose equal rights must be furthered and protected. At the same time, utilitarianism was explicit in promoting additional protection for those traditionally less powerful in the social, legal, and political arena.

However, it might be premature to consider utilitarian philosophy as only a positive legacy when examining the moral condition of contemporary society. For example, Annas (1977) reassesses Mill's work on the subjection of women and observes that some of Mill's assumptions about men's views of injustice were not only unwarranted during his time but also reflected Mill's understanding of social power.

Mill did not argue clearly for either a reformist approach—based on the equality of women to men—or a radical approach—based on women's differences due to social oppression and neglect. Instead, he mixed the approaches, leaving in intellectual limbo the question of whether only legal reform or a more widespread reform of social institutions was necessary.

Annas observes that in *The Subjection of Women,* "Mill (1970 [1869]) is sure what he is against, but he is not sure whether he is committed to a radical or a reformist approach, and in trying to have it both ways blurs what he is saying" (1977:192). She contrasts this work with an early essay, "The Enfranchisement of Women" (1970), which is more forceful and clearer in its assessment of the need for a radical approach to the subjection of women. This early essay, published under Mill's name, has often been attributed to Harriet Taylor. In any case, Annas argues, Mill's later inconsistent position—reflecting his eagerness to do justice to all sides—was unable to offer an argument that would take into account the imbalance of power between men and women so that social reform could occur.

In summary, feminist revisions of utilitarian philosophy allow us to better understand their contribution to our moral view of contemporary society. These analyses also help us to reassess the strength of utilitarianism regarding power inequalities vis-à-vis more recent, narrow interpretations.

Assessing Bias in Current Knowledge in Business Ethics

In this second task of revision, feminist authors call attention to the misogynistic and patriarchal biases embedded in the principles that underlie all disciplines. This type of revisionary task is already known in business ethics (even if not very well represented in the textbooks) through Gilligan's (1982) questioning of Kohlberg's concepts of moral development. Other such feminist analyses of this sort have criticized Rawls, for his emphasis on abstract individualism, and Kant, who will serve as our example in this section.

Kant's view of the categorical imperative is discussed in business ethics textbooks as representative of deontological theories. More specifically, it is argued that it is a universal principle that "everyone should be treated as a free person equal to everybody else . . . everyone has a moral right to such treatment, and everyone has the correlative duty to treat others in this way" (Velasquez, 1988:90). Furthermore, all persons should be treated in such a way that their existence as free rational beings is promoted. Velasquez claims that a major criticism of this theory is that it is not precise enough to always be useful, and that even if it were consistent in its principles, it can lead to immoral behavior.

Feminist criticisms of the moral principles in Kantianism are more precise. Different from critiques of utilitarianism, where feminist analyses have uncovered stronger feminist dimensions, feminist critiques of Kant's moral philosophy demonstrate the male bias in this approach. The revision of Kant's record has appeared in various forms, but all of them point toward the strong rationalistic approach in Kant, which, at the same time, calls into question the possibility of equal rationality for all members of society.

Blum, for example (1982), indicates that Kant's moral rationalism is male dominated because qualities of character traditionally exalted as male are placed at the center of Kant's scheme. Therefore, this philosophy is the reflection of a male-dominated society and clearly sanctions male superiority. The argument is further explicated by Mendus (1987) and Grimshaw (1986), both of whom go to the philosopher's texts to uncover their biases.

Mendus's assessment of Kant's moral position focuses on his arguments about women's potential for becoming free rational beings. First, a woman may be accorded only the status of passive citizen; she may not, by self-improvement or advancement, aspire to the status of active citizen. Second, a woman has limited potential because of her intrinsic nature, which is exemplified in the marriage contract, in which a woman relinquishes her equality and allows a man to dominate in public life in exchange for her domination in domestic life. A woman must agree to these terms because only through marriage can she gain freedom. This dependent view of women's freedom is justified on the basis of woman's nature, identified with inclination rather than reason.

Mendus's major critique, however, is not of Kant's treatment of women. Rather, her analysis serves to contextualize Kantianism within historical and social parameters. Her critical focus is on the inability of contemporary moral theorists to notice that Kant was simply a narrow-minded bourgeois in eighteenth-century Germany, who even if he was honest was unable to propose anything beyond the social conventions of his time and place. Furthermore, Mendus decries the consequences of uncritically following Kant's philosophy. This lack of criticism helps sustain an individualistic stance toward a morality whose central (patriarchal) tenet is that someone must dominate and someone must give way.

Grimshaw's (1986) argument follows a similar line, but is more explicit about Kant's support for certain virtues as requirements for morally worthy actions. She observes that in "Of the Distinction between the Beautiful and the Sublime in the Interrelations of the Two Sexes" (1960 [1763]) Kant ascribes to men, among others, the following potential characteristics: profundity, abstract speculation, fundamental understanding, reason, universal rules, and capable of principles. For women potential characteristics, among others, are compassion, sensitivity, benevolence, complaisance, particular judgment, and incapable of principles.

One might argue that Kant was merely describing the differences between men and women according to the stereotypes of his time and that he was simply presenting them as complementary. However, the problematic nature of these descriptions appears in Kant's discussion of moral worth *(Groundwork of the Metaphysics of Morals)* (1948[1785]), which can arise only out of duty. For Kant, to act out of duty necessarily implied acting out of principle—something men were capable of but women were not. No other characteristic could define moral worth.

Now, let's go back to business ethics. We notice that the arguments about Kantianism in this discipline do not reflect on the context and assumptions underlying Kant's moral theory. Business ethics criticizes Kant's theory solely on the basis of internal consistency and pragmatics, thus resulting in statements such as:

> What arguments can be given to show, for example, that a corporation's interest in financial gain is more or less important than the health of its neighbors? The answer to this question will determine whether or not a corporation's right to use its property for financial gains should be limited in favor of its neighbors' right not to have their health injured. All that Kant's categorical imperative is meant to tell us is that everyone must have equal moral rights and that everyone must show as much respect for the protected interests of others as he or she wants others to show for his or her own. It does not tell us what interests people have, nor what their relative importance is. (Velasquez, 1988:96)

While Velasquez is attempting to discuss the limits of Kantianism, the question that needs to be asked first is, "Under what premises is this a valid example?" Paradoxically, this example is a moral dilemma *only* if we accept Kantian premises, despite the fact that it is presented as something that Kant's philosophy cannot help solve.

According to the previous discussion, Kant proposed that moral judgments stem from principles, which can be exercised only by active citizens (nonwomen). Active citizens exercise these judgments within the public sphere, which is dominant over the private. Thus, the example of a corporation's right to financial gain versus the right of its neighbors' health makes sense and is legitimate as a moral dilemma only because superiority of moral judgments in the public versus the private domain is implicit. In no other way could the health of any one citizen be proposed as a dilemma in relation to corporate rights.

Moreover, that corporate rights can be argued under the maxim that everyone must have "equal moral rights and that everyone must show as

much respect for the protected interests of others" hinges on a philosophical posture of abstract speculation—a male characteristic in Kantianism. Otherwise it would have been difficult to consider a corporation
as an "equal everyone." Kant's guiding logic of "autonomous selves" is an
abstraction that supports the definition of "corporations" and "neighbors" as equals, and later supports the "responsibility of business" as only
that of any*body* else—no more, and sometimes less. Kantianism, taken
uncritically, positions the corporation on a plane of equality with abstract
individuals. We should underscore that it is irrelevant that Velasquez was
careful to insert the pronouns "she/he" and "his/her" in his argument,
since the whole problem is established, a priori, under Kantian masculinist premises.

Now, if we consider the unprincipled's (according to Kant) characteristics of sensitivity, compassion, benevolence, and particular judgment as
guiding values, it is possible to argue against the logic of this example as
a moral dilemma. For instance, one would hold the health of concrete
selves as a primary right, based on a logic that considers the private
domain as a major value. Under this alternative logic the example would
have been dissolved.

To summarize, feminist analyses that assess biases in current knowledge underscore the patriarchal logic *already embedded* in approaches to
reasoning and knowledge that we take for granted. These analyses also
call into question the exclusion of alternative approaches and make
explicit the historical and social roots of such exclusions.

Making "New" Theory in Business Ethics

The foregoing arguments, then, have brought us to the last feminist revisionary task. This task emphasizes the possibility of alternative epistemologies that will regain the silent voices of knowledge. For example,
our preceding argument about the dissolution of a moral dilemma
under the logic of "the unprincipled" moves us in that direction. The
major issue here is whether an alternative feminist ethic is possible, and
what that might accomplish.

To illustrate our argument we will make the general observation that
business ethics textbooks seem to have a strong preoccupation with providing clear frameworks in which different types of issues can then be
classified and discussed. For example, Hoffman and Moore (1990) open
their text with an ethical framework for application in business, arguing
that they are committed to being *comprehensive, impartial,* and *systemic.*
But what do they mean by this?

Consider, for example, the question of how decisions are made about
what should be included in a business ethics textbook. In Hoffman and
Moore's, where "comprehensiveness" is an explicit commitment, the
only issues pertaining to women within business contexts (women being
at least 50 percent of the population, and the majority in many occupa-

tional groups) are limited to hiring practices and to two cases, DuPont's policy of exclusion and the Procter and Gamble Rely tampon case. (The latter case is presented as a eulogy to corporate social responsibility because P and G *eventually* decided to retire the product from the market, in spite of inconclusive date—that is, there was no strong statistical evidence pointing to the harmful effects of the product because not enough women died.)

We observed that several topics which intersect organizational issues with issues of concern to contemporary women are mostly absent from Hoffman and Moore (as well as from other contemporary business ethics textbook we examined). Among these topics are sexual harassment in the workplace, working families and child care, single mothers and job opportunities, new technologies and reproductive rights, and children as consumers. We also noted that there are other, more general social issues of current concern that are seldom represented. Among them are the relationship between homelessness and unemployment, race and ethnicity concerns pertaining to minority representation in managerial positions and to language requirements in the workplace, animal rights and laboratory testing, and corporate responsibility toward public education.

At still another level, we noticed that some textbooks include sections on economic systems and describe our economic system, capitalism, only in positive terms. Further, these descriptions position the business sector as the centerpiece of U.S. social and economic life. We were surprised, however, to find no examination of the effects of the capitalist system—and its concomitant conception of "the good life"—on major and supposedly nonbusiness areas of society such as military, political, and public information activities. For example, how can this economic system shape policy regarding military intervention in world events? What role does military subcontracting play in our society? What is the effect of PACs on political finances? How does financial strength impact the opportunity to elect some candidates and not others? What might be the consequences of privatizing "public information"? What can happen when "news" programs are turned into profit centers?

We tried to understand the rationale that may have been followed to select certain topics and not others in representing "comprehensiveness" in business ethics. And we concluded that the topics chosen—and the ways these topics were treated—defined the limits of "comprehensiveness." In business ethics "comprehensiveness" seems to stay at an abstract enough level that it is impossible to upset the current business vision of property rights, contractual obligations, and free market activities.

If "comprehensiveness" has certain limits, it isn't farfetched, then, to question what is meant by "impartiality" in these textbooks. Hoffman and Moore (1990) are explicit in this claim, so we looked at their book first. They base their impartial stance on the fact that they offer points and counterpoints for different issues. However, there is no feminist ethics standpoint represented here, even though the Kohlberg/Gilligan controversy, for example, would have been an excellent area for a point-counterpoint presentation.

We noticed also that Hoffman and Moore, as well as others, have considered the role of the multinational organization as a subject of interest for business ethics, particularly regarding South Africa and the third world. On the other hand, opinions about these issues are expressed from the U.S. or Western point of view. Third world citizens do not seem to have a say in these discussions; and women's and children's exploitation in Southeast Asia and Mexican-American border plants is seldom mentioned in the texts (but see Russell, 1988, for an exception). What if not only the arguments but also the topics selected for inclusion were different when observed from the "local" point of view?

Thus, to assume that these textbooks are impartial may lead us to overlook the fact that "impartiality" is just one rhetorical device among others. For example, we may be led to overlook the fact that often these books present "whistle blowing" as a risky act on the part of an employee without questioning the unequal power bases in the organization that make it risky. We may also not see that some cases which purport to emphasize the importance of statistical evidence to support the existence of discriminatory practices end up supporting the opposite position because the statistical "evidence" cited is partial and/or dated. All of this makes us ask, "Impartiality in business ethics, from whose point of view?"

Finally, we wanted to understand what is meant by "systematic." According to Hoffman and Moore (1990), it seems to mean going from the general, abstract, and theoretical principles to the particular, concrete, and specific aspects of issues and cases. We find that "systematic" is primarily defined as "relating to or consisting of a system" (*Merriam Webster's Collegiate Dictionary*, 1988:1199). We look under "system" and find that it is defined as "a regularly interacting and interdependent group of items forming a unified whole." We think, then, that we finally understand what is meant by "comprehensive" and "impartial" under the premises of being "systematic." The implication must be that we cannot discuss issues that make the "unified whole" fall apart. We must circumscribe a logic in which only certain questions can be asked, only certain information is relevant, and only certain people can participate.

Unfortunately, nowhere do the textbook authors tell us what moral theory informed their selection of "ethical systems." What makes it possible, for example, to present the moral philosophies of Kant, utilitarianism, Rawls, Nozick, and Kolhberg while ignoring the positions of Dewey, Russell, Sartre, and MacIntyre or Chodorow, Gilligan, and Harding on the question of ethics in philosophy?

And that brings the issue home. Where are *we* standing to make the arguments that we are making here? We must confess that we are neither "systematic" nor "impartial" nor "comprehensive." Moreover, following Baier (1985) and Walker (1989), we must confess our suspicion of any moral theory if by that is meant "a fairly systematic account of a fairly large area of morality, with a keystone supporting all the rest" (Baier, 1985:55). Paradoxically, we claim to be arguing from the "epistemological grounds" of a feminist ethos.

Although "feminist ethic(s)" may be better represented by the imagery of "always in the making," we might be able to articulate here some dimensions of ethical discourse from feminist positions. For example, Walker defines feminist ethics as

> one which clarifies the moral legitimacy and necessity of the kinds of social, political, and personal changes that feminism demands in order to end male domination, or perhaps to end domination generally. Another conception of feminist ethics is that of one in which the moral perceptions, self-images, and senses of moral value and responsibility of women have been represented or restored. (1989:15)

In another attempt to define feminist ethics, Andolsen, Gudorf, and Pellauer (1987) state that

> feminist ethics is rooted in this new effort by women to name our own experiences in the public world. (xiv)

> The process of turning private troubles into public issues involves many moral judgments about our society . . . and when we make such judgments, they are not abstract statements. They are based upon sensitivity to the stories of women's lives. . . . Furthermore, telling our stories to each other and making judgments about injustice and justice leads women into *action* . . . a whole host of new organizations and institutions which have transformed the social landscape. . . . Sharing our experiences, naming the injustices in our lives, we imagined a new future, one in which society respects the human worth of women and promotes our well-being. . . . (xvii)

Aside from the social change implied in these accounts, moral discourses in the field of feminism often argue for moral epistemologies that are interactive, including elements of discovery, expression, interpretation, and adjustment between persons, rather than being theoretical instruments for impersonal decisions (e.g., Walker 1989; Andersen, 1987; Benhabib, 1987). More specifically, feminist moral epistemologies are likely to consider moral judgments and moral understanding as grounded in actual contexts of particular others (e.g., Held, 1987; Murdoch, 1970) rather than in general cases of abstract others as is typical in other moral philosophies. Although the most common understandings about feminist ethics have been those of an "ethic of care" (e.g., Tronto, 1987; Gilligan, 1982) and of "maternal ethics" (e.g., Chodorow, 1978; Rich, 1977), these have been amply criticized in their attempts to provide a "positive account" of what may be only particular experiences of a few women or a group of women (e.g., Kittay and Meyers, 1987; Grimshaw, 1986).

However, one should not confuse the notion of contextual judgments with individualistic premises. Feminist ethics is seldom individualistic. The conditions of oppression and deprivation are located in social structures, which have been culturally and historically constituted. Thus, feminist moral discourses are often strong critiques of other moral discourses that promote the fiction of autonomous moral agents. This fiction, they argue, disguises the power relations that maintain the structures of oppression in place (e.g., Benhabib, 1987; Baier, 1985).

For example, Walker (1989) has articulated a feminist moral epistemology that is based in *moral understanding* instead of *moral knowledge.* This alternative promotes the interdependence of attention, contextual and narrative appreciation, and communication in the event of moral deliberation. It then locates these elements in contrast with the universalist/impersonalist tradition, which pursues a scientifically complete and systematically reflective form in morals. Walker argues that when we contrast one with the other it is possible to notice that the claims of the universalistic/impersonalistic view—that the adequacy of moral understanding increases as this understanding approaches systematic generality—is just the opposite. That is, from the alternative epistemological position we see that the adequacy of moral understanding *decreases* as its form approaches generality through abstraction.

What makes this critique possible is not an alternative, shadow image parallel to the impersonalistic view but "instead a point of departure for a variety of different problematics, investigations, focal concerns, and genres of writing and teaching about ethics" (Walker, 1989:20).

In these arguments, then, other issues come to the fore because in most cases feminist ethics is presented not just as an academic genre circumscribed by an institutional tradition but rather as a form of social action, ongoing and always incomplete, that cuts across disciplines, activities, and institutional limits. For example:

> Feminist modes of social analysis require us to look beyond the ordinary limits of the fields of ethics (narrowly construed) and beyond the disciplinary boundaries of the usual university curriculum. Sexism works as a whole; we cannot accept disciplinary lines which force us to see it only in narrow fragments. . . .
>
> Furthermore, we cannot accept rifts between knowing and doing or among separated areas of life. . . . In ethics, this means that we cannot accept artificial dichotomies between "personal ethics" and "social ethics" or "public ethics." (Andolsen, Gudorf, and Pellauer, 1987:xx)

With these commentaries we have reached the limits of the epistemological activity of revising. We are now entering the realm of another activity—reflecting. Reflecting allows us to argue against certain logics embedded in business ethics textbooks, permitting them to make, with impunity, statements like the following:

> Those who study the facts of cases invariably want more facts. They see a solution as dependent on knowing more than is known about what transpired. If

additional data can be discovered, they think, the problems can be handled and the dilemmas disentangled. A related temptation is to doctor the known facts, thus presenting a hypothetical or new case, rather than an actual case. Both the temptation to put off decisions by searching for more facts and the use of hypothetical facts can have a place in case study, but generally these maneuvers should be avoided. Cases are often interesting because only limited information is known or can be known. One is called on to treat the problem under these real-life conditions of scarcity of information. Professional business works under such conditions day in and day out. There is every reason to want to understand that context as it is, and not merely as it might be in some possible world. (Beauchamp and Bowie, 1988:52–53)

In this passage we hear echoes of Gilligan's (1982) "morally developed" Jake, who immediately knew that Heinz should steal the drug for his gravely ill wife. One more time, the "different voice" of Amy—who wanted to extend the case and obtain more information before choosing between two morally undesirable positions—is silenced due to her "moral underdevelopment."

REFLECTIONS: LOOKING BACK AT "MORALITY IN ORGANIZATIONS"

Our revisionary activities on business ethics textbooks have left us with a few impressions. We do not claim that one can arrive at these impressions only through a feminist critique, but the latter is certainly one way. Our impressions are as follows:

1. Most business ethics textbooks are strong on rational/analytic viewpoints. Whereas they claim to offer only guidelines for a process of moral reasoning, they offer clear normative approaches by excluding alternative and critical philosophical viewpoints and critiques of the rational/analytic tradition. There is a monologic embedded in business ethics.
2. The discursive approaches in these texts claim to be based on ethical issues, but they often fluctuate between legal and moral arguments. In general, legal arguments are used to sustain corporate rights and minimize employee claims; moral arguments are employed to question the legal grounds of corporate obligations. Such discourse often rationalizes, and the tone is one of apology for the managerial viewpoint.
3. The ethical posture supporting this discourse is centered around an assumption of equal interests—that is, individuals' self-interest—while avoiding a recognition of power inequalities. Most situations are presented as individual moral dilemmas to be solved by individual moral agents. At the same time, social, historical, and contextual conditions, which may impede some forms of institutional action and foster others, are downplayed.

4. As each text locates itself in a "growing field"—promoted as very important for the health of organizations—we notice the familiarity of the discourse. There is, indeed, a "market value" discourse attached to this "new, and differentiated product" called business ethics. Each volume is a product that attests to the power of our free-market practices.
5. Business ethics discourse is, therefore, a stronghold of the business sector status quo in our society.

This view of the field is perhaps very negative, and we wish it weren't so. Still, we believe it is important to reflect on the situation we have described, even if it might be pure speculation. We want to move out of our analysis of textbooks and ask, "What institutional conditions promote this kind of discourse?" Or, "How is it possible that business ethics—with its mantle of 'business conscience'—lacks a critical edge?"

Feminist theorizing helps us approach these questions because its reflective enterprise, which examines the institutional conditions that promote or block certain discursive and disciplinary practices, has become an important part of feminist epistemology. Even though the content of feminist knowledge has captured a great deal of attention in academic circles and publications, we need to ask, "What are the consequences of creating knowledge within the structures of the academy?" Thus, as part of feminist epistemology there is also the emerging reflexivity of a sociology of knowledge (Morawski, 1988).

Bringing feminism into the traditional curriculum has thus meant, at the same time, exposing the invisible paradigms that rule what is taught, how it is taught, and the relation of the "what" and "how" of teaching to the ideologies of dominant groups in society (e.g., Furman, 1990; Andersen, 1987; Reinharz, 1985; Schuster and Van Dyne, 1985). Similarly, the social construction of science has been explicitly addressed in feminist writings. Some feminist theorists have tried to promote images of scientific work as integration of hand, brain, and heart (Rose, 1983) or spinning and quiltmaking (Rose, 1988) or craft-structured inquiry (Harding, 1987) or nonhierarchical science (Bleier, 1984), but these ideas have had little impact. As many people now recognize, difficulties in changing the scientific discourse cannot be understood without addressing the prestige of the scientific enterprise in the university and society, and the related emphasis on "being scientific," which seems required of many disciplines outside the natural sciences (e.g., Stacey and Thorne, 1985).

Thus, is it even possible to come out of this paradox? Isn't "doing knowledge" part and parcel of the reproduction of patriarchal conditions of power/knowledge embedded in the "scientific enterprise" (e.g., Diamond and Quinby, 1988)? Embracing feminist revisions also means, then, embracing a reflexivity that constantly assesses the relation between "knowledge" and the "ways of doing knowledge." The assessment evaluates approaches to knowledge as they reproduce or change power relations and patriarchal models.

A good example of feminist writings that focus on the relation between "doing" and "saying" in moral knowledge making is, again, Margaret Urbin Walker (1989). After discussing how institutional arrangements and certain dominant approaches to moral knowledge are connected, she reminds us that they "may project a sort of 'moral colonialism' (the 'subjects' of my moral decisions disappear behind uniform 'policies' I must impartially 'apply') precisely because they were forged historically with an eye to actual colonization—industrial or imperial" (1989:23). Walker then proposes another kind of moral epistemology, one that encompasses reflexivity over specific conditions in the production of moral philosophy. It

> reminds us that styles of moral thinking are not primarily philosophical brainteasers, data begging for the maximally elegant theoretical construction, but are ways of answering to *other people* in terms of some responsibilities that are commonly recognized or recognizable in some communities. Philosophical representations of these styles will both reflect and reinforce the relations of authority, power, and responsibility they encode. Hence, for moral philosophy to be sincerely reflective, it must attend focally to questions heretofore considered "philosophically" inappropriate: questions about the rhetoric and politics of ethics. (1989:23)

Following Walker's advice, we focus on some concrete representations of business ethics as they have become institutionalized in the past several years. Two issues are important indicators of the rhetoric and politics of business ethics—first, the way the current state of business ethics is represented as the product of *progress*; and, second, the way this new business ethics is clearly differentiated from any prior attempt at the same. For example, Karen Paul (1987) describes the evolution of the field and creates a date of inception. She cites an article by Duddy (1945) in the *Journal of Business*, which "appears strangely prescient. He pointed out that, for businessmen, the exercise of individual rights brings about corresponding obligations to the society that guarantees these rights" (Paul, 1987:7). Paul goes on to trace the development of the field since that time by focusing on issues that gained centrality in the following decades, particularly from the time of Ford and Carnegie Foundation reports that evaluated the state of business schools in 1959.

This recent "memory" of the field seems curious to us. Paul's focus seems to be on the institutionalization and legitimation of business ethics in the business curriculum and in the academy or, said differently, on the professionalization of business ethics. Her narrative also lets us know that topical interests have changed with changing ideologies in the past decades.

As Paul recounts, during the 1960s popular discontent with business institutions grew because of the obstinacy of business when faced with challenges from the civil rights movement, because of the complacency of business with regard to its involvement with the Vietnam war, and

because of the insensitivity of business to the concerns of environmental-
ists, women, and consumers. University courses were then developed that
focused on socioethical issues, with several institutional contingents coop-
erating in the effort, including the American Assembly of Collegiate
Schools of Business (AACSB) and the Academy of Management. Paul's
story then changes pace. We don't know what happened to the concerns
of the sixties as they vanished inside the institutional story. Were they
taken care of? We are not told. The story proceeds to discuss institutional
matters into the 1980s and describes the encounters between philosophy-
oriented and management-oriented sides of the discipline, facilitated by
scheduling meetings of the Society for Business Ethics just prior to the
Academy of Management meetings, beginning in 1986.

After underscoring how strikingly different are the philosophical and
managerial approaches to business ethics—the first one rigorous, theoretical, logical, and abstract; the second practical and concrete—Paul
makes us notice that "given the strong differences in intellectual traditions, analytic modes, and discipline styles and cultures, the extent of
rapprochement occurring between the two groups in recent years is rather
significant" (1987:15). And we agree, significant, yes, but not surprising.
In the next two pages, under the topic of the changing climate of business environment which ends the article, Paul tells us that

> the past two years have brought about deregulation in many key areas of the
> economy. We now have a celebration of the potential of private enterprise, act-
> ing unfettered by excessive federal regulation, to produce the economic
> resources that permit increased opportunities for personal achievement and
> economic growth.
>
> In the field of business environment, the mood has also shifted, looking
> with more sympathy at the problems of the private sector in the past decade.
> During the earlier years, there was an inclination to assume the economic via-
> bility of business, and the central issues of the field tended to revolve around
> questions of legitimacy and justice. Now more emphasis is placed on the per-
> formance of business in an increasingly competitive world economy. . . .
>
> During the early 1970s, abundance and just distribution were seen as
> critical issues in the study of the U.S. economic system and the social responsi-
> bility of business. Just distribution remains a concern, now on a global scale,
> but the assumptions of continued abundance have been shattered by a decade
> of economic uncertainty. New ideas from the neoconservative philosophers
> have strongly challenged the liberal tradition that has dominated in the acad-
> eme, even in business schools, for the past five decades. The appeal of the
> quasi-socialist systems of the Scandinavian nations has been replaced by the
> allure of the successful Japanese system. . . . (1987:16–17)

After reading this paragraph we can understand how the significant *rapprochement* between the philosophical and the managerial sides of business
ethics has occurred. It seems to have been the product of an exchange
between neoconservative discourse and increased opportunities for personal achievement and economic growth. We also understand that it will

be impossible to address the still unresolved issues of the sixties with these discourses.

This understanding is reinforced by reading "Ethics and Values in Management Thought" by Bremer, Logan, and Wokutch (1987). The authors explain that business ethics comprises a micro and a macro dimension. The microethical dimension, on the one hand, presupposes the existence and fundamental goodness of the present business system and fits well in the typical business school culture. The macroethical dimension, on the other hand, questions the desirability of particular economic arrangements and entertains the possibility of radical change (Bremer, Logan, and Wokutch, 1987:78). The authors acknowledge that in the United States the microethical aspects dominate, with the macroethical side seldom considered.

The authors recommend, however, paying more attention to macroethics because this approach is alive and well in Europe, Latin America, and other centers of academic thought and theory. As they see it, the topics touched upon by macroethics become vital for business courses as international business grows in importance. Yet, the possibility of a discourse that addresses the national and unresolved issues of the sixties seems to be placed out of bounds through an institutional decree that juxtaposes "macroethics" and "international."

In summary, in observing the institutional conditions in which discourses of business ethics seem to have recently proliferated, we notice that while they have become professionalized as a separate and legitimate field, they have also become narrower and more consistent with the dominant business discourses and interests. Paradoxically, contemporary business ethics seems to be a practical and concrete result of the need of the business field in general to be seen as rigorous, logical, theoretical, and abstract—that is, a marriage of convenience.

In the meantime, we regret that this recently invented "memory" of the field has chosen to forget that business ethics has been a concern of colleges and universities at least since the turn of the century. At that point the first college courses on the subject were instituted (School of Commerce, New York University, 1913), books were written, and lectures delivered (e.g., the Barbara Weinstock Lectures on the morals of trade, University of California, Berkeley, were initiated in 1904), and these activities have continued ever since (e.g., Christian, 1970).

The new "memory" ignores that throughout these decades there was a real concern on the part of businesspeople and business academics to convince society that business and ethics can go together. For example, John Graham Brooks in his 1909 Weinstock Lecture, "The Conflict between Private Monopoly and Good Citizenship," asserted that individualism and competition have resulted in privileged monopoly, suggesting that regulation was needed. He praised President Theodore Roosevelt for his policy of conservation of resources, above private and corporate interests, for the future and for the whole people. Recall also that Roosevelt's policy on conservation of resources was used by F. W. Taylor to legitimate his arguments in *Principles of Scientific Management* (1911).

It seems to us that suppressing the pre-World War II years in business ethics as prehistoric serves no other purpose than to make us forget that during all these years the business field had to demonstrate to society that it was not above ethical considerations. The burden of proof was on business to demonstrate that it could actually promote and provide the social good, as Follett (1925), Barnard (1938), and even *Fortune* (1935) illustrate so well.

Not until after World War II was there any intention to separate the "knowledge" and "values" sides of business, as it appeared then in Simon's (1947) support for logical positivism and further promoted by the Ford and Carnegie Foundation reports. Thus, what we see now in current business ethics is the reproduction—under the guise of moral reasoning—of the patriarchal scientific stance so much decried by feminism because it excludes from the process perhaps the most important questions:

> what actual community of moral responsibility does this representation of moral thinking purport to represent? Who does it actually represent? What communicative strategies does it support? Who will be in a position (concretely, socially) to deploy these strategies? Who is in a position to transmit and enforce the rules which constrain them? In what forms of activity or endeavor will they have (or fail to have) an application, and who is served by these activities? (Walker, 1989:24)

In conclusion, the consequences of feminist reflexivity over epistemological narratives in business ethics would also imply political engagement over the limits of moral knowledge making. It would imply the necessity of examining why dominant epistemologies have become embedded in certain institutional arrangements and preferred rhetorical modes and why they have appeared under particular historical conditions. It would also imply questioning the interests these epistemolgies have been serving under the guise of knowledge.

The ethical questions we need to ask first are not about employer/employee, organization/environment, minority/majority, or rights/obligations, as if they were external to our texts and our academic institutional arrangements. Rather, we need to ask first, "What are the dichotomies that have come to delimit the current texts of business ethics?"

REWRITING "BUSINESS ETHICS"

We must confess at this point that all our prior writing of this essay was in preparation for this section. We were preparing the space for deconstructing "business ethics."

The way we proceeded in the previous sections followed the deconstructive moves of identifying a binary opposition (*presence* of patriarchal discourse/*absence* of feminist critique) and reversing it, making the feminist critique very central to our text. In this sense we were trying to show that the patriarchal discourse was not sustained by its essential "truthfulness" but, instead, by what it ignored or tried to suppress.

Our job is not finished, however. If we leave the text now, we could be accused of a similar essentialism. On what basis are we claiming the "rightfulness" of a feminist critique? What makes our story any better? A deconstructive approach must not only reverse the opposition, it must also displace it.

In order to do this our narrative should change in a way that locates business ethics and some feminist criticism in the same discursive space. In so doing we hope to illustrate how they share and sustain a current field of relationships: academic disciplines in late capitalism in the United States.

We argued that a particular type of discourse (rational/analytic, conservative, supportive of the business status quo, individualistic) pervades business ethics. We argued at the same time that feminist epistemologies could "correct" these kinds of discourses. We said that the current state of business ethics has a mode of institutional existence that sustains and legitimates its discourse. And we proposed that feminist reflections on institutional arrangements and histories can help us understand that the institutionalized discourse of business ethics was not "truth" but a "cozy arrangement."

However, we can also say now that both business ethics and feminist criticism have only "academic voices"; they share the space of the university by doing no more than debating academic issues—"moral reasoning" notwithstanding. Meanwhile, the poor have become poorer and the rich richer, underemployment is rising, discrimination is widespread, children enroll in the military because they need tuition money, homelessness is on the increase, we have a hole in the ozone layer and don't even know why.

Many of our classrooms have become a continuation of our television sets, video games, and spreadsheets. They are information centers that are expected to provide either facts or entertainment (and better both); they are not the real world. As teachers, we worry that we may be too passionate in our opinions. We don't want to be "ideological"; we try to provide pros and cons and to sound neutral. Our writings are safe, we want to be published, we need to get tenure.

These are the very material conditions in which we academics find ourselves today: a place in which much scholarly discourse has become irrelevant, incapable of contributing to a debate toward "a good society."

Some people may say that the cycle is only temporary, but many more suspect that it is perhaps the last cycle of a downward spiral: the end of modernity. It is a spiral that we did not start but that we have all helped to sustain while riding on it. In general, we have all contributed to maintaining the Enlightenment's illusion of progress: that the social sciences, the humanities, and the natural sciences, in their separate spheres, were capable of creating justice, beauty, knowledge, and freedom. In the process we have also contributed to the differences on which all these positive terms were to be constructed: injustice, ugliness, ignorance, and slavery.

Although we believe that these conditions are the end of the line for modernity, we observe that the current discourse of business ethics, as well as some oppositional feminist discourse, is holding onto modernity in a nostalgic attempt to either "save the Enlightenment project" or "critique the Enlightenment project" without even noticing that "the Enlightenment project" is not there anymore.

Our legacy of that project is a society involved in a politics of Knowledge. "Knowing," "expert opinion," "information" seem to be primary goods. For example, business ethics topics like "comparable worth," "affirmative action," "pollution," and "whistle-blowing" qualify as areas that pose moral dilemmas primarily because they are debatable on an assumption of possible knowledge. Deciding whether particular jobs are worth the same hinges on the possibility of *knowing whether they require the same knowledge.* The fairness/unfairness of affirmative action is debated on grounds of *merit due to more/less knowledge.* Arguments centering around pollution are sustained on the possibility of *knowing how to control it better/cheaper.* The whistle-blowing argument revolves around *control of information.* But what if knowledge didn't matter? What if it weren't possible?

If we think of knowledge (with a small "k") as cultural and historically located, we can perhaps understand that we debate, for instance, comparable worth because we accept a theoretical and historical construct—the Market—as transcendental knowledge. The Market does not exist now, and it probably never did. Only because we take for granted the Market's existence do we need to rationalize and measure jobs. But what if we question whether there is a such a thing as the Market? Unfortunately, that is not how we, contemporary academics in the United States, proceed.

Whereas business ethics presents a measured discourse of neutrality and the pros and cons centering around the Market, proceeding as if it were sure of the Market's existence, the rest of us in the business schools keep ourselves busy teaching and researching ways to strengthen Market institutions, and the economists keep themselves busy building models and theorizing about the Market. Together with the rest of our society, we are all now helping to export our magical invention to our newly discovered friends in the East. After all, we have Knowledge.

What if in the meantime we created a debate around the noxiants of Knowledge? What if Knowledge is bad for you? This is a debate that can be initiated only in the academic space. It all started in that space, and it is here where the norms of "neutrality," "objectivity," and the "authority of science" should start to be questioned. While most of us do not have the authority to elucidate in our classrooms, for example, whether unemployment is right or wrong, we certainly have the authority to show

how the type of economic system and the market we support relies on unemployment as a matter of course. We may then be able to trace how the notion that we have "the right" to "downsize" or to close a plant, came to be part of our "common knowledge." We may also be able to warn against policies that transcend time, culture, and region in the name of Knowledge.

Succinctly, we are arguing here that our forms of doing knowledge, with their uncritical separation and specialization, prevent each of us from doing anything about a better society while at the same time strengthening, through all of us, the conditions that maintain the power of an illusory status quo. What would happen if we did knowledge differently?

We think that the space of "difference" is where ethics, management/organizational theory, and feminist theory can reconstitute themselves together, if temporarily, in a more critical form. Postmodern feminist theorizing has already moved in this direction. For example, some postmodern feminist discourse has renounced the "women's voices" perspectives—often criticized as essentialist—by replacing the unitary notions of "woman" and "feminine gender identity" with plural conceptions of social identity that treat gender as one relevant strand among others (e.g., Fraser and Nicholson, 1990).

Kathy Ferguson's *The Feminist Case Against Bureaucracy* (1984) is a good example of a feminist critique of organizational theory—inspired by Foucault's poststructuralism—that uses "the feminine" as a deconstructive strategy rather than as an essential characteristic of women. What comes to the fore in Ferguson's work, as well as in Joanne Martin's (1990) feminist critique of bureaucracy, is the multiple patterns of subordination/domination that sustain the apparent neutrality and unity of a traditional organizational form. Under these premises it doesn't make sense for business ethics to argue cases like the "Challenger" disaster and the B.F. Goodrich brake pads as merely moral dilemmas. Rather, together we should reflect on issues such as, What kinds of organizations our society sustains and for what purposes? With what consequences? And how do we contribute to it?

Other feminist postmodernist works have challenged the narrowness in the construction of Knowledge by arguing for a multitude of viewpoints—rather than alternatives—in any knowledge claim, even if the multiple points of view are contradictory (e.g., Nicholson, 1990). But instead of leaving the situation as unresolvable, or as an intellectual exercise in impartiality, these works proceed to demonstrate the partially ambiguous and ambivalent grounds under which many Knowledge claims are adjudicated. On what basis are claims adjudicated? What strategies make adjudication possible?

For example, Joan Scott (1988) demonstrates how conceptualizing equality and difference as alternatives for women's claims obscures the fact that each already contains the other. She shows how the construction of the 1979 Sears sex discrimination case, adjudicated in favor of Sears, was based on opposing these two views rather than on reconstructing the argument around the perfectly feasible case of equality *and* difference. What won the case for Sears (ironically, under that favored feminist claim of "difference") was the oppositional discursive strategy of equality/difference, acceptable in our culture and supported by many women. Rhetoric matters because rhetorical strategies sustain and are sustained by other dominant social practices. Rhetoric can gloss over contradiction, partiality, and injustice under the mantle of Knowledge. Would we have too many doubts about what is right and what is wrong in the "Challenger" and the B.F. Goodrich cases if we didn't have a rhetoric that constructs them as moral dilemmas and that requires rational arguments?

One way or another feminist poststructuralists, together with other postmodernist writers, have come to realize the connection between Knowledge and the places and ways in which Knowledge gets done. One way or another they have come to locate many of the noxiants of Knowledge in the micropractices of textual construction and have engaged in deconstructive activities. And it is in the deconstructive space of the text where we think feminism, business ethics, and organizational/management theory must engage each other.

Two observations need to be made at this point. First, deconstruction has often been criticized for "having only to do with texts," but "text" here means discursive strategies and other signifying practices around which meaning—through difference—is constructed not only in the written text but in our society. Second, we focus here on the written text because that is the ultimate site of Knowledge in the academic community. The ways in which we structure and construct texts signify Knowledge. How we write and what we write matters.

With that in mind, we illustrate our approach to deconstruction with a segment taken from a business ethics textbook—which is the rhetoric that students would read and take as Knowledge. This activity—this "rewriting"—*is* a postmodern political engagement. It is through this form of analytics—which exposes how the textual structure performs—that we could turn our classrooms into an active site of knowledge for "a good society," over and over again.

For purposes of illustration we have chosen the introduction to a chapter on corporate responsibility:

> Most discussions of business ethics begin with horror stories of business wrongdoing: Company T has polluted the environment, Company U has engaged in fraudulent Eurobond trading, Company V has been found guilty of overcharging the public for gasoline, Company W has been kiting checks, and Company X is charged with sex discrimination. The *Wall Street Journal* will often carry over 100 stories a month of this sort, from which we might infer that there is a basic pattern of questionable practices in business.
>
> However, as business persons constantly point out, many companies also behave in ways that are normally commendable. In their best seller *In Search of Excellence*, Thomas Peters and Robert H. Waterman argue that, among other

things, many of the most successful companies remain close to their customers and consider their employees their most important product. For example, Frito Lay provides a level of customer service that in the short run cannot be justified on economic grounds: "It (Frito-Lay) will expend several hundreds of dollars sending a truck to re-stock a store with a couple of $30 cartons of potato chips. . . . The institution is filled with tales of salesmen braving extraordinary weather to deliver a box of potato chips or to help a store clean up after a hurricane or an accident." Hewlett-Packard does not fire employees in recessionary or hard times; everyone shares the pain by taking a pay cut, occasionally with "free" days off to cushion the blow. The Dana Corporation did away with time clocks. At Delta Airlines a committee of flight attendants chooses the uniforms. At IBM, the company philosophy is respect for the individual. This list of commendable policies adopted by corporations could be almost endlessly expanded. The horror stories together with the honor-roll stories suggest a very mixed picture of business living up to their responsibilities.

In the first section of this chapter the articles explore questions of the nature of corporate responsibility and the extent to which corporations can be held responsible. The second section focuses on the debate over duties, if any, that corporations have to various persons or groups. (Beauchamp and Bowie, 1988:56)

We want to make it clear that we chose to deconstruct this paragraph out of convenience because it was short but centrally located as the introduction to a chapter. We could have taken other paragraphs from any of the business ethics textbooks and done the same. We are not pointing to what any particular authors have done but to the intertextual conditions that make *meaningful* and *understandable* our organizational texts as Knowledge. The paragraph just quoted is perfectly acceptable within our disciplines. And that is precisely our point. Why? And with what consequences?

First, we will separate the text into two columns and show how oppositional constitution makes the text meaningful (see opposite page):

Now, we can easily see that the two columns are not really oppositional. Any company could have done, at the same time, the activities described in both columns. In fact, we can claim that the record is not mixed but very negative. Can we accept as a positive that salesmen have to brave the weather for two $30 cartons of potato chips? That they clean up stores? That employees take pay cuts and days off without pay in exchange for doing away with time clocks and choosing their uniforms, while companies write in their philosophical statements that they have respect for the abstract "individual"? Can we see these as "endless commendable policies" (another abstraction) while a very concrete number (over 100 companies a month) are charged with environmental pollution, fraudulent bond trading, gasoline overcharges, check kiting, and sexual discrimination? And can we accept that the impact for society of the positive versus the negative column balances out? We believe that our students would do more than just buy into the rhetoric of "a mixed record." They are likely to infer that the balance is positive and that corporations should be left alone to do the right thing.

Corporate Responsibility

Positive: Honor Roll Published in *In Search of Excellence* Peters and Waterman	Negative: Horror Stories Published in *The Wall Street Journal* Journalism
Frito Lay • Spent several hundred dollars for 2 $30 cartons of potato chips • Salesmen brave weather to deliver potato chips • Salesmen help store cleanup	Company T • Polluted the environment
Hewlett-Packard • Does not fire employees • Employees take pay cuts • Employees take "free" days	Company U • Engaged in fraudulent Eurobond Trading
Dana Corporation • Did away with time clocks	Company V • Found guilty of overcharging the public for gasoline
Delta Airlines • Flight attendants choose uniforms	Company W • Has been kiting checks
IBM • Company philosophy is respect for individual	Company X • Charged with sex discrimination
Commendable policies: endless	Horror stories: over 100 a month

Suggests: very mixed picture
Can corporations be held responsible?
Do corporations have any duties to various persons or groups?

Why? Because the humanistic rhetoric of our organizational behavior courses, reinforced by the individualistic and psychologizing discourses of our society, is very well represented in the business ethics rhetoric. In our organizational behavior and theory courses we have told students that a good manager is a good person who motivates employees by helping them understand that serving the client is good for them and for the business: an achievement-oriented salesman will go out there and do it right on his own. Good companies—our knowledge rhetoric continues—do as the Japanese do, do not fire or lay off (but furloughs are O.K.; somebody has to pay); time clocks are a relic of Taylor's era, and we have better motivational techniques, such as "participation" in decision making (e.g., choosing one's uniforms through committee work). And whatever we do, we must remember that individual differences matter, so remind the students that you respect that.

Thus, the positive side has been personalized, or made *present.* The good companies have names, they are easy to remember, and so are their good deeds; they could be part of a manager's everyday life. Plus the stories come from a reliable source—a well-known book, a best seller, that proclaims to know excellence; and a well-known author and speaker who is paid bundles for his advice. Moreover, honor roll is positive and real in a school context.

The negative side is effaced, or made *absent*. Aside from describing very elusive, abstract ideas that are not every manager's daily life—pollution, fraud, overcharging, kiting, sexual discrimination—the culprits don't have names. Who are companies T, U, V, W, and X? The information is journalistic, already a questionable source since the images of journalism and sensationalism have often intersected in our society. Journalistic style has also been counterposed (as less factual) to scientific writing: the former associated with rigorous theory testing, let-the-facts-speak-for-themselves, universalizable, durable; the latter suggesting the impressionistic, the subjective, the easily dated. And there is no authorship, only the newspaper's name. You can throw a newspaper away—it is inconsequential. Besides, horror stories are fiction—they happen only in the movies.

But the larger question is, How can we write this way and get away with it? We can and we do because a textbook is knowledgeable; it can tell the difference, it can tell the Truth through authors and teachers—the experts. The author function authorizes our words and helps us reinforce the power relations that are already there. Could the above text be written differently? Could the authors stand in an opposite position, call the names of the culprits, and show the manipulations through which corporations reenact slavery? Could they call such a text business ethics?

Our answer is, most likely not. It would have been called propagandistic and ideological. If published, it would have probably been through an alternative press, the ones that do not sell many textbooks in business schools because they do not give too much thought to the Market.

But we do not think that, for our purposes, these texts need to be written any differently. We think that business ethics texts, *as they stand today,* can be very useful in teaching "deconstructively." (See Fig. 2c.) We can imagine these texts as depositories of our current business organization/management theory/ethics knowledge. We can imagine rewriting our business courses with them. We can imagine teaching organizational theory and behavior with them as the core text. Deconstructing business ethics in the classroom can help us show how all our courses—and all of us academics in the business schools—belong to an intertext that promotes the society we *do* have, with all its undesirable consequences. At that point we may be able to explore with our students "*unknown* contradictory multiplicity" and be "irrational" in trying to make our world better.

But in order to do that, we also have to question our own stance in regard to authorship, knowledge, and truth. We have to call into question our patriarchal tradition where all of us—male and female teachers and

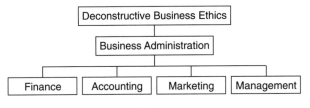

Figure 2c.

authors, mainstream and critical—stand to be able to "speak Knowledge." And here we can resort back to a commentary by Jacques Derrida, who has sometimes remarked that deconstruction is women's writing: "Because, indeed, if woman *is* truth, *she* at least knows that there is no truth, that truth has no place here and that no one has a place for truth. And she is a woman because she herself does not believe in truth itself, because she does not believe in what she is, in what she is believed to be, in what she thus is not" (1978:53).

It is with the deconstructive figure of "woman/*mujer*" that we want to end this text, playing on the multicultural multiplicity of our authorship and our sex that is not one (Irigaray, 1985). But suddenly, as we reflect upon the fact that *mujer* is not just "woman," we remember that we must tell you something more about "*predicando la moral en calzoncillos*." This saying doesn't really translate as "preaching morality in your underwear." It can be said only from a *mujer* point of view. Or, better, from the point of view of those third world *mujeres*, sitting behind their stands in the marketplace, because in these sites women can still have a good time ridiculing the fellows who wanted to "preach morality in their boxer shorts (*calzoncillos*)." Meanwhile, here in "developed North America," liberated women of the Market, who might be tempted to feel sorry for those *mujeres* as victims of machismo—may be able to engage in "serious debates" about "moral dilemmas" only by employing the language of the patriarchs.

4

Postmodernism, Feminism, and Organizational Ethics: Letting Difference Be

Kathy E. Ferguson

Feminism's relation to business cannot be founded on cooperation. Feminism cannot become a tool for business to develop fairer practices or to pursue its goals more efficiently. It cannot improve business because feminism's quarrels are not with the excesses and abuses that pervade business organizations but with the very premises that underlie standard operating procedures. It does not point to unfairness within the system because that would presume the possibility of fairness at the level of the system. Feminism does not question the efficiency or effectiveness of business practices but the moral and political legitimacy of these practices: not how best to use the power that business accords certain groups of people (owners and managers, for example) but *why* these people are thus empowered. It does not challenge bad business but business as usual.

The definitive tone of dismissal in the above statements might seem to close the very doors this volume seeks to open, denying both the possibility and the efficacy of a link between feminism and business ethics. But this is not necessarily the case. The field of business has a tendency to co-opt its critics by absorbing them into its orthodoxies, where market values and positivist epistemologies reign. A critique that is somewhat extravagant and makes some questionable generalizations may be necessary in order to clear the path for other arguments—arguments that can challenge rather than perpetuate the paradigms that prevail in the field. Such challenges are a necessary part of any effort to do business ethics differently.

Feminism's vision of the world is incompatible with the world that business has created. This is not to dismiss feminism as utopian and irrelevant but to suggest that feminism must raise a broad spectrum of questions. It must struggle against myriad hegemonic institutions and discourses to make its arguments, both in this essay and in the world. We face everyday events, actions, and encounters that have devastating consequences for women, for children, for all human beings, for the earth and all its life. Rather than simply rehearse the statistics, let's look at concrete examples:[1]

one
two
three
four
five
six
one
two
three
four
five
six

Every 6 seconds somewhere in the world a child dies. Most children die from readily preventable conditions, primarily malnutrition and diarrhea. They die because their parents or their communities are too poor to provide them with clean water, adequate food, and basic health care. This situation could be reversed if the enormous inequities between industrialized nations and the third world were confronted, rather than perpetuated, by what is euphemistically called development. One every 6 seconds.

one   one
two   two
three three
four   four
five   five
six   one
one   two
two   three
three four
four   five
       one
       two

Every 5 seconds cattle ranchers in Central America and the Amazon valley destroy an acre of rain forest for the sake of raising beef for the lucrative export markets in industrialized nations. The habitats of thousands of plants and animals, including human animals, are disappearing. This course of destruction could be stopped if the dominant voices in the human world did not view the nonhuman world as, in Heidegger's phrase, "standing reserve"—if human beings required themselves to interact with the natural world rather than seize it for their own use. Every 5 seconds.

five
six   three one
one   four   two
two   five   three
three one   four
four   two   five
five   three   six
six   four   seven
one   five   eight
two   one   nine
three two   ten
four   three one
five   four   two
six   five   three
one   six   four
two   one   five
three two   six
four   three seven
five   four   eight

Every 10 seconds a quarter of a million dollars is spent worldwide on the military. Every dollar poured into the abysmal toilet of war preparations is a dollar stolen from dying children, smoking rain forests, and other sites of suffering and destruction. Every 10 seconds.

We must denaturalize the political circumstances in which we find ourselves in order to theorize about these tragedies. Instead of looking at infant mortality, ecological destruction, and military waste as unfortunate or unintended side effects, feminism brings them to center stage as crimes of indifference, the logical outcome of the world that business as usual has created.[2] To redirect thinking in this way

one	one	one
two	two	two
three	three	three
four	four	four
five	five	five
six	one	six
one	two	seven
two	three	eight
three	four	nine
four	five	ten
five	one	one
six	two	two
one	three	three

calls for a substantial shift in our understanding of responsibility, reason, politics, ethics, and other categories of collective life. I understand that business is not the only culprit responsible for producing these injustices: governments are eager to do their share, as are religions, the military, schools, and other conduits of destruction. My project is to implicate business squarely within the discursive and institutional constellations that produce disaster for women, children, and the planet and to interrupt this hegemonic order in the name of feminism.

But what kind of feminism? Let me step back a moment from these perhaps inflammatory claims and define some key terms. "Feminism" is an umbrella term for a huge family of ideas that are often sharply at odds with one another. One important distinction is that between liberal feminism and its more radical cousins. Liberal feminism, also known as equity feminism or humanist feminism, calls for the equal treatment of women within existing institutions. Taking the parameters of the existing arrangements largely for granted, liberal feminism shouts a loud "me too" at the wall of arrogance and exclusion that marginalizes women. Liberal feminism's reforms often enhance the opportunities available to those classes and colors of women who can claim access to traditional institutions. I am bracketing this face of feminism not because I want to dismiss it but because it is the face of feminism that the business establishment finds most palatable. It is represented in *Ms.* magazine's praise of Control Data for its enlightened management practices:

> Control Data is among those enlightened corporations that offer social-service leaves. . . . Kit Ketchum, former treasurer of Minnesota NOW, applied for and got a full year with pay to work at NOW's national office in Washington, DC. She writes: "I commend Control Data for their commitment to employing and promoting women. . . ." Why not suggest this to your employer? (Spivak, 1987:91, quoting "A New Way to Work for Women," 1982:30)

Meanwhile, in one of Control Data's South Korean plants, 237 women workers went on strike for higher wages:

> Six union leaders were dismissed and imprisoned. In July, the women took hostage two visiting U.S. vice-presidents, demanding reinstatement of the union leaders. Control Data's main office was willing to release the women; the Korean government was reluctant. On July 16, the Korean male workers at the factory beat up the female workers and ended the dispute. Many of the women were injured and two suffered miscarriages. (Spivak, 1987:89, quoting "Was Headquarters Responsible?" 1982:16).

While the reforms that liberal feminism can deliver are often significant to the managerial women who benefit from them, they have little to do with altering the structures that produce global gender inequities (for example, multinational operations in free trade zones, run-away shops relocating to exploit cheap female labor, or repressive third world regimes propped up with Western aid) or with changing the world in a feminist direction. Businesses that support upward mobility for selected managerial women while relying on a disempowered female workforce may earn praise from liberal feminists, but they do little to satisfy more radical feminist critiques.

The feminism I speak from is more radical because it finds the existing power structures unacceptable no matter who is at the helm. It is informed primarily by two competing impulses: one to create a "woman-centered" understanding of the world and a contrary one to deconstruct the distinction between margin and center. The relation between the two is complex, full of tension and opportunity. Both impulses frame the questions of moral and political life around the problematic of gender, but in different ways. In the first view, men—male power, male identities, masculinity as a set of practices—are seen as problems; in the second, the gendered world itself is a problem. Both stances bring gender into view as a powerful organizing principle of social life, but the first one reverses patriarchal gender priorities whereas the latter explodes them. The development of women's voices, sometimes called gynocentric theory or feminist standpoint theory, entails diving into a world divided between male and female experience in order to critique the power of the former and valorize the alternative residing in the latter. It is a theoretical project that opposes the identities and coherencies contained in patriarchal theory in order to identify a different set of identities and coherencies—that is, a different and better way of thinking and living. In the second view, feminists pursue the deconstruction of gender, stepping back from the opposition of male and female in order to loosen the hold of gender on life and meaning. This project renders gender more fragile, more tenuous, and less salient both as an explanatory and evaluative category. Feminist standpoint theory creates a woman's point of view in order to reject male orderings of the world, while the purpose of gender deconstruction is to reject the dualism of male and female.[3] Realizing the persistent tension between feminist standpoint theory and feminist deconstruction, I am, nonetheless, going to treat feminism as if it were a coherent category with stable boundaries within which unanimous agreements had been reached. I shall take these liberties in order to bring other questionable categories into focus. Feminism, its internal struggles acknowledged, will be posited here as a launching point from which to unpack other categories and render them problematic.

I will draw upon ideas from both sides of feminism, but as the title of this essay suggests, I will favor the face of feminism that connects to postmodernism. The postmodern movement within feminism comes to the defense of difference in opposition to "the founding of a hysterocentric to counter a phallic discource" (Spivak 1983:184). The deconstruction of gender is done in the name of a politics of difference, an antifounda-tionalism defending that which resists categorization, which refuses to be corralled within familiar categories. While nearly all feminists at some level oppose binary oppositions, postmodern feminists are the most emphatic in their call for an opposition to sexual dualism itself, in the name of "the multiplicity of sexually marked voices," or relationships that "would not be a-sexual, far from it, but would be sexual otherwise: beyond the binary difference that governs the decorum of all codes" (Derrida, 1982:76, quoted in Moi, 1985:76).

Here again is an obscuring of differences within a category in order to have a more or less comprehensible point from which to argue. Such obscuring is a big problem not simply because there are many different, often contending, arguments included in postmodernism but also because the very creation of the category is problematic. To create a thing called postmodernism or poststructuralism, which one can then be for or against, is to risk taming the rebellion against categorization expressed therein. I frequently use the term "genealogy" to speak of the intellectual terrain labeled postmodern in academic debates, both to evade the ideological closure that often comes with the term and to recall the Nietzschean influence. The denaturalization of meaning claims and the critique of origins should not be reduced to another "ism" on the ideological menu. Nonetheless, for purposes of this essay I will call upon both feminism and postmodernism to stand still, to quell their internal disturbances, and to keep the peace within their own ranks so that we may examine the problems inherent in another set of ranks, those of business and business ethics.

On to the other crucial categories of inquiry. I take "business" to be shorthand for the world that international capitalism has created: a world of transnational corporations, of the electronic flow of capital, of governments recruited to serve the interests of corporate profit and penalized when they do not, of endless consumer wants generated by advertising, of the commercialization of life around the cash nexus. I take business ethics to be an academic enterprise that tends on the whole to legitimize the world of business—or else to be ignored by it. In a curious way business ethics is a lot like liberal feminism. It seems largely to take the system for granted and to look for ways to introduce into that system new and improved methods of operation: flextime for women supervisors or workshops on stress management carry a political status similar to that of lessons in Rawlsian or Kantian moral reasoning for managers. Business ethics resembles liberal feminism in another way: each provides a career niche for certain members of their respective constituencies (upwardly mobile women or unemployed philosophers) in the more lucrative arenas of management or business administration. Yet neither does much for the women whose class, color, or culture bar them from managerial positions or for the kinds of philosophy or philosophers who do not readily accommodate the needs of business. Liberal feminism and business ethics stand in a similar relation to business: they take for granted precisely what more radical feminism throws into question.

From the perspectives that a feminist postmodernism makes available, the question is not what to do about business when it acts "unethically" but how to critique business when it is being "ethical" according to its own standards, raising what Heidegger (1977) and others have called the question of the frame. The questions that we can ask about the world are enabled, and other questions disabled, by the frame that orders the questioning. When we are busy arguing about the questions that appear within a certain frame, the frame itself becomes invisible; we become *enframed* within it. Heidegger observes that the frame makes claims upon our questioning that we have trouble hearing: "Man stands so decisively in attendance on the challenging-forth of enframing that he does not grasp enframing as a claim, that he fails to see himself as the one spoken to. . . . The dominant frame orders our thinking in such a way that alternative orders are silenced: "But enframing does not simply endanger man in his relationship to himself and to everything that is. As a destining, it banishes man into that kind of revealing that is an ordering. Where this ordering holds sway, it drives out every other possibility of revealing" (308–309). Those who are enframed within the moral and political universe of business tend to see only those battles that their practices name as worthy. Enframing is challenged when elements on the fringes or in the basements of a particular frame (say, feminism as fringe or basement of the modern business world) become more audible.

Let us consider an example of such audibility: the critique of international "development" practices offered by Vandana Shiva (1988) in her book *Staying Alive*. Trained as a scientist, Shiva abandoned the field to do political, economic, and social analysis of international development—the system that enables the destruction of traditional peoples in the name of progress. It is commonplace to hear that international development on a capitalist model hurts women, that it destroys or devalues women's traditional extra-market labor, undermines their capacity to care for themselves or their families, and transfers economic and political power to men (see Staudt, 1990). Shiva's project is to push these consequences to the center of the analysis rather than marginalizing them as unintended and temporary outcomes of an otherwise worthy practice. By attacking the "sacredness" of modern scientific knowledge and economic development, Shiva shows these to be "not universal categories of progress, but the special projects of modern western patriarchy" (Shiva 1988:xiv). The violation of nature by what Shiva calls "maldevelopment" is associated with the violence done to the women who depend on nature to sustain themselves, their families, and their communities. Shiva's book is an attempt to articulate how rural Indian women experience and perceive ecological destruction and its causes and how they have initiated processes to arrest the destruction of nature and begin its regeneration (1988:xvi).

To advance her argument, Shiva sketches the everyday world of village women in India, whose daily life practices entail close interaction with trees, land, and water to obtain food, clothing, and shelter for their families. She shows how the patterns of these women's lives are being annihilated by the initiatives of the economic "developers" and their plans for "progress." Rural Indian women's traditional practices regarding water use and conservation are now being displaced by scientific water management systems with their emphasis on cost/benefit analysis and productive utilization of water. For the new water managers, the delicately interconnecting ecosystems are invisible; for example, water that runs into the sea is wasted, regardless of its long-term contribution to maintaining the water table. At the same time, the forestry industry is destroying the environments in which local women traditionally gather food and fuel. For the forest managers, trees that are not marketable from an "industrial materials standpoint" are "clearly weeds," no matter what their contribution to the local food supply (Shiva, 1988:64, quoting Bethel, 1984). Peasant women are being cut out of the food chain by the so-called green (commercialization of food crops) and white (dairying) revolutions. Labor traditionally done by women to sustain life is disqualified from consideration, whereas the work of "experts" counts as productive:

> It is assumed that "production" takes place only when mediated by technologies for commodity production, even when such technologies destroy life. A stable and clean river is not a productive resource in this view: it needs to be "developed" with dams in order to become so. Women, sharing the river as a commons to satisfy the water needs of their families and society are not involved in productive labour: when substituted by the engineering man, water management and water use become productive activities. Natural forests remain unproductive until they are developed into monoculture plantations of commercial species. (Shiva, 1988:4).

Shiva chillingly describes how the green revolution has fostered female infanticide and feticide: commercialization results in higher wages for men than for women (often twice as high), which translates into a lower value for women's labor, both market and nonmarket; this, coupled with the expense of providing girls with dowries, increases the cost of girls to families while reducing their worth. When a traditional society is invaded by the discursive and institutional world of business, women and children lose.

Another example of a feminist fringe made audible comes from Sara Ruddick's (1988) analysis of the practices of mothering in her book *Maternal Thinking.* In Ruddick's view the experiences of mothers take on a philosophical significance, and she suggests the political possibilities residing therein. To do so, Ruddick wrests mothering out of the arena of sentimentality and kitsch, away from the hegemonic views of a society quite ready to become maudlin about mothers but unwilling to legitimate much power for women. Maternal thinking, at its best, is found to have certain central qualities: it is ongoing, processual ("though we desperately needed to act, it was abundantly clear that our nighttime conclusions simply yielded the next afternoon's questions"); it is practical ("We were not reflecting for the sake of reflection; we needed answers") (Ruddick, 1989:11). Done well, maternal thinking requires a kind of control that limits itself and strives to make itself unnecessary. It calls for a scrutinizing of the world that looks unobtrusively for danger without unduly limiting exploration. It requires the muting of narcissism and the appreciation of "alternative excellences and virtues" (108). It gives birth to an attentive kind of love that Ruddick calls "holding" (78–79), a connection somewhat like empathy but not so self-oriented: "knowing another *without* finding yourself in her" (121). It relies on feelings, properly assessed, to direct and explain action, thus establishing feeling as a form of knowing:

> Rather than separating reason from feeling, mothering makes reflective feeling one of the most difficult attainments of reason. In protective work, feeling, thinking, and action are conceptually linked; feelings demand reflection, which is in turn tested by action, which is in turn tested by the feelings it provokes. Thoughtful feeling, passionate thought, and protective acts together test, even as they reveal, the effectiveness of preservative love (70).

Ruddick's category of "thoughtful feeling" (70) undermines the male-ordered dualism of reason versus passion; the practices of mothering make available the constitution of a self-in-relation that thinks her feelings and feels her thoughts.[4]

The particular relations that Ruddick most closely examines are between mothers and children. She emphasizes the child as actor, not as raw material to be managed. Ruddick speaks of the "child's body, from its birth" as "enspirited" (83). In granting subjectivity to those beings usually excluded from philosophy except as the recipients of authority, victims of power, or carriers of the next generation's responsibilities, Ruddick names a site for the production of powerful intersubjectivities and also brings into view a perpetually silenced other—children.

Ruddick connects mothering to peace politics. Mothers are not seen as inherently peaceful but as beings whose work requires them to make *efforts* toward being peaceful. She emphasizes that mothering is a struggle; mothers struggle with fulfilling their own commitments, with their failures and temptations, and with or against the demands of others upon them. Ruddick sees the skills and practices of mothering as offering "resources for creating a less violent world," but no guarantees (136; see also 57).

One such resource can be found in an alternative notion of responsibility. The male-ordered concept of responsibility is narrow in its range of meaning. One can be responsible in the sense of having caused something to happen—that is, being personally to blame for an event. (By this logic, affirmative action is reverse discrimination because individual white men living today did not cause slavery or patriarchy in the past.) One can also be responsible in the sense of entering into a contract that calls for certain payments in exchange for goods. (For example, liberal theorists often speak about the rights and responsibilities of citizenship.) Feminists argue for an expanded and reconstituted notion of responsibility as the need to *respond*, to extend oneself, to take care. While not abandoning the idea of individual agency, the concept is broadened to be more collective and more relational. One is responsible not only for what one has done, or even for what one has not done, but for what is *required* (see Sophia, 1984:58; Cook and Kirk, 1983:5).

Shiva's analysis of economic "maldevelopment" and Ruddick's discussion of mothering may seem far cries from the postmodern face of feminism, with its emphasis on fluidity of categories and avoidance of closure. Shiva deconstructs "development" and "progress" as Ruddick does "mothering" and "fathering," but they let other unities, such as third world women or nature, pass unscrutinized. Although the disjunctures between Shiva's and Ruddick's brands of feminism and those with more postmodern tendencies is substantial, they share a common ethical gesture: they both incline toward an ethics of letting difference be. Shiva and Ruddick arrive at this ethic by emphasizing differences *between* women and men or between adults and children or between the first world and the third. Postmodernism arrives at this ethic—at least at the possibility of this ethic—by a different route. By focusing on the differences *within* particular identities (a woman, for example) or meaning claims ("progress," for example), postmodern feminism explodes these claims from the inside. This intersection raises numerous questions about the relation between efforts to put women at the center and efforts to deconstruct centers; recognizing these questions, I want nonetheless to set them aside to focus on what might be found at the end of these journeys toward difference.[5]

The postmodern approach to an ethic of difference begins with its counter-ontological claims: postmodernists typically deny that there is any order out there to be discovered. The world is a place of flux and discord to the postmodern thinker; it offers, as Foucault remarked, no legible face and is indifferent to our need for a resting place in truth. The genealogical thinker is suspicious of appearances not because they conceal an underlying reality but because underneath the disguises laid down by power, in its self-justifying ideologies, she finds another layer of disguise. We make up our claims to truth, Nietzsche stated, then we forget we made them up, then we forget that we forgot. Claiming that there is always more to being than knowing, the genealogist sees the positivist's search for a correspondence between word and thing as hopeless. It is hopeless because the empirical codes that govern positivism are based on a cultivated ignorance about the inherently metaphorical nature of language. Similarly, the genealogist views the interpretivist's search for attunement with some higher unity (for example, history, the laws of nature, progress, or the goddess) as dangerous, since it stretches itself toward some truth that is held to be out there waiting and fails to notice its own participation in constituting what it then claims merely to have discovered. Instead of searching for unity or taking refuge in positivism, the genealogist opens herself to the discordances and discontinuities discernible within a field of meaning.

Interpretive and positivist thinkers usually start from the undemonstrable premise that there is a fit between human desires, human categories of understanding, and the world that humans inhabit. Genealogists, who begin from the equally undemonstrable position that there is no fit but only resistance and slippage among what we want, how we think, and where we are, do not necessarily scorn the desire for an order, only the assumption of it. The genealogical insistence that the world does not come made for our categories, that there is no necessity unfolding itself through history or science or the goddess, can be a radically disturbing claim. The claim is disturbing because it destabilizes the "reality" side of the still necessary but now problematic appearance/reality distinction that supports both interpretation and positivism. The claim can also be radically liberating, since arguments that language constitutes, rather than merely describes, the world open the way for efforts to structure the world differently in discourse. And it can also be a quite humbling claim, opening the way to acknowledgments that the world is not "for us" and that our touch upon it should be light.

The genealogical project has a constant eye out for the appearance of the will to truth or the will to power over truth. This suspicion inspires, among other strategies, the substitution of verbs for nouns in genealogy's rhetorical practices: to speak, for example, of *valorizing* or *privileging* a point of view or table of values is a way of calling attention to the act that one is performing in valuing that phenomenon over others. This linguistic move denaturalizes the attribution of worth by emphasizing that the higher status has been accorded rather than discerned. Genealogy seeks to unsettle the settled contours of knowledge and power in order to make way for disunities and misfits—to let difference be. Genealogists tend to employ disruptive epistemological codes intended to throw doubt both on positivism's Joe Friday approach to knowledge ("Just the facts, Ma'am") and interpretivism's determination to fit everything into a coherent narrative. Luce Irigaray (1985), for example, disrupts the orderings upon which both positivism and interpretivism arise through her reliance on analogy. Analogy can disrupt the comfortable lull of familiar narratives by bringing together pieces from different stories. In "The Mechanics of Fluids," a chapter in her book *This Sex Which Is Not One*, Irigaray draws an analogy between the resistance of fluids to a mechanics based only on solids and the resistance of women to the dominant symbolization of male discourse. In fluids she finds "a physical reality that continues to resist adequate symbolization and/or that signifies the powerlessness of logic to incorporate in its writings all the characteristic features of nature" (Irigaray, 1985:106–107). The complicity between accepted rationality and solid mechanics excludes fluids, just as that between reason and male discourse excludes women; women/fluid is continuous, diffusible, and traversable, evading boundaries and identities. By juxtaposing the contrasting configurations of mechanics and of gender, Irigaray's "textual impertinences" create an analogical space in which a new set of connections might be made (Shapiro, 1985:195).

Genealogy often does its work indirectly and is sometimes accused by its opponents of not doing much work at all. The word "deconstruction" suggests an unfortunate architectural metaphor, implying that genealogy only tears down meaning, never offering anything one can affirm. But genealogy does more than serve as the wrecking crew of political theory, although that would be no small contribution: it calls our attention to that which has been omitted, suggesting an ethic of difference. By pursuing a relentless history of particulars, and giving examples of misfits and anomalies, genealogy is "compelling us either to find ways to draw these misfits into the fold or to acknowledge the element of dissonance or artificiality within unities themselves" (Connolly, 1987:155). Genealogy insists upon recognizing the marginal, especially that within individuals or meaning claims that must be policed, denied, and repressed in order to present a consistent and solid identity to the world. Genealogy's ethic of difference "counsels us to come to terms with difference and to seek ways to enable difference to be. It is an ethic of letting difference be. It calls into question the project of perfecting mastery of the world on the grounds that, given resistance built into the order of things, the project would reduce everything to a straightjacket while pursuing an illusory goal" (Connolly, 1988:161).

Calls to let difference be reflect not the "fuzzy shrug of the shoulders of pluralism" but an active attention to multiplicity[6] (Callaghan, 1990:10), not the claim that all claims are equally valid but the call to attend to all calls to order with a sympathetic ear for what does not or will not fit. This ethic does not dispense with the need for governing norms or intelligible rules for ordering collective life, but it does call attention to the status of those norms and rules as contestable outcomes of negotiations, as artifice rather than discovery.

Enhanced appreciation of difference, both internal and external, can come from many sources. It can issue from learning the light touch needed to guide another life without crushing it, as Ruddick (1989) says about attentive love: "Attention lets difference emerge without searching for comforting commonalities, dwells upon the other, and lets otherness be. Acts of attention strengthen a love that does not clutch at or cling to the beloved but lets her grow" (122). And further, mothers train themselves "to look, imagine, and then to accept what is different" (123). Alternatively, appreciation of difference can grow from stretching oneself toward the life worlds of precapitalist or precolonial peoples, from imagining living in a cosmology in which the world comes alive through the stories of one's ancestors (Silko, 1977). Shiva (1988) encourages such stretching by giving an account of rural agricultural practices in which these practices are presented not as less rational than those of the modernizers, but as differently rational. Or appreciation of difference can issue from a genealogical understanding of the arbitrariness of all categories and the costs of all demands for stability and order. The desire to let difference be, to lighten the hand of order so that difference can reside in greater safety and with greater honor, can come from more than one direction.

The call to let difference be may seem to lead to political quietism, to be an invitation to protect all positions and postures, including those that oppress people. But one can combine appreciation of difference with a call for change; more specifically, one's appreciation of difference can insist on a call for change. The world business has created calls vociferously for innovation, but resists difference. The modern business world is always in need of new stuff, but it immediately brings it to order around the prevailing norms and rules. Letting difference be does not entail indifference to oppression and suffering nor a tolerance for oppressors as just another difference. Loosening the hand of order and abating the drive to mastery require us to let be the differences that let difference be while opposing those who call for greater uniformity and regulation. A society fully attuned to this ethics might not be able to tune out the clamor of suffering and outrage around it: a child's death every 6 seconds, an acre of rain forest destroyed every 5 seconds, a quarter of a million dollars wasted every 10 seconds. Pushing past tolerance to appreciation of difference, both that between us and that within us, takes us at least part of the way toward realizing a feminist postmodern ethics.

II

Critical Responses
to Feminist Theory
and Business Ethics

5

Radical Feminism and Business Ethics

George G. Brenkert

What can business ethics learn from feminism? This question, of course, is too abstractly posed. I suggest two specifications. First, there are various kinds of feminism. Liberal and radical feminism are two prominent forms represented by the four main chapters in this volume. I shall consider the question just posed by concentrating on the implications of radical feminism. But even radical feminism comes in different stripes: marxist, deconstructionist, anarchist, and so on.[1] The radical feminism portrayed in this volume by Calás and Smircich; Ferguson; and Martin and Knopoff is linked to deconstructionism. Accordingly, I understand the question above to refer to radical feminists who set their stakes by deconstructionism.[2]

Second, if business ethics can learn the same things from a variety of sources (including other forms of feminism), then it need not pay special attention to radical feminism. It could accomplish the same ends by other means. Business ethics would not have to be modified by the tenets particular to radical feminism.[3] Hence, we should ask, What can business ethics uniquely learn from radical (deconstructionist) feminism?

The answer is, I believe, a very mixed one. Radical feminists correctly point to a number of important problems in business and to limitations of current business ethics. They suggest several useful methodological techniques for analyzing business (ethics) texts. Nevertheless, the ethics they offer in the place of current business ethics is disappointing. The metaphysical and epistemological grounds for their ethics are subject to serious dispute and are of questionable relevance to the views they propose. Indeed, I shall suggest, radical feminism might well learn a few things from current business ethics.

RADICAL FEMINIST CRITIQUES OF BUSINESS AND BUSINESS ETHICS

Radical feminists associate manifold problems with business and business ethics. Contemporary business, they argue, is linked with the subordination and exclusion of women, the destruction of rain forests, infant mortality, and military waste (Ferguson: 81). It is an example of the will to power or the will to dominate (Ferguson: 89). Accordingly, Ferguson claims that feminism and business are utterly incompatible (Ferguson: 80). Furthermore, contemporary business ethics is not a critic of this situation but its defender. It has a "cozy arrangement" with business (Calás and Smircich: 72). It is conservative, it avoids certain issues crucial to women, and it draws on traditional ethicists, who unwittingly use male assumptions (Calás and Smircich: 58–61). Consequently, business ethics is not an effective critic of contemporary business; it has only an "academic voice."

Though I do not wish to focus on these criticisms, three comments are important. First, such criticisms are essential to what drives not only radical feminists but other (liberal) feminists as well (Calás and Smircich: 4). They are part of the raison d'être of feminism. Further, many of these criticisms are insightful and important reminders to those doing business ethics. Among such criticisms I would list (1) Kant's limited views on women (Calás and Smircich: 58–61); (2) the historical and personal connection between the founders of utilitarianism and early feminists (Calás and Smircich: 56); (3) the importance of considering the morally problematic nature of the institutional structures within which specific moral problems arise, and not simply the moral problems themselves; and (4) the omission of issues of particular concern to women in standard business ethics texts—for example, the glass ceiling and sexual harassment (Calás and Smircich: 22).

Other criticisms, however, are questionable and, at the least, need much greater exploration and defense. Among these I include the following claims: (1) any individualistic-based orientation toward utilitarianism violates the premises of classical utilitarianism, whose interest was social reform (Calás and Smircich: 57); (2) Kant was "unable to propose anything beyond the social conventions of his time and place" (Calás and Smircich: 59); and (3) business ethics is a form of the scientific method (Calás and Smircich: 53).

Considering only the criticisms that seem valid, it is clear, first, that most of these points have been, or could be, made by others without the philosophical commitments and other views of radical feminists.[4] Thus, these are not contributions that radical feminism uniquely offers to business ethics. Still, those who are directly affected by, and sensitive to, injustice, discrimination, and bias (among other things) may more forcefully bring to the attention of those not so affected the moral sufferings they experience. The contribution radical feminists make through such criticisms is not that they theoretically do what others cannot do but that they practically do what others may not be inclined to do. Thus, although we would not have to adopt the methodology or other commitments of radical feminists to accept their criticisms, we may still learn from their drawing our attention to issues that others might too easily neglect.

Second, it is important to remember that business ethics itself is not a monolithic enterprise. Radical feminists sometimes forget this. For example, Ferguson refers to that entity that calls itself "business ethics" (Ferguson: 84). In short, she hypostatizes "business ethics" into a thing, some solid creature she can then take apart, or deconstruct. Surely this is mistaken. Though Ferguson urges upon us an ethics that would let differences be, she denies the differences that exist among those doing business ethics. It is quite clear, however, that there is a wide moral and political variety of business ethicists: conservative, liberal, libertarian, radical, and reactionary. There are utilitarian and Kantian business ethicists; those who approach moral matters on a very concrete case level and those who work on the very abstract level; those who are empirically inclined and those who operate more a priori; those who support classical free market views and those who reject these views. And, not the least important to recall, business ethicists come in male and female genders. To the extent that radical feminists do not note these differences, they deal abstractly with their subject matter.[5]

Third, central to the radical feminist critique of business ethics is that business ethics lacks a critical edge. Since business ethics, they contend, tends to accept the structure of contemporary business practices, it can look only at minor moral ripples in the flow of business as usual. Hence, it kowtows to current business interests. Accordingly, Ferguson says that she takes business ethics "to be an academic enterprise that tends on the whole to legitimize the world of business, or else to be ignored by it" (Ferguson: 84).

Now, whenever a discipline assumes close relations with that or with those it would critically evaluate, there is always a danger of being blinded to weaknesses and deficencies or of being coopted by favors and influence. Surely business ethics (or business ethicists) has succumbed, in various ways, to these hazards. Accordingly, to maintain its integrity business ethics should distance itself somewhat from its subject matter.

Yet, the appraisals of those who get close to the institutions and persons they evaluate may also be more concrete and informed as to the real situation of what they investigate. Hence, their appraisals may be better grounded. Consequently, business ethics should develop close relations with its subject matter.

The tension between these two aspects of business ethics is typical of any applied field. Radical feminism reminds us of the hazards such close association can bring, but not its rewards.

Part of the reason for the one-sided view of the radical feminists is their interpretation of business ethics as the ethics of business (under-

stood simply as free enterprise, or American capitalism in the late twenti-
eth century). Such an understanding of business ethics necessarily limits
business ethicists to being quasi-apologists of that social-political-eco-
nomic order. This is, I suggest, a misconception of business ethics.

Rather, business ethics must be understood to be the ethics of the productive sector of society.[6] As such, business ethics may look much more
deeply, broadly, and critically at current business practices. It need not
be limited, by definition, to assuming some form of the current business
system. To urge this point is simply to remind us of the generality of
ethics and of the Aristotelian view that links ethics with political philosophy. Radical feminists do business ethics a favor when they challenge
those who simply act to rationalize the status quo. They do business
ethics a disfavor when they suggest that such rationalization is the proper
characterization of business ethics.

FEMINISM AND DECONSTRUCTIONISM

The preceding criticisms on the part of radical feminists are aimed at
overturning and transforming business and business ethics. In the
remainder of this essay, I shall concentrate on the revisions that radical
feminists seek and the grounds they offer for these revisions. It is here
that their commitment to deconstructionism is particularly important.

Radical feminism claims that through a deconstruction of the central
categories and concepts in important texts and discursive strategies we
arrive at an ethics of difference. This is variously stated. Ferguson speaks
of an ethics of letting difference be. Calás and Smircich call it the celebration of differences. Clearly, all their other criticisms and discussions
are aimed at announcing this new, postmodern feminist ethics. How are
we to understand this ethics?

The ethics of difference must be viewed in contrast to the current
"ethics" of business, which radical feminists see as involving subordination, domination, and the exclusion of others and their differences.[7]
Inasmuch as business ethics, male-dominated business, and bureaucracy
seek to exclude and oppress the differences that women represent, they
do not let differences be. Hence, one meaning of this ethics of difference is that the differences, represented by persons who are excluded or
restricted in the workplace and by business ethics, should have a voice.
The characteristics or differences of these excluded groups and classes
ought to be represented.

However, the ethics of difference does not simply demand for women
the opportunities men have had. Nor does it insist that particularly "feminine" characteristics be allowed expression or existence within business.
Rather, radical feminism seeks to overturn dichotomies and binary oppositions such as male/female, public/private, and so on. The issue is not
simply that certain "feminine" traits or issues are to be represented in

the workplace and business ethics but that, for example, the dichotomy of masculine and feminine should be dissolved and replaced with a set of relationships and conditions that transcend it.

Accordingly, radical feminists owe us an account of "differences" and what would transcend the differences bound up with the male/female dichotomy. Which present differences may we admit, and which should we reject and seek to root out? How are the new differences that replace old dichotomies to be characterized?

Ferguson assures us that we are not to let be those differences that involve oppression and suffering (Ferguson: 91). These differences are to be eliminated. Thus, the radical feminist does not advocate political quietism. Instead, we are to loosen "the hand of order and abate the drive to mastery" (Ferguson: 91). We are to oppose "those who call for greater uniformity and regulation" (Ferguson: 91).

But this is all terribly vague. First, the sentence just quoted might have been uttered by those who hold a variety of political viewpoints, from conservatives to libertarians and ultimately other radicals. And yet radical feminists would not, seemingly, agree with all of these groups. But then how are we to interpret this basic ethical stance? Radical feminists tell us very little on this score.

Second, the basic premise or principle of the ethics of difference, that is, "let difference be," sounds passive rather than active. Ferguson does say that such calls to let difference be reflect "an active attention to multiplicity" (Ferguson: 90).[8] But this phrase does not carry its meaning on its face. She immediately explains that she does not intend to imply that all claims are equally valid but rather that we should "attend to all calls to order with a sympathetic ear for what does not or will not fit" (Ferguson: 90). In short, when the call to order goes out one is sympathetically to listen for what does not fit in. But such an active attention to multiplicity may still simply amount to preventing the imposition of order. It need not imply anything beyond that.[9]

This conclusion is supported if we consider that Ferguson also speaks of an enhanced appreciation of difference issuing from the light touch needed to guide another life without crushing it (Ferguson: 90). But this "guiding" gets little content. Drawing on the role of mothers, Ferguson says that mothering involves "acts of attention," such as looking, imagining, and accepting what is different (Ferguson: 90).

This interpretation of the ethics of difference is striking, I suggest, because it links it with classical liberal views rather than with radical ones. Traditionally, liberals have sought to remove impediments from the actions of people rather than provide support for them. Lightening the hand of authority, rather than providing the means for certain forms of life, has been its driving force. Whether this undercuts the normative thrust of radical feminists is for them to decide. But if we are to learn from radical feminists, we need to know to what extent they wish to foster, promote, or support differences in ways other than simply eliminating that which ordinarily stands in their way. In short, we need to know whether radical feminists simply support a form of negative freedom or some form of positive freedom. That is, do they simply seek to remove coercion and various constraints from individuals, or do they also seek to enable and empower individuals to determine their own lives and courses of action?[10] Both efforts, not simply the first, are required, I suggest, by the problems radical feminists (and others) have pointed out.

Third, there is another way to try to pry open the content of an ethics of difference. A deconstructed business ethics, we are told, would not have simply an academic voice (Calás and Smircich: 72). Radical feminists complain that both current business ethics and feminist criticism have only "academic voices" and do "no more than debate over academic issues" (Calás and Smircich: 72). These academic debates occur even as, Calás and Smircich contend, "the poor have become poorer and the rich richer, underemployment is rising, there is widespread discrimination, children enroll in the military because they need 'tuition money,' homelessness is increasing, we have a hole in the ozone layer . . ." (Calás and Smircich: 72).

This is, however, a peculiar criticism because radical feminists also complain that current business ethics is "supportive of the business status quo" (Calás and Smircich: 63). Now, I suppose business ethics could be the latter by simply being an academic voice; but the sense that radical feminists give is that something more than keeping to itself is involved. But if business ethics is supportive of the status quo, then it would not seem simply to be an academic voice.[11]

What does the claim about an engaged business ethics reveal about the content of an ethics of difference? Calás and Smircich claim that such a feminist business ethics would confront problems of unemployment, poverty, discrimination, and so on (Calás and Smircich: 72). However, they also say that it would do this "in the academic space" (Calás and Smircich: 73) by addressing a broader range of topics and doing so in a way (e.g., as an advocate) that makes no pretensions of neutrality.

In short, an engaged, deconstructed business ethics is one that would discuss and analyze a broader range of issues than current business ethics. It also would raise issues about the validity of various epistemological and metaphysical assumptions Western philosophy has shared since the Enlightenment (see the next section). However, there is no guarantee, as far as I can see, that this means that business ethics—or any other academic discipline—can have a greater effect than it presently has. In addition, without further direction as to what an ethics of difference involves, it would seem simply bent on replacing certain characteristic views and topics with others. That is, it is not prepared to let differences be so much as it is to transform the differences that are allowed to stand. But this returns us to the need, as we noted above, for a theory concerning the nature of differences.

In short, the feminist ethic of letting difference be is an important call to recognize persons who are subordinated and/or excluded from various areas of (business) life. However, this radical ethics is inadequately defined and developed. Before it can offer business ethicists an approach to redirecting their own activities, a great deal more must be said.

THE METAPHYSICS OF POSTMODERN FEMINIST BUSINESS ETHICS

Understanding the radical feminist ethics of difference requires understanding its grounds (Ferguson: 87). By looking to the justification for this ethics, we can explore the fundamental reasons radical feminists believe that contemporary business ethics has been irrelevant and why a light touch is required upon life, other people, and the world about us (Ferguson: 89).

Underlying the ethics of difference is a metaphysics and an epistemology that reject what Calás and Smircich call "the Enlightenment project." Postmodern feminism holds that there is no order "out there" waiting to be discovered and captured by our knowledge (Ferguson: 88). There is no ultimate truth apart from ourselves. There is no necessary fit between human desires and categories of understanding and the world that humans inhabit. In short, "the world does not come made for our categories; there is no necessity unfolding itself through history, science, or some goddess" (Ferguson: 89).

Instead, there is resistance and slippage between what we want, how we think, and where we are. The world is a world of flux and discord. Behind appearances are forms of power (Ferguson: 89). We create our knowledge within this context. Thus, it is involved in the various struggles in which we take part.

In this situation there is the possibility that we can constitute the world differently. The forms we impose on the world involve various interpretations and valorizations (Ferguson: 89). The knowledge we claim is bound up with the places and ways in which knowledge gets done (Calás and Smircich: 75).[12] Both knowledge and reason have a contextual nature. Calás and Smircich reject any theory of knowledge and reason that portrays them as transcendent. It is in this metaphysical and epistemological context that radical feminists claim that it is mistaken (Ferguson: 89)—a manifestation of the will to power over truth (Ferguson: 89)—to seek to impose a single unitary order. This is not to say, it should be recalled, that postmodern feminists assert that no order is needed (Ferguson: 91). Some order is important. Not all claims are equally valid (Ferguson: 91). But then, which claims are valid? What kind of order is required?

First, radical feminists appear to believe that simply because the world does not come "preordered" or made for our categories, our touch upon the world must be light (Ferguson: 89). In short, they directly derive their ethics of difference from the preceding metaphysics and epistemology. Because the world is not fixed for us, because we must bring our interpretations to it, and because the world resists the imposition of a single order, we ought to let differences be.

But this conclusion does not follow simply from the preceding metaphysics and epistemology. Indeed, it appears to be a classic case of deriving an "ought" from an "is"—a move that business ethicists have long pointed out is invalid. Simply because the world is one of flux and we must, unavoidably, impose our distinctions and interpretations upon the world, it does not follow that "our touch upon it should be light" (Ferguson: 89). An alternative view might be that we should vigorously try to dominate and master that world as well as the humans within it. Certainly, Nietzsche did not draw the conclusions that radical feminists draw from a metaphysics that sounds, at times, quite like his. And even if we are to learn "the light touch needed to guide another life without crushing it" (Ferguson: 90), there is a wide continuum here, of which not crushing the life out of something is only one part (indeed, one end).

Second, radical feminist metaphysics contends that the world resists the imposition of order. This is not to say that it resists the imposition of all order, only that it resists the imposition of a single, unitary order. Now, suppose that radical feminists held that the world's resistance to order *necessitated* that we let difference be. If this were the case, then letting difference be would not be a moral doctrine but would simply amount to recognizing the unavoidable. Any attempt to impose a single, unitary order would be doomed to failure. But then radical feminists would hardly have to exhort us to let difference be. We could do not otherwise. However, since we have (supposedly) not let difference be—that is what radical feminists are alleging—then the mere resistance of the world to the imposition of unitary order neither necessitates that we accept the feminist ethics of difference nor provides a sufficient reason to do so.

Third, Ferguson actually says that the "enhanced appreciation of difference . . . can come from many sources" (Ferguson: 90). She lists three: (1) learning the light touch needed to guide another life without crushing it; (2) stretching oneself toward the life worlds of precapitalist or precolonial peoples; and (3) a genealogical understanding of the arbitrariness of all categories and the costs of all demands for stability and order.

What Ferguson understands when she says that the enhanced appreciation of difference can "come from" these three sources is unclear. It may simply be a psychological statement. However, an ethics of difference requires more than this: it requires a philosophical or justificatory source.

Reflecting on this list, one sees that unless one already appreciated differences or were willing to let difference be, neither of the first two could serve to enhance one's appreciation of differences. Accordingly, an appreciation of differences might come only (in a philosophical sense) from the third source—the genealogical understanding. Ferguson uses "genealogy" to refer to "the intellectual terrain labeled postmodern in academic debates" (Ferguson: 84). Consequently, this source returns us to the metaphysics and epistemology of radical feminism we considered above. But we have already seen the difficulties in deriving an ethics of difference simply from the metaphysics and epistemology of radical feminists.

It should be noted that Ferguson also suggests another basis within (3) for a radical feminist ethics—namely, "the costs of all demands for stability and order" (Ferguson: 91). This important suggestion of a utilitarian appeal, however, goes undeveloped in her essay. It does not appear in that of Calás and Smircich. Further, it seems a weak reed upon which to base the radical feminist claim. Many people in business would claim that they are already making allowances for the costs of demands for stability and order as well as change.

Finally, it is questionable that those who view knowledge as separated from historical contexts and specialized are "prevented . . . from doing anything about a better society" (Calás and Smircich, 74). Surely many people who view knowledge as objective, independent of historical contexts, and so on, have done a great deal that has mattered historically. Those influenced by Plato, Kant, and Husserl (to name only three) have had significant historical influences. One need not subscribe to radical feminist deconstructionism in order to do "anything about a better society."

CONCLUSION

What radical feminists can teach us about business ethics forms a very mixed lesson. They point to undoubted lapses, suppressions, and exclusions in current business and business ethics, as well as in traditional philosophical theories. However, their contribution is more the expression of the interests and concerns of those who have been systematically oppressed by or excluded from much of public life rather than the particular methodology they bring to such expression.

The ethics of difference that lies at the heart of the radical (deconstructionist) feminism represented in this volume remains amorphous. Indeed, it is striking that radical feminists criticize contemporary business ethicists for having little effect, and then suggest by way of response that we should "let difference be." One would have hoped for something more concrete and direct. Business ethics can hardly be effective if it does not know how to determine which differences are to be protected and fostered and which are to be extirpated or suppressed.

Further, it is doubtful that one can derive the revisions needed in business and business ethics only by way of the radical feminist epistemology and metaphysics. Many people might agree with the substantive criticisms of business and business ethics that radical feminists offer and even accept some of the methods of analysis by which they derive these results, but reject their epistemology and metaphysics. Accordingly, radical feminism needs to pay much more attention to the relation of its claims concerning ethics and its underlying metaphysical and epistemological views. Current business ethics has little to learn, at this point, from the associations that radical feminists have drawn so far.

Finally, these difficulties suggest that radical feminism needs to pay much greater attention to problems moral philosophers have traditionally sought to resolve. In short, feminist postmodern ethics needs business ethics (and its knowledge of the "foundations" of ethics) as much as business ethics needs feminist postmodern views. The two might well learn from each other.

6

Morally Informed Iconoclasm: A Response to Ferguson's "Postmodernism, Feminism, and Organizational Ethics"

Thomas J. Donaldson

Seldom has an author provided her respondent with a greater convenience in shaping his response. Yet, you will see that this convenience reveals, starkly, how far apart she and I are. In the first paragraph of the chapter we encounter the claim that "feminism's relation to business cannot be founded on cooperation. . . . Feminism cannot become a tool for business to develop fairer practices or to pursue it goals more efficiently. . . . [and] feminism cannot improve business, because feminism's quarrels are not with the excesses and abuses that pervade business organizations but with the very premises that underlie standard operating procedures" (80). The thrust of my response can be expressed by changing each of the three "cannots" in this passage to "cans." That is, feminism *can* take up a relation to business that is founded on cooperation. Feminism *can* become a tool for business to develop fairer practices or to pursue its goals more efficiently. And, in some instances, feminism *can* improve business, because, as Ferguson notes, feminism's quarrels are not with the excesses and abuses of business but with at least some of its standard operating procedures.

I wish to make two points and then suggest a reformulation of the concepts of business articulated in Ferguson's essay. First, the strategy the essay takes of increasing moral sensitivity by "letting difference be" is not a promising one. To put matters bluntly, the ethic of difference turns out not to be a true ethic. Second, postmodernism, in its essential and traditional form (i.e., through the philosophical attitudes of Derrida [1982] and Heidegger [1977]), lacks the ability to generate, ground, or even take moral judgments as meaningful. Hence, the project undertaken in the essay of mixing postmodernist, deconstructionist, genealogical philosophy with a woman-centered critique of the sort offered by Shiva (1988) and Ruddick (1989) is thrown off balance.

I begin with the former point, namely, that the hope to increase moral sensitivity by letting difference be is illusory. There can be no doubt that for Ferguson moral sentiments are at issue, and moral nihilism is regarded as off limits. Early in the essay we are reminded that every 6 seconds somewhere in the world a child dies. Most children, we are reminded, die from readily preventable conditions, primarily malnutrition and diarrhea. And in the concluding paragraph we read that "loosening the hand of order" requires us to let difference be. "A society fully attuned to this ethic might not be able to tune out the clamor of suffering and outrage around them . . . every 6 seconds . . . every 5 seconds . . . every 10 seconds" (91).

To be sure, this is an intriguing claim. Jettisoning structures and eliminating order will make us more sensitive to malnourished children, to the destruction of the rain forest, and to rampant militarism. The metaphor here is worth marking: structures and order are like noise, like "clamor"; eliminate the clamor and you can hear the softer sounds of suffering.

The problem is that poststructuralism contains no means of stifling the amoral or immoral clamor while allowing us to hear the moral sound of suffering. For, as many have observed, it contains no intrinsic means or source for making moral judgments. From a moral point of view it can recommend only that we loosen some moral structures, or at the extreme, if you will allow me to stretch the analogy, that we put on earmuffs. Earmuffs, alas, block out both the small cries and the clamor.

At two points, the essay is precariously close to recognizing this concern only to back away. The author wonders if the word "deconstruction" implies that genealogy might only tear down meaning, never offering a person anything one could affirm (90). And later she notes that the call to let difference be may seem to lead to political quietism, to a position that protects all points of view, including those that oppress others (91). We want either to remove structures or let difference be, but, of course, we don't want to do all of either. Consider some of the conceptual structures with which we may choose to analyze moral issues in the third world: developmental economics, dependency theory, human rights theory, exploitation theory, ecological theory, neoclassical economic theory, and anthropological theory. Some of these structures are morally sensitive, some are not. The point is, the act of deconstruction or of letting difference be contains no means of moral *discrimination* among these theories.

We seem to find help in the exhortation to take a "relentless look at particulars," but we must remember that depends on the particulars being examined and on how they are interpreted. No theoretically void interpretation exists. The interpretation of particulars absent traditional theory will be made by the same people, with the same dispositions, the same frailties, the same thirsts, and the same hungers. I see no reason to think that a reinterpretation of particulars will be any more enlightened morally than existing interpretations.

It is also said that genealogy does not have to be a political wrecking crew and that "one can combine appreciation of difference with a call for change" (91). Now, I assume here that we are not insisting on just *any* kind of change but rather on the kinds of changes that lessen rather than enhance "discrimination," "exploitation," and "mastery." But stop and think; where did these words come from? They are moral concepts—precisely moral concepts—and they are not inherent in the essential task of deconstruction unless, of course, we expand deconstruction to include them. And if we define deconstruction to include them, then we should reflect upon and evaluate what we are including. This is moral theory.

For this reason the woman-centered, often economically caustic critique of Ruddick (1989) and Shiva (1988) are odd, and ultimately inconsistent, companions of poststructuralism. In describing Shiva's relating of the green revolution to infanticide and feticide, Ferguson explains that "commercialization results in higher wages for men than for women . . . , which translates into a lower value for women's labor, both market and nonmarket; this, coupled with the expense of providing girls with dowries, increases the cost of girls to families while reducing their worth" (1988:12). This is a far cry from blindly letting difference be. Should we deconstruct this as we might neoclassical economic theory? (In fact, Shiva's view appears to be an implication of neoclassical economic theory.) Presumably we should not, but *why* should we not? Is it because we have a moral concern for the powerless people caught up in a seemingly inevitable process of impoverishment and decreasing self-respect? I hope so. But then this is *moral* talk, *moral* theory, *moral* insight. It is not merely deconstruction. It is not simply letting difference be. And it deserves to be unpacked and examined. If I can borrow from the style of postmodernism, let me say that I am recommending bringing postmodernism's moral assumptions from the periphery to the center.

In fact, of course, I wish to applaud the strongly moral tone of Ferguson's shamelessly postmodern essay. But may I suggest a change in the presentation of concepts, of ideas that might avoid the postmodern syndrome of generating moral concepts ex nihilo? Why not explicitly acknowledge that the deconstructionism in the context of the essay is a heuristic tool to be used in combination with preexisting, undeconstructed moral concepts such as "dominant, male-generated" and "human rights." From this perspective the methodological imperative is to loosen up structures, not from all sources; not from, say, Shiva, Ruddick, or a woman's cooperative in Mexico but from dominant, male-generated structures such as cost-benefit analysis and game theory. In this manner moral consistency is gained for the relatively meager price of a more pedestrian and less radicalized approach. If made, this change would redefine the emerging concept of "feminist postmodern ethics" mentioned at the end of the chapter to one of "morally informed iconoclasm," that is, informed by what the philosopher Charles Taylor calls "hypergoods"—for example, rights, equality, caring, freedom. By definition, hypergoods are goods used to critique and evaluate other goods.

Let me make a further suggestion. Ferguson defines "business" rather broadly as "the world that international capitalism has created: a world of transnational corporations, of the electric flow of capital, of governments recruited to serve the interests of corporate profit and penalized when they do not; of endless consumer wants generated by advertising, of the commercialization of life around the cash nexus" (84). I believe that definitions should, like appetizers, come at the beginning of the meal; in turn, this seems a bit much to swallow.

May I suggest a simpler definition: business consists of the existing practices and institutions through which men and women coordinate their activities to create goods and services. And I wish to add the moral claim that business fails unless it enhances the quality of human life, the equality of human worth, and the extent of human caring. Once made, these changes allow us to revise the "cannots" of the essay's first paragraph to "cans." I conclude, then, by noting that feminism *can* take up a relation to business that is founded on cooperation. For example, feminism can cooperate in any project, institution, or process of institutional destruction and change that leads to greater respect for the marginalized and disenfranchised. I conclude that feminism *can* become a tool for business to develop fairer practices and to pursue its goals more efficiently. That is, feminism can demand fewer white male faces in the corporate board room and more in the secretarial pool. And I conclude feminism *can* make business more efficient by allowing unused talent a chance to make a difference. In sum, feminism *can* improve business because, as Ferguson notes, feminism's quarrels are not with the excesses and abuses of business but with at least some of its standard operating procedures.

7

Look What Sister's Done to My Theory, Mama: A Defense of Kantian Ethics

Jesse Taylor

In her chapter Kathy Ferguson argues that gender differences have ethical implications sufficient to warrant gender categories of ethical theories. The categorical nature of gender differences, according to Ferguson, establishes a necessity of "an ethic of difference" as a fundamental property of ethical theory. Ferguson's construction of "difference" is composed of a "care"-based ethic and a "reason"-based ethic. Following Sara Ruddick (1989), she advances the view that "'thoughtful feeling' undermines the male-ordered dualism of reason versus passion" (Ferguson: 87). Thus, I take it that Immanuel Kant's ethic is at the center of Ferguson's conception of the "male-ordered dualism."

For a number of reasons I find an ethic of difference, as such, troubling; however, I concentrate here on demonstrating that Ferguson's arguments for an ethic of difference are flawed. Specifically, I wish to show that failure to take into consideration the full scope of Kantian ethics has created a failure to come to grips with Kant's ethics, as an ethic of difference. Instead, Ferguson rejects the Kantian dualism in favor of the less tidy dualism constructed on the basis of gender. If I am successful in exposing conceptual difficulties inherent in Ferguson's analysis, other difficulties I associate with her position will prove irrelevant. My arguments will indicate (though not establish) that an "ethic of difference" involves confused ideas of ethical theory, epistemology, and ontology. However, this does not mean that the issue I take with Ferguson is without considerable general agreement regarding her insights on "difference." I reject the idea that "difference" so conceived sufficiently warrants an "ethic of difference," as Ferguson proposes.

In an attempt to pinpoint the thrust of Ferguson's analysis, I developed the following fictional scenario to illustrate more fully the key implications of her constructions of genders. I seek also to flush out Ferguson's views on the role of "difference" in the construction of ethical theory.

Imagine a little boy painstakingly investing his energies in the development of a theory in which theoretical adequacy[1] is intimately related to theoretical universality. The boy believes that such "universality" can be achieved only by satisfying a truth standard to a greater degree than competing theories. Let us also suppose that this boy is a postmodernist who has been influenced heavily by Derrida (1978) and other advocates of "value-laden conceptions of truth." Thus, we may assume that the boy knows that value-neutral truth can be simulated only with the help of universal principles. An important goal in constructing ethical theory is for the theory to work for all of us. When this objective is accomplished, the boy is happy. On a broader perspective, the theory contains uniformity, consistency, simplicity, universality, necessity, and truth, all co-existing in a harmonious "frame."

Suppose that the boy has a sister. Suppose, further, that sister's voice is absent as a definition of brother's theory. In this event, one would not be surprised to learn that sister is uninterested in theory elegance, for example, universality, consistency, and simplicity, as described earlier, because such characteristics relate to brother's theory. Sister has perhaps decided that her brother's theory is "too narrow" to work for her; in this sense, we can see how sister might be troubled by brother's claim that his theory is universal. The universality of the boy's theory stands in the way of sister's ability to address her own moral standing as it relates to her experiences outside the framework her brother employed in his theory construction. Hence, there is a conflict.

Sister does not want to destroy brother's theory (she has feelings for her brother, even though she does not see herself in him), so as a peace offering she suggests that girls are different. Such an offering has liberating properties for both of them. Accordingly, brother's notion of universality does not hold in her case, since cases like hers served no role in brother's idea of a moral theory to begin with. This neglect on the part of brother creates a kind of tolerance that allows brother's theory to remain universal, but only with the modification *universal for men*. Sister believes that her modification will allow their different theories to co-exist. Brother, however, believes that co-existing theories undermine necessity or the elements of truth that are used to create the appeal of theory. As necessity is undermined, so is theoretical adequacy, and other frame-making properties are harmed as well. Brother does not want his theory to lose appeal, so he rejects sister's notion of what I refer to now as theoretical relativity. Sister, on the other hand, rejects brother's theory in spite of brother's appeals to accept it (it just doesn't fit). Sister develops her own theory. Theoretical relativity comes into being. Brother's theory is no longer necessary—its monopoly on truth is lost. Brother is upset. His training and identification with a gender that has long enjoyed historical dominance in the area of theory construction demands production of moral theories with absolute value. By reference to such a background, "it was the only thing that brother could do all right, but it turned out all wrong."

Mama[2] is aware of the conflict; she also knows that at any moment her son will come to her to relate the details of sister's flagrant disregard for his theory construction. Brother believes that his theory would reign supreme in a competitive setting involving only other boys; thus, he does not believe that sister has the capacity to be a serious rival in the domain of theory construction, since the advantages of training and history are not on her side. In this sense, sister is merely a pain in the rear.

The boy goes to his mother and begins to tell her how his sister has rejected every principle that would allow moral communication between them. He adds that sister's rejection was spiteful rather than rational (a violation of the Kantian dualism), since the usual theoretical conditions of adequacy had been met. Those conditions have never included women's experiences, and theories did not seem to be undermined as a result. Mama then asks her son, "What precisely is your problem with sister's rejection of your theory?" and, "What would you like me to do about it?" The son replies, "The only reason sister rejected my theory from spite was because she had no good reason. Had sister stuck to reason, she would have discovered that my theory was all right. Indeed, it was the only thing that I could do all right, but she's made it come out all wrong. So please, Mama, make sister be reasonable."

If Mama consoled her son by assuring him that he can work things out with his sister, she would be showing favoritism to him by suggesting that there is some rational principle (where such a principle is a male construction) that is universal between the siblings. Yet, to retort that girls are simply different would be to favor sister's principle of difference. So, as peacemaker, Mama reminds her son that the truth content in his theory is, after all, a simulation—that is, a hybrid of his experiences, wishes, training, and so on. Moreover, those constructive categories have profound gender implications. Sister's truth simulation will also reflect some gender characteristics, not as a matter of choice but rather of "difference." Mama takes pains to emphasize that difference in the context under consideration belongs to life rather than to theory. Hence, brother should let the difference be. For Mama, this is the end of the matter.

It seems appropriate to ask at this point, How has Mama resolved the conflict between sister and brother? Perhaps an appropriate response is the following: Mama has given her son a reason for not blaming sister for theory relativity. Blame implies fault, but Mama has shown that between brother and sister there is only "difference." Thus, difference is not a feature of a moral theory in, say, the way in which respect may be said to be a feature of such a theory. Rather, difference belongs to conditions that make the framing of theories possible. Here I want to throw light on the relation between truth and theories in general, though my focus is specifically on ethical implications. I believe that sister's appeal to difference relies on a universal truth commitment to a greater degree than brother's.

Somewhere amid the controversy involving epistemology, ontology, and gender is a moral issue that I believe distorts the theoretical requirements for moral philosophy in general and for the gender implications of moral philosophy in particular. According to Ferguson, a concept of "universality," as characterized here, presupposes commensurability of gender "identities." Since women and men differ psychologically, sociologically a supposition of universality is without the support of a reliable transgender identity relation and is therefore unfounded. Ferguson writes, "The development of women's voices, or a gynocentric theory or a feminist standpoint entails diving into a world divided between male and female experience in order to critique the power of the former and valorize the alternative residing in the latter" (83).

Kant also recognized the necessity of a connection between ethical principles and identity characteristics of moral agents. He maintained that moral actions are always determined in relation to a principle; consequently, such actions are considered restricted to beings with an understanding and a will capable of sustaining a serviceable concept of "ought"—indeed, "every rational being reckons himself qua intelligent being as belonging to the world of understanding, and it is simply as an efficient cause belonging to that world that he calls his causality a will." Kant believed that understanding involves a faculty of reason, which is capable of restraining human behaviors in compliance with principles. In considering the possibility of a categorical imperative, Kant remarked: "What makes the categorical imperative possible is this, that the idea of freedom makes me a member of the intelligible world, in consequence of which, if I were nothing else, all my actions would always conform to the autonomy of the will; but as I at the same time intuit myself as a member of the world of sense, they ought so to conform"[3] (quoted in Green, 1957:337). If I may appeal to a Kantian schemata for ethical theory in order to contrast Ferguson's view, I take her position to be that it is understanding rather than reason that has gender ramifications. Ferguson does not associate gender properties with reason as such, only with so-called framing mechanisms that govern the form of reason. Thus, she may well consider women rational in the Kantian sense, but stipulate that their rational capacities are situated in a cognitive frame that has been shaped by their experience and training. The moral incommensurability Ferguson speaks of (via difference) comes into play as a result of her view that cognitive dispositions orient experience and are not therefore themselves subject to experience-determined modalities. I take this view to be similar to Kant's conception of understanding. Accordingly, gender-structured orientations leave us without assurance that ethical principles are universal with respect to gender. Following Heidegger, Ferguson espouses the idea that "the questions that we can ask about the world are enabled, and other questions disabled, by the frame that orders the questioning. . . . [T]he frame itself becomes invisible, we become enframed in it" (85). Practically speaking, therefore, it appears feasible for men to design their own ethical theory and women theirs. Where the theories differ, we simply let the difference be, in deference to the psychological impossibility of employing reason to reconcile that difference. Indeed, such differences are not merely gender based but extend to race, and perhaps to individuals, although I suspect Ferguson is not quite this liberal in letting difference be.

In an important respect, the problem with the so-called ethic of difference involves deciding what differences matter from an ethical point of view. If we accept the view of a frame basis for theory generation, we are immediately saddled with two critical problems. The first is ethical relativism, because every individual is a unique cognitive system with unique framing propensities. It would seem, therefore that consistency would require the principle of difference to apply in all cases in which ethical relativism is identified. Individuals change their personal moralities over time, yet if we take the concept of difference seriously, persons whose moral orientations change would be allowed to claim only that they are different moral agents, not that they are better or worse persons. The second problem is that the idea of letting difference be tends to equate the concept of moral justifiability with that of psychological disposition. Traditional ethical theory has assumed a lack of an identity relation between right actions and those an agent is perhaps cognitively disposed to perform. For example, traditionalists such as Kant responded to the moral/psychological dichotomy by suggesting that the former is rational and the latter natural. Ferguson's position, by contrast, suggests that there is no categorical difference between the rational and the natural. She is committed to the idea that moral orientations must first be compatible with framing properties and only secondarily with serving a regulatory role in conduct. The wisdom here may be formulated thus: human beings are, after all, a natural kind, and so reflective thinking is a natural function without the freedom Kant presumes it to have. Thus, it is quite possible that where meaningful psychological differences exist between beings capable of reflective thinking, there are meaningful differences in the form of that thinking as well. Hence, understanding is fashioned by formal or aesthetic properties rather than by material ones.

A logical consequence of this view is that Knowledge itself has a structural or aesthetic basis that is psychologically determined. This basis permits knowledge to be accessible to one psychological type but inaccessible to others, since the form of knowledge is ultimately shaped by understanding. Ferguson seems committed to the view that the concept of reason is not context free within a community of rational agents bearing different psychological properties. The traditional concept of reason must be modified to mean "reason in psychological system 'W' or 'M'," where "W" and "M" represent the psychologies of women and men, respectively.

Epistemologically speaking, the position implied by Ferguson as a reliable basis for an ethic of difference assumes, as Chomsky (1980) has suggested, that knowledge is "causal" rather than empirical or "innate" (in the traditional sense). Human understanding, therefore, of the data of experience largely reflects structures of the mechanisms that make experience possible. These structures can be cultural, historical, political, educational, and so on. When all is said and done, they create the result that the output of truth does not necessarily resemble the input of data. At most, successful epistemology can throw light on how the mind works, since the same data presented to different cognitive processing systems (within the human ranks) constitute different knowledge. Knowledge is nothing more than the activity of the human mind working on input data. This reduces epistemology and ontology to psychology. The question of "What is there?" for instance, now becomes second to that of "How does the mind process input data?" Of course, Ferguson replies to this question by referring to the "Heideggerian frame"—a reply that is simply made up from the appropriation of frame-making categories.

Ferguson's ethic leaves us in a rather unpleasant existential moral kingdom. All knowledge is subjective—that is, determined by unique cognitive processing systems. However, Ferguson's idea of subjectivity appears different from that of the existentialists: hers appears to be founded upon a psychological determinism, whereas the existentialists espouse a notion of freedom.

The two conceptions of subjectivity are similar in that both view individuals as monadic unities. Our understanding of the individual qua individual is never fully accessible to the other. Yet, by virtue of that other inaccessibility, there is a truth to which only the individual has access, via one's unique cognitive processing mechanisms. Though quite personal, subjective truth is on an equal epistemological footing with all truth: from it we learn how the mind operates on input data. As Ferguson notes, Jane Flax makes this point in a slightly different manner: "Truth is merely the name of a property that all true statements share, or a kind of honorific we give to practices or ideas that accord with our assumptions. It is not possible to have an interesting philosophic discussion about such notions" (1990:201).

Truth constructed from practices, assumptions, values, and so on, lacks traditional properties philosophy has commonly assumed it to have—namely, justification and truth content. Ferguson suggests that the conventional dimension of worldviews is contingency governed. This makes knowledge "disposable." Should we find that our relation to the world is not to our liking, we may be at liberty to cultivate a worldview in which relationships turn out more to our favor, since truth and justification are on holiday. Truth from that disposed world (the world of disfavor) continues to exist as truths for that world, but the world itself is now different, and those truths can no longer be given the "honorific."

I do not believe that Ferguson's conception of difference warrants an ethic of difference as such but rather an ethic in which difference is a component of the theoretical framework for ethics (as, in fact, it is in Kantian ethics). But if coming to terms with difference is a significant task of morality, then it is not clear that going beyond Kant is desirable. I shall return to this issue shortly, but for the moment I will focus on the ontological implications of Ferguson's alternative position. Aristotle (see *De Anima*) was the first Western philosopher to use the concept of species to define the ontological status of organisms. The definition was a functional one in the sense that organisms displaying unique functional characteristics were categorized as members of the same functional or species group. Aristotle also maintained that the "well-being" of an organism is tied to its ability to function in accordance with species-specific propensities. Given the diversity of species functions, the notion of happiness must be applied in a manner consistent with natural function. In this view, therefore, meaningful conceptions of happiness would not forbid an organism from being what it is by its nature, even if we add to the Aristotelean conception of nature a sociological component. Indeed, an organism is happiest when its behavior is in agreement with its function as a unique "natural kind." Apparently, the ethic of difference maintains that because there are differences between women and men, it is not possible to have an ethic that can effectively foster the happiness interest of both genders. It should be noted, however, that gender-determined conceptions of happiness take Aristotle a step beyond his insights with respect to uniqueness. Aristotle never argued that gender differences are relevant to the function that determines the nature of happiness for a species. I do not believe that this is an oversight on the part of Aristotle; I would attribute to him the belief that gender is embedded in the idea of a natural kind. This position, however, does not imply that thinking as a natural function of human beings does not have gender-specific characteristics. Indeed, thinking has idiosyncratic characteristics as well, and these are in part a likely consequence of the fact that every individual is a unique psychological system. However, the mere fact that there are differences within a species does not change the definition of happiness for that species—only its application. I believe there are good reasons for resisting the inclination to admit multiple ethics merely because a unique natural function manifests itself differently according to gender dispositions. The danger here is that the ethic of difference establishes different categories of being for men and women rather than illustrates two ways of participating in the same category of being. If we were to accept a moral dualism of the kind Ferguson proposes, there would be no basis for assuming that the concept of difference that she advances is universal with respect to both moral realms. On the other hand, if as a principle letting difference be is gender neutral, then it is not, strictly speaking, an ethic of difference as such but a principle that assumes some degree of identity with respect to the nature of human understanding independent of gender; thus, the principle should be capable of sustaining a gender-neutral generalization. Perhaps Ferguson wants merely to favor the principle of letting difference be as an aspect of feminist ethics. But, if this is the case, it has no necessary bearing on male behavior, since male characteristics may favor a different manner of establishing relations. How would the feminist go about discouraging men from being what they are by nature without denying them their happiness in the Aristotelean sense? Ferguson offers a moderate attempt to address this issue, but her argument is unclear. She says, "The call to let difference be may seem to lead to political quietism, to protect all positions and postures, including those that oppress others. But one can combine appreciation of difference with involvement for change; more specifically, one's appreciation for difference can insist on involvement for change" (91). But Ferguson does not provide a framework within which this "involvement for change" is to occur. Perhaps the issue here involves "truth" in the universal sense to a greater degree than difference. Thus, it would appear that the foundations for ethical theory must first meet epistemological and ontological standards, and psychological standards only secondarily. But Ferguson maintains that truth is a product of a manner of thinking rather than a result of thinking. Major differences in ways of thinking that are perhaps gender determined may produce significant differences in the concept of truth. Yet all such truths are on an equal epistemological footing. I do not see how Ferguson proposes to avoid the problem of "political quietism" (91).

A major mistake Ferguson makes as an advocate of an ethic of difference is her assumption that Kantian ethics is constitutive of individual identities. Kant's ethics were inspired by three basic insights: (1) that happiness is not an object of our knowledge, (2) that individual conceptions of happiness *differ* (in some cases, significantly), and (3) that persons are ends in themselves. These insights define the task of morality as one of respecting an individual's conception of happiness as if that happiness were one's own. Kant's concept of duty comes into play to evoke a requirement that all individual rights (i.e., claims to conceptions of happiness) must be respected. In an important sense, therefore, Kant is saying that our differences can be permitted only if there is a universal realm within which our rights and duties can be articulated with uniformity. This uniformity, however, does not constitute personal identity; it merely creates necessary conditions that make the flourishing of personhood possible. In this respect, morality does not have truth content; ethical principles are designed to respect individual autonomy, whereas autonomy as such is not subsumed under those principles. As Sartre suggested, this leaves persons free to make themselves within those restrictions constituting their limitations. However, Sartre rejected Kant's limits to freedom as imposed by the categorical imperative, although he accepted the Kantian notion of freedom itself.

Ethical principles are restrictive, but restrictions are justified only in the spirit of preserving the equal status of all persons as persons; they are not intended to forbid differences among persons. An autonomy-limiting principle that is not linked to the rights of other individuals assumes a knowledge which is cognitively inaccessible to the human organism and is thus unfounded. For Kant, all moral behavior must be rational behavior to avoid the possibility of serving the interest of a group or of an individual at the expense of others. To test that behavior is reason determined, it must be demonstrated that the principle of action (or maxim) was drawn from a law rather than a feeling (or inclination). For Kant, this showed that the agent has no personal advantage or bias involved in the determination of the agent's choice to act morally. Thus, feelings are forbidden from the realm of morality as components of moral worth, but not as components of human worth. As Kant remarked:

> When we are speaking of laws of duty [not laws of nature] and, among these, of governing men's external relations with one another, we are considering a moral [intelligible] world where, by analogy with the physical world, attraction and repulsion bind together rational beings [on earth]. The principle of mutual love admonishes men constantly to come nearer to each other; that of the respect which they owe each other, to keep themselves at a distance from one another. And should one of these great moral forces fail, "then nothingness [immorality], with its gaping throat, would drink the whole kingdom of [moral] beings like a drop of water" [if I may use Hallar's words, but in a different connection]. (1964a:116)

The principle of mutual love brings persons together as a community of intelligible beings. Insofar as persons engage in intelligent discourse, human qua human behavior is without nature content; rather, it belongs to the understanding as a kind of intuition that nests the essence of human existence. The phenomenon of intelligence creates an interface between persons and nature—that is, a contingency-shaped identity, which permits a freedom that makes autonomy possible and responsibility necessary. Human autonomy is not shaped by nature. Thus, empathy for the human condition must be accomplished by humans. Without others, we are alone. Kant assumes that no one wants to be alone, so we have a duty to love other human beings as subjects of a common existential status. The principle of distance rests on the assumption that persons are "bundles of biases" (*Groundwork*) fashioned by individuality. Lest we maintain a distance from one another, our biases will determine the character of our relations. When this happens, there is the danger of treating beings with dignity as if they are mere objects: that is, the "gaping throat" of immorality would "drink the whole of the kingdom of moral beings." Ferguson's remark that "Ruddick's category of thoughtful feeling undermines the male-ordered dualism of reason versus passion" (87) points ultimately to a preference for principles over passion as a hedge against the natural propensity to be biased. Employed for the task of morality, reason is not functioning to attain truth but to mark off a kingdom wherein persons can exist as persons in spite of their differences, not to abolish their differences.

In concluding, I am in general agreement with Ferguson and others about gender-specific dispositions. I believe also that men tend to ignore these differences during theory construction, perhaps because of what Maria Lugones has referred to as an "arrogant perception" (1987:4). However, in my view gender differences have cultural, social, and psychological implications, but not ethical ones—at least not in the sense that difference warrants a different ethic. On the other hand, I do not wish to suggest that a Kantian ethic is the only alternative to an ethic of difference, although I believe that Kant was successful in specifying some of the "must" characteristics of an ethic. For example, ethical theory must include the categories of universality and impartiality, though not necessarily of the sort Kant prescribed.

A principle of impartiality comes into play from what I have referred to as the common existential status of persons as subjects destined to determine themselves. The presumption of equality at work in this context is a kind of impartiality that views individuals as foundations unto themselves. But beyond that—indeed, by virtue of that equal status—many differences are evidenced within the human community. Kant's mission in ethical theory was never to design a common foundation for personhood but rather to provide a common foundation that would admit difference. Of course, Kant thought "reason" (as defined in the First Critique) was our best hope of identifying universality within a kingdom of self-determining agents, but he could have been wrong about reason as such, and right about the universality requirement. Viewed in this light, perhaps we would do better to treat the categorical imperative as a hypothesis, that is, as a universal without necessity rather than as an indispensable condition or as a truth. Remember, Kant's assumptions about the role and character of reason were drawn from eighteenth-century epistemology, but as feminists, African-Americans, and others have since indicated, that Kantian notion is perhaps founded upon a bias of the kind Kant himself was trying to avoid. We should not assume that Kant was being dogmatic on this issue.

Hypotheses are always open to revision; they might even be abandoned for reasons of evidence and/or interest. However, they are useful in providing a tentative universal context within which to weigh moral precepts, while at the same time leaving a window open through which that context may be modified. Even if harmony of moral percepts is never fully determined, we can continue to exist as a human community on the strength of some hypothesis about what that harmony is—provided, of course, that we have a method of measuring the adequacy of our hypothesis. I suggest that such a measure exists comparatively against other hypotheses, and categorically by reference to the status of humans as a community of self-determined beings. Knowledge of truth is not assumed by any hypothesis, but that does not mean that truth content is unnecessary to support knowledge claims. Consequently, we have a standard for revising hypotheses, but we are not dogmatic in being dependent on specific hypotheses such as the categorical imperative as formulated by Kant.

I have argued that we are hypotheses dependent with respect to ethical theory and that the idea of an ethic presupposes an identity relation of some kind, although the idea does not presuppose that we know immediately what that relation is, or even that we can know it. However, simply because "ultimate truth" might be beyond our cognitive grasp, we should not infer that truth as such is irrelevant to the economy (or, for that matter, the survival) of the human organism. A truth hypothesis must envelop the harmony echoed by difference, and in so doing truth, specifically moral truth, is difference dependent but not difference determined.

To return briefly to Mama's resolution of the conflict between sister and brother, Mama appeared to have stopped short of truth as harmony and attempted to find it in difference. However, in difference there is no ethic, merely difference. As such, the conflict partially characterizes every member of the moral community. Had Mama distinguished between epistemology and truth, she would have observed that the former is psychologically governed, but the latter is not. In benefiting from this distinction, Mama would have informed her son that his is not the only access to truth and that the universality he desires in theory must come from the blending of his and sister's perspectives. Thus, it is a property of neither. We do not "make" the world, as Ferguson suggests, we merely "encounter" it from different perspectives and dispositions. Truth, therefore, is not entirely a human property. Hence, epistemology offers no guarantees of truth attainment, only of limited access. To understand what a given "access" means, in some comprehensive context, it is necessary to see how it converges with difference.

8

Meaning, Rules, and Bureaucracy: Comments on Martin and Knopoff on Max Weber

Edwin Hartman

TRUTH CLAIMS AND OBJECTIVITY

My account of Knopoff and Martin's chapter comes from a point of view characteristic of analytical philosophy, but it is a fundamentally sympathetic one. Where arguments seem to be missing from their account, they can be inferred from what they say elsewhere, or supplied. To do either is a form of interpretation, even deconstruction. This device of using an author's words or methods against the author is an old one, and it is particularly tempting to use here. But using some of their methods *on* Martin and Knopoff themselves does not amount to using them *against* them, and it is really the former that I aim to do, as the sincerest form of flattery. But insofar as Martin and Knopoff have ruled that philosophy is not to be at issue, I shall not cooperate.

Let us start with the following passage, in which the authors say of deconstruction, apparently sympathetically, that it "questions the validity of all absolute statements about what is 'true,' claiming instead that multiple interpretations of what is true or ideologically desirable are always possible. In contrast, ideologies make a truth claim" (35). Now ordinarily I do not like this sort of statement. It is difficult to distinguish the activity of making statements of almost any sort from that of making truth claims, and Martin and Knopoff say nothing to make it any easier. Attacks on metaphysical realism—whether through actual arguments or, more frequently, not—seem to me not very good or even very coherent, and as often as not self-refuting. Do Martin and Knopoff really mean *all* absolute statements? Absolutely all? One might also ask for clarification, or even defense, of the implicit truth claim that multiple interpretations of what is true are available. Might some of these interpretations be wrong? How do we distinguish a good interpretation from a bad one?

As it turns out, these rhetorical questions do not go entirely unanswered. The authors' arguments give the quoted words some muscle, and finally some plausibility. That is, they can be interpreted as successfully making a truth claim, and not one that is ideological in a silly way. I do not think one need bend over backwards in making this interpretation, but it requires extrapolating from some whose argument has a similar style. We can get at one of the roots of much of what Martin and Knopoff say by way of warning against absolute truth claims, but not by making them out to be subjectivists or relativists. That is, they need not be taken as implying that one argument or claim is as good as any other.

The warning against absolutism one might take as suggesting, what Martin and Knopoff would find congenial, that there is no ultimate algorithm for deciding between competing theories. We do have some guidelines for choice—falsifiability, economy, generality, and so on—but in at least two ways these guidelines are not ultimate. First, they are themselves no more than empirical, in the sense that they have developed over time along with successful theories, rather than in advance of theories that have been propounded successfully, apparently as a result of following them; and we take them seriously only insofar as we think science in its current state is more successful than its predecessors. Second, there will always be arguments about the priority of the guidelines and their application to sets of competing theories. But to say that there is no neutral standpoint from which theories can be evaluated is not to say that we cannot criticize theories and find them one-sided or inept or just wrong. And Martin and Knopoff seem to agree that the deconstructor does not herself stand on some neutral ground apart from all theories, immune to deconstruction. Yet even then there may be value in their deconstruction.

The more radical view, that we cannot show that a theory is wrong or is better than another unless we can show which theory is ultimately right, is as old as Plato. The view that this radical view is false is as old as Socrates, whose mode of deconstruction has much admirable in it. Yet for all his skepticism Socrates believed that one must be personally committed to one's position in arguing about morality.

RATIONALITY

One can make similar observations about rationality, though Martin and Knopoff seem to put a rather different construction on it. The term "rational" is a kind of honorific term, like "scientific"; its use does not imply that we have agreed on a great many claims or methods that any sane person must readily accept. The criteria for the term's application will vary: they will attach to a certain opinion on how we ought to argue, and that opinion in turn will attach to a certain view of the world. This is not to say that irrationality is good or indistinguishable from its opposite. We can on some occasions legitimately distinguish between what is rational and what is not, even though our notion of the rational, like that of the scientific, will change over time as we learn more about what distinguishes good arguments from bad ones. No doubt one basis for saying that women are irrational is that men get to decide what is rational and what is not.

REACHING THE END OF THE ARGUMENT

To Martin and Knopoff's claim about how silence speaks volumes I have a similar response. What one does not say can indeed be significant, but one cannot mention everything, and there is no ideologically neutral way of deciding what to put into one's account and what to leave out—which is not say that any omission is as justifiable as any other. Jerry Falwell could argue that Martin and Knopoff's account by its resounding silence marginalizes a Christian approach to organizational ethics and thereby valorizes secular humanism. That sort of criticism is helpful on balance so long as it is not taken to be in itself a conversation-stopping proof of anything. What it is supposed to do first of all is raise questions. Apparently Martin and Knopoff hold—reasonably—that deconstruction is a form of conversation that never reaches the final word, the point at which all has been said; hence, their use of the phrase "a full deconstruction" should be ruled a slip rather than a knockdown. All this suggests that there are certain arguments that are virtually impossible to terminate conclusively, but these may be won or lost when one side or the other tires of wheeling in some ad hoc device that can defend any theory or explain any counterevidence.

A corollary to the view that there is neither any neutral place on which to stand to adjudicate among theories and interpretations is one that Martin and Knopoff seem to violate in describing their deconstructive practice, though possibly not in their actual practice. There is no such thing as *the analysis of* anything. Contrary to what Martin and Knopoff suggest, you cannot take a text or anything else apart into its ultimate building blocks, because there are no ultimate building blocks of anything. Nor, to make a similar point about words, can you always analyze or restate a position or a theory in neutral terms that both the theorists and their opponents are bound to accept. But to make their case Martin and Knopoff need not claim to have carved Weber at his joints.

MEANING AND TRUTH

That there is no single way of giving an analysis or an interpretation of anything is one consequence of a piece of news that resonates through much of contemporary philosophy: the dichotomy between statements true by definition and those true by virtue of what the world is like is untenable— as are many traditional dichotomies. There is no such thing as the readily assignable *meaning* of a word or a sentence, no clean separation of definitions and substantive claims. It is partly because we cannot give a good account of the nature of meaning that deconstruction can press its views of how our words mean, though those views are often difficult to discern in any detail, stated as they are indirectly, negatively, and ironically.

The overlap of meaning and truth implies that understanding a conceptual system that may be different from one's own is not entirely separable from accepting the truth of the sentences that constitute it. (On this point see Quine, especially 1960, and on related topics Davidson, 1984.) So when the sponsor of a new way of looking at the world says to a dissenter, "You just don't get it," she raises the question whether one can separate understanding from assent, hence dissent from misunderstanding. Indeed, one cannot do so perfectly cleanly; but if they differed not at all, then all our disagreements would be misunderstandings, and that is not a hypothesis to be invoked lightly. There is a distinction here, not a dichotomy, for the concepts of assent and understanding admit of degree and overlap. (Distinctions are nowadays considered good and dichotomies, which are clean and exhaustive, bad; but alas the difference between a distinction and a dichotomy is a distinction, not a dichotomy.)

RULES AND NUMBERS

Skepticism of this sort applies naturally to rules, which are, of course, a central feature of Weberian bureaucracy. Consider what Martin and Knopoff's account shows us about them. We credit Wittgenstein (1953), a favorite among the deconstructive, with having argued that following rules is not as easy as people who consider meaning unproblematical (call them strict constructionists) make it sound. To begin with, we must agree on how rules should be applied. To reach agreement we may invoke further rules that guide us in applying those first-order rules; but then we may disagree on the application of the second-order rules, and so on, unto infinity. So we must not assume that any activity can be wholly rule-bounded, but it does not follow that rules are nothing.

At the last Ruffin Lectures, Robert Solomon (1994a) attacked moral philosophers' overconfidence about rules and offered an Aristotelian account of virtue as a superior guide to moral action. The notion of virtue has problems of its own, but it is clear how little the rule orientation of the scribes and pharisees has to do with genuine morality, for the same reason it has little to do with genuine organizational effectiveness (to mention an ideologically provocative concept).

Perhaps the ultimate in Weberism is a fondness for quantification as a solution to our problems of uncertainty and imprecision. As a former consultant with experience in job evaluation and performance assessment, I can attest to the fascination that quantification holds for many managers, who incline to the hard, precise, clear, rational, verifiable, solid, comprehensible, valid, objective, firm, scientific, rigorous, logical, and bottom-line oriented. We find the same attitude among those who believe that rules are sufficient as well as necessary for management, and it fails for some of the same reasons. Quantification of the value of various things does not save us from the hard work of making decisions about how to evaluate work, allocate resources, and so on. Usually quantifying just makes these decisions, implicitly, unconsciously, and not very well. It is not altogether surprising that the single exception to the fondness for quantification seems to be comparable worth, which some managers and their ideological allies reject because it involves illegitimate quantification.

THE REAL PROBLEM IN WEBER

I do not think Weber's problem is one about women in the first instance. To state the matter broadly, it is a naive faith in the possibility of getting things right, born perhaps of a realization of how easy it is to get things wrong. Its political expression is a naïveté that partisans of democracy deplore. We find the right rules, the right organization design, the right means of reward and punishment, and the result is a political or administrative system so good that it need never change. It is a foolish kind of utopianism to suppose that anyone could design such a system or would want to live in one, though utopians from Plato onwards have banned change from the ideal state on the grounds that, since *ex hypothesi* it is ideal, any change will automatically be for the worse. It is all based on the kind of epistemological naïveté that Martin and Knopoff on the whole deplore and avoid, which is the traditional empiricist view of language, rules, analysis, and the nature and scope of science. And of course rationality, of which Weber gives an essentially Humean account: it is the most efficient choice of means to some end, which in turn is chosen on no rational basis and cannot be defended rationally. (For further criticism along these lines, see MacIntyre, 1981.)

The underlying problem about Weber has little to do with women directly, though I have little argument with Martin and Knopoff's view of the consequences of Weber's views and methods for women. But while his empiricism and the utopian structure built on it may be used against women, so may the opposite orientation. Most managers are aware of what can go wrong in the application of rules. In fact, partly because they are aware that no situation can be wholly rule-bound—not that they would put it that way—the men simply invoke the rules where they want to and invoke intuition where they don't. Men are quite capable of insisting sometimes that rules are rules and we have to be fair and on other occasions saying that of course we have to be reasonable and not rigid, as when hiring friends or setting salaries. Neither men's adherence to rules nor their departure from them is by itself the problem.

Surely male bonding is a greater threat to women than the hyperobjectivity of men, which is usually primarily a matter of lip service. Old boyism and even good old boyism are so well entrenched in some cases that Weberism would represent an enormous improvement. The grace and sympathy that Martin and Knopoff commend are no further removed from rationality than is the way the guys behave. In fact, it is my impression that female managers tend to differ from males in that the females are the ones who get their work in on time, behave decorously in meetings, and abide by the rules, in part because they are more readily punished when they do not. But it is true that insistence on the rules is typically a conservative move, and it is the men who usually have the power worth conserving.

Notice how the inadequacy of rules in this situation argues for the inadequacy of legislative remedies for women's grievances. Emphatically I do not argue that such an approach is futile. That would be to let myself be seduced by a false dichotomy: passing laws versus working on people's hearts and minds. One can do both; the point is that one can be content with neither.

Weber sees the problem of bad organizations as being a matter of the inadequacy of the rules, rather than slavish adherence to rules or cynical use of them. It does not follow that there is a subtext having to do with the subordination of women. To say Weber is the enemy is to cut just part way to the truth, as our earlier philosophical ruminations suggest: too great a reliance on rules, objectivity, and so on, is a sin equal to giving too little attention to these, and either may be and has been used against women. Weber thought he was saying that competence should be what counts. The notion that he was thinking about women at all seems at best poorly attested, though arguably he should have been.

Here we verge on the crucial but difficult issue of how we know that something, in Weber's case *das ewig Weibliche*, is the subject of a subtext. One can hardly be confident of how to identify a subtext if one cannot give a sound account of the notion of meaning and if on top of that there is a problem about relying on rules, whether for interpretation or anything else. But an interpretation may be more or less good; or at the very least, there is a time to listen and a time to invoke the hermeneutic of suspicion. Many of Martin and Knopoff's claims seem to rest on some views about ways of interpretation; the reader would like to hear more about those views. One might object that that is a lifetime project. This is probably true, but let us then not be confident on any occasion that we have identified a subtext.

Martin and Knopoff have directly or implicitly attacked rules, dichotomies, meanings, and utopias; they seem to be recommending reasonableness, distinctions, conversation, and better organizations in their stead. The false view of language, the world, and morality that underlies Weber's treatment of bureaucracy is broader than its sexist consequences and would continue to be problematic even if sexism were eliminated.

Here is another reason for doubting that women are the primary target, though they may be the primary victims. Just as problems about meaning have shown us we need to be wary of anything that parades as *the* analysis or deconstruction of a text, we must be suspicious of the claim that there are some properties unarguably natural for or essential to anything. I interpret [*sic*] Martin and Knopoff as attacking the facility with which we claim that any property naturally applies to anything. In that spirit, we should be suspicious of the claim that women are naturally soft, graceful, good at raising children, or anything on the right-hand side of Martin and Knopoff's list. As Elm argues in chapter 10 of this volume, Kant is just wrong in claiming that women are irrational.

It is true that, as things are, bureaucracy works against women, for example, by separating public from private. But that is not inherently a problem about bureaucracy. In fact, if companies did make special provisions having to do with daycare and so on just for the sake of women, then they would be perpetuating precisely the stereotypical sex roles that ought to be the real target of complaint here. That would be a kind of Felice Schwartz solution. A hundred years from now Weber will have no sexist consequences if by then cultural change has created self-fulfilling expectations of men doing their share of the work at home and women not having a recognizably feminine style of work or men a recognizably masculine one. Carol Gilligan's work (especially 1982) may then appeal only to historians of a particularly specialized kind. But Weber's views will probably still be a problem.

In Sum

This collection of mild complaints about what Martin and Knopoff have written and applause for some promising arguments and suggestions on which I would like to hear more comes to this: that Martin and Knopoff's chapter, in its necessary brevity, can only hint at the subtle and complex structure that lies beneath its provocative surface, at the powerful lessons they teach us, at enlightening conversations only begun.

9

Phallocorporatism

Daniel R. Ortiz

> *[M]an is the more aggressive, rational, . . . analytical-minded sex. . . .*
> *Woman, on the other hand, represents stability, flexibility, reliance on*
> *intuition. . . . Where man is discursive, logical, abstract, or*
> *philosophical, woman tends to be emotional, personal, practical, or*
> *mystical. Each set of qualities is vital and complements the other. . . .*
> Phyllis Schlafly, *The Power of the Positive Woman* (1977:20)

The four central chapters in this volume take aim at very large targets: corporate structure, bureaucratic ideology, and Western epistemology itself. Tired of what they see as the apologetics of traditional business ethics and the namby-pamby prescriptions of mainstream assimilationist feminisms, these chapters offer radical critique. Rather than identifying and palliating the many manifestations of gender oppression in business, they seek to cut to the very core by bringing to our attention the structural oppression of American corporatism.

Their overall ambition is to challenge phallocorporatism: the related practices, values, and ways of understanding that underwrite the existing economic order. These constructs, ranging from work expectations that prevent employees from spending time with their families to privileging objectivity in business analysis to valuing autonomy in business ethics, are phallocentric, the essays argue, because they reflect only male experience. In short, they are socially constructed notions that assume men as the measure of all things. Typical hours and conditions of employment, for example, assume that employees have no child-care responsibilities. Since women by and large still provide the care for children in our society, these terms of employment covertly assume that employees are male.

These chapters challenge phallocorporatism by denaturalizing it. They employ postmodernism to make us see current business practices and values as contingent, to recognize their status not as truths but as artifacts of culture. They then proceed to unmask the interests that these cultural constructs further. The constructs are not neutral but, instead, reflect and promote the values and well-being of some persons over those of others. Indeed, the politics of these constructs is simple to discern. Like most social institutions, the constructs favor those who created and control them—in this case, men. The chapters reflect the authors' hope that once we see through the objectivity and neutrality these traditionally accepted practices pretend to and come to see the practices as furthering men's interests, we can begin to replace them with other constructs less hostile to women's needs and aspirations.

These are laudable and radical ambitions. Paradoxically, however, three of the central chapters (Kathy Ferguson's excepted) fail because they are not radical enough. By failing to apply their postmodernist analysis thoroughly, the chapters end up reconstructing business practices along lines that recapitulate the problems of patriarchy. In particular, each of these three essays adopts to some degree the perspective of relational feminism, a theory holding that women speak in a different voice than men. This different voice, which embodies traditionally subordinated values like connectedness, care, responsibility, and contextuality, stands opposed to the patriarchal values that the essays believe prevail in business.

The problem stems from the reluctance of the essays to view relational feminism itself critically. By failing to understand it as yet another social construction, the essays fall into a dogmatic relational fundamentalism that ultimately undermines their feminist ambitions. Their stance not only violates some of their own "feminist" assumptions but, more dangerously, threatens to shore up traditional notions of women's identity. In short, while the essays do well to denaturalize phallocorporatism, they are wrong to erect relational fundamentalism in its stead. By failing to stay the course of postmodernism, the essays prove troublingly conservative in the end.

Of the four central chapters, Robbin Derry's makes the most limited use of postmodernism. Through interviews she seeks to explore the conflict businesses create for women between their own identities and their work roles. Derry finds that most women in business feel that they must sacrifice their identity in order to succeed. If they want to "make it," they must subordinate their own unique voice to the organization's. They must, in short, silence themselves.

Derry's postmodernist streak appears in her analysis of prevailing business practices. She believes that these practices are purely contingent, as a good postmodernist would, and further that they reflect a male point of view. Men have constructed business and business ethics in their own image, she argues, not on any neutral or objective basis, and they have made women live up to male models of behavior. She also argues that earlier feminists misconceived the business problem. Earlier assimilationist feminists, who argued that equality meant treating women the same as men, did women a true disservice. Instead of changing business to accommodate women, they merely encouraged women to compete with *men* as *men* to reach *male*-defined goals. Theirs was a project both futile and oppressive—futile because women should not be expected to compete successfully with men on men's own terms and oppressive because women must give up their own identity to try to succeed. It is better for feminism to change the corporation to make room for women, Derry implicitly argues, than to change women to fit existing business roles.

Derry's particular notion of women's identity would require a major change in business practices. The feminist approach, to Derry, "sees morality as increased connectedness and responsiveness rather than greater distance and autonomy" (28). Were women empowered *as women* in business, they would replace hierarchies with "organizational webs" (15) and emphasize reciprocal communication between parties. They would encourage "sharing information" (15), "building trust" (15), engaging in "collaborative dialogue" (15), and improving family-oriented policies (15).

Derry, moreover, has much hope for implementing this vision. Unlike the other writers, she sees no unavoidable conflict between achieving business goals and respecting women's identity in the workplace. As she puts it, "women have strengths and abilities . . . which can contribute to organizational strength, once their [different] voices are heard and celebrated" (29). Hers is a feminism even the shareholders would embrace.

Joanne Martin and Kathleen Knopoff aim at an even larger target. By exploring the tensions and omissions in Max Weber's theory of bureaucracy, Martin and Knopoff find that bureaucratic ideology itself, the set of values underlying the structure and existence of corporations, devalues women's experience. In particular, Martin and Knopoff uncover a series of dichotomies structuring Weber's work and, by implication, current business practices. On the left stand qualities traditionally valued in business; on the right their devalued opposites:

Valued	Devalued
Objective	Subjective
Rational	Irrational
Expert	Untrained
Abstract	Case-by-case
Dehumanized	Humane
Detached	Involved
Impersonal	Personal
Unemotional	Emotional
Authoritarian	Nurturant
Unequal	Egalitarian
Graceless	With grace
Unsympathetic	Sympathetic
Untouched by gratitude	Moved by gratitude

To Martin and Knopoff, these dichotomies all point toward a hidden assumption; the devalued characteristics are all, traditionally, more likely to be associated with women than with men (92). In other words, they believe that the principles which structure corporations are largely male. Businesses oppress women, in this view, not so much because they demand that women renounce their unique identities in order to be successful, as Derry argues, but more because business values deny women's experience and ideas about how to organize human experience. The values of the corporation, not merely its practices, enshrine and protect male supremacy.

Martin and Knopoff stand in a somewhat equivocal relationship to Derry. They both reinforce and undercut her at the same time. They reinforce Derry by finding that corporations devalue and exclude women's experience in yet another way. Whereas Derry locates masculinist privilege in business structure, Martin and Knopoff locate it in the ideology which underpins that structure. In a sense, they argue that the problem lies on an even deeper level. To the extent they suggest that corporate structure is an epiphenomenon of ideology, however, Martin and Knopoff undercut Derry. For their argument raises doubt about whether we can make room for women's unique voices within corporations if we do not first discard the masculinist ideology upon which corporations stand. Can we reform structure without first reforming ideology?

Martin and Knopoff offer a curious answer. Although they strongly criticize corporate ideology, they seem pessimistic of achieving any change at this level. Instead of offering up strategies to combat bad ideology, they suggest reforms much like Derry's: changing everyday business practices to make the workplace more hospitable to women. Their concrete suggestions include ending more than full-time work commitments; altering training requirements; and permitting flexible hours, part-time work, job sharing, and leaves of absence (46). Why do Martin and Knopoff, who locate the problem deeper than does Derry, work to cure it in exactly the same way? Are they radicals at heart who are resigned to unfairness because of the great depth at which they believe oppression resides? Or do they propose chipping away at discriminatory work requirements rather than reforming the governing ideology itself because they believe smaller, concrete changes in work structure are a necessary prelude to ideological renovation? Their answer is unclear.

Marta Calás and Linda Smircich locate gender oppression at an even deeper level. Whereas Derry sees oppression in corporate structure and Martin and Knopoff see it in the ideology generating that structure, Calás and Smircich see it in the epistemology, the way we think and understand, that underwrites ideology itself. In other words, while Derry and Martin and Knopoff criticize masculinist practices and values, Calás and Smircich criticize the masculinist ways of knowing that support both practices and values. As a discipline, they believe, business and, in particular, business ethics valorize concepts like rationality, comprehensiveness, impartiality, systematicness, scientism, objectivity, autonomy, abstraction, and universalism, all of which together constitute what Calás and Smircich call "patriarchal logic" (61) or the "patriarchal scientific stance" (71). These concepts, they assert, are masculinist through and through.

Calás and Smircich call for feminist revisions of these ways of knowing. They seek "alternative epistemologies" (64), particularly "feminist moral epistemologies" (64), which would reflect women's attempts to name their own experience. And like Derry and Martin and Knopoff, Calás and Smircich have a particular idea of what such feminist alternatives would look like. Despite their postmodern distrust of claims for a univocal women's identity, they would move toward an interactive relational epistemology, one in which "moral judgments, and moral understanding [are] grounded in actual contexts of particular others" (64) and one that would emphasize the fundamental interdependency of human existence. In short, Calás and Smircich hold to a unitary epistemology of women that valorizes all the qualities traditional (masculinist) epistemology disparages. Like Martin, they affirm for women the qualities traditional constructions have long subordinated.

Calás and Smircich stand in the same uneasy relationship to Martin and Knopoff as the latter authors do to Derry. On the one hand, Calás and Smircich extend Derry's and Martin and Knopoff's critique by showing how patriarchy pervades the most fundamental ways in which we know and experience the world. On the other hand, if Calás and Smircich are right, Martin and Knopoff's attempt to reform corporate ideology and Derry's attempt to reform corporate structure are doomed because they overlook the masculinist epistemology on which ideology and structure stand. How can we "feminize" business if Western epistemology, which underwrites it at every point, remains masculinist through and through? No matter how deeply feminism presses, the phallus rears its ugly head.

A more troubling problem is the particular notion of women's identity all these writers adopt. To a significant degree, all three chapters affirm relational feminism as women's identity. In this theory, most famously developed by Carol Gilligan (1982) in *In a Different Voice,* women and men tend to approach experience and morality differently. Puzzled as to why women scored lower than men on tests of moral development, Gilligan conducted research into how people reason their way through hypothetical and real moral dilemmas. In her studies, Gilligan discovered that the values of abstraction, rationality, autonomy, universalizability, and rights, which morality has traditionally celebrated, describe only one moral perspective.

It is, moreover, a moral perspective associated with men. Girls and women, Gilligan argues, reason differently. They value connectedness, not autonomy; they organize relationships through webs, not hierarchies; they generate morality from responsibility to those in need, not from individual rights; and they look at moral dilemmas concretely, not abstractly. Whereas men tend to follow a logic of justice, women tend to heed an ethic of care. Under this view, women reason differently than men, not less well, and their poor performance in earlier studies should not surprise us since those studies measured masculinist ways of thinking.

It should be clear how thoroughly the three chapters adopt this relational perspective. Derry, for example, insists that women have a "unique voice" (11), a voice that speaks in webs, not hierarchies (11), and that shares information, builds trust in clients, and draws co-workers into collaborative dialogue (15). It is, moreover, a voice that "require[s] greater attention to individual needs, desires, traits, strengths, advantages and disadvantages, rather than eschewing such information in an attempt to achieve blind justice and impartiality. This feminist approach sees morality as increased connection and responsiveness, rather than greater distance and autonomy" (28).

Martin and Knopoff adopt relationalism just as explicitly. At one point she cites Gilligan as exemplifying "precisely those qualities that Weber is dismissing with disdain" (41). More important, her list of feminine concepts devalued by bureaucratic ideology—the subjective, the irrational, the humane, the personal, the emotional, the nurturing, and the sympathetic (41)—largely coincides with Gilligan's ethic of care.

Calás and Smircich are just as complete, although perhaps more diffident, in their embrace of relational feminism. Although they refer to relationalism as one of "the most common (and vulgarized) understandings [of] feminist ethics," note its controversial essentialism, and call for feminism to assume a postmodern form that "renounce[s] the 'women's voices' perspectives . . . by replacing the unitary notions of 'woman' and 'feminine-gender identity' with plural conceptions of social identity" (74). In the end they advocate constructing women's identity in much the same way that relational feminism itself does. Their alternative epistemologies favor contextualism over abstraction, community and interdependency over autonomy, and responsibilities over rights (64). They may renounce relationalism as women's *moral* identity, then, but they certainly affirm it as their *epistemological* one.

Affirming relationalism as women's identity is troubling for several reasons. First, it essentializes women by claiming for them all an identity that only some, perhaps privileged, women may possess. Even Gilligan herself now claims that relationalism accurately describes only a minority of women. According to her more recent work, just as many women exclusively exhibit traditional masculinist qualities as exclusively exhibit relational ones, while a third group of women, also of equal size, exhibits both (Gilligan, 1987). Unless these relationalists mean to make hefty normative claims about what women's identity *should* be like and are willing to write off many women now as mere victims of false consciousness, their affirmation of relationalism as women's identity is somewhat troubling.

Second, even if most women did possess this unique relational perspective, it is unclear what attitude feminists should take toward it. Relationalism could accurately describe women only because it represents the identity that men have allowed women to assume. As Catherine MacKinnon writes, "Women value care because men have valued us according to the care we give them. . . . Women think in relational terms because our existence is defined in relation to men" (MacKinnon, 1987: 39). In MacKinnon's view, women's "different voice" is a male construction. Since men have given women this unique perspective, it hardly sounds right to call it women's own. In fact, in this view, affirming such an identity as women's does not liberate women but instead perpetuates more effectively men's domination over them. It leads the slaves themselves, not just the masters, to celebrate the identity the masters have allowed them to assume.

Finally, relationalism is highly susceptible to political misuse. In the hands of those who would relegate women to the sphere of domesticity, relationalism proves a powerful tool—as the quotation by Phyllis Schlafly at the beginning of this chapter suggests. If women's "nature" is to nurture, perhaps women's "natural" role is that of mother. As Joan Williams (1989) has noted, although relationalism can serve as a powerful critique of traditional capitalist ideology, claiming relationalism as women's identity, let alone celebrating it as such, provides powerful arguments to those who would keep women in the home and family. Dissenters from traditional women's roles could be told—now with some feminist "backing"—that domesticity represents women's strength and special identity.

All of these troubles, particularly the political ones, spring from the fundamentalism of the essays. Although the essays powerfully unmask accepted business truths as social constructions, they simply accept without question the truth of relationalism for women. Women's relational identity stands as a given, as a kind of metaphysical fact. Unlike the institutions of patriarchy, relationalism cannot be challenged and so stands largely immune to political analysis. Like the patriarchs before them, these writers naturalize the identities and values they champion.

Ferguson alone avoids these dangers, shunning the others' conservatism by pursuing postmodernism through and through. Ferguson asks us to adopt a postmodern business ethic, which calls upon us to recognize the marginal and to "attend to all calls to order with a sympathetic ear for what does not or will not fit" (90). At bottom, she asks us to celebrate and encourage diversity, not for its own sake but because it will better enable us to reenvision ourselves and to reconstruct our primary social institutions, including business. Most important, she, unlike the other writers, does not affirm any particular construction of women's identity, let alone traditional ones. Rather, she seeks to reinforce in us ways of thinking that question, disrupt, and destabilize whatever particular notions we hold.

Ferguson's argument may disappoint some. By arguing more for an attitude toward identity construction than for any particular construction of identity, she may appear hopelessly wishy-washy. Unlike the others, she gives few concrete prescriptions. Ferguson's reluctance to affirm any particular identity for women, however, is actually her strength. Hasty, specific constructions, like those the others argue for, may betray women's identity rather than fulfill it. Ferguson's vision of identity construction has little content because at this point any content would represent an imposition. How can women affirm their own identity before men have freed them to discover it? Men have defined so much of women's history and identity that describing an undominated women's voice is simply impossible—for now. Until we let women be, free them to discover, name, and create their own differences, Ferguson suggests, we cannot construct a feminist identity.

Luckily, Ferguson tells us how to begin our project. She describes several ways of opening ourselves up to difference. By reading accounts like Vandana Shiva's (1988) *Staying Alive* or Sara Ruddick's (1989) *Maternal Thinking*, for example, we can begin to see how some women's best understandings of their own experiences challenge received notions of identity and of business practice. In this way, we can come to question our own notions, open ourselves up to difference, and ultimately revise our own ideas.

Other means stand available as well. As the method of several of the essays suggest, by looking at the historical development of our own practices and values we can come to a realization of their contingency and so open ourselves up to difference. History can thus denaturalize our institutions, enable us to consider alternatives, and furnish us with materials from which to build. Similarly, other feminists suggest consciousness raising as a means for discovering difference. Through this methodology, women explore the gaps between the roles society has created for them and their own experiences, needs, and desires. By discovering how they themselves resist the descriptions society provides, women can better understand and challenge existing constructions of identity.

Any approach like Ferguson's will not bring quick results—only better ones. Men have so controlled women's history that women cannot simply assume an identity unaffected by male domination. Even women's own experiences, needs, and desires, the materials out of which they would start constructing such an identity, reflect the history of identities that men have given or permitted them. This is why we must be careful before making broad claims about women's identity to consider both the extent to which men have constructed the identities we would ascribe to women and how well these identities suit the aspirations of those whose lives they would prescribe. Any other course would be naive and would run the risk of reinscribing the traditional notions of women's identity that we should be trying to escape.

We should be similarly careful before rejecting all existing constructions of male identity and business practice as patriarchal. Even if notions such as rationality, autonomy, and rights have been constructed and controlled by men, who have often wielded them against women, women should not simply dismiss these constructions as forms of oppression. It would be better for women to consider whether these tools and descriptions, along with all others, can be useful to them. Some of these constructions may be useful, some not, but they represent a source of possibilities that we should allow women to consult.

Rejecting these descriptions wholesale, as relational feminism does, can only impoverish women, for it denies them a rich source of materials from which to construct their own identities. It is not inconceivable that at least some women may want to appropriate some of these descriptions and claim them as their own. Relational fundamentalism would foreclose this possibility. In the name of women's uniqueness, it would sharply delimit the ways in which women can reimagine and re-create themselves. As in patriarchy, their identities would belong to others than themselves. We need to get beyond these orthodoxies—both the patriarchal and fundamentalist ones. Both sides' descriptions of women are too simplistic and confining. Rather than impose a new, more complicated orthodoxy, however, we should, as Ferguson asks, attend to difference. Only by transcending orthodoxy itself, by rejecting formal prescriptions of gender and individual identity that others would impose, can we fully exploit the possibilities for individual and social re-creation.

III

New Directions for Business Ethics

10

Feminism in Business Ethics: Equal and Different

Dawn R. Elm

This chapter seeks to point out the injustice done women in our society by virtue of the common idea that women must be like men to be considered equal (and therefore of any value) to men. There is a tide rising throughout the United States today that provides the beginning of recognition of the idea that women do not have to be the same to be considered equal to men. Books like Helgesen's *The Female Advantage* (1990), Gilligan, Ward, and Taylor's *Mapping the Moral Domain* (1988), and MacKinnon's *Toward a Feminist Theory of the State* (1991) are symbols of this tide. The irony of this conception of "equality" is its juxtaposition with stereotypical slurs such as "You're a woman; you just don't understand" or the criticism that women are too "emotional" or "passionate" to be rational regarding intellectual inquiry (or any other traditionally "rational" activity).

There are at least two reasons to disregard these conceptions of women. First, women may be passionate and still contribute meaning to intellectual pursuits. Consider the passion of Nietzsche, a man who was insane when he wrote many of his treatises. Passion does not necessarily exclude reasonable thought.

Second, women may also be more rational than men. This could be possible for two reasons: Men do not have a corner on the market of rationality, since they commit irrational acts as frequently as women (as a brief look at criminal activity statistics demonstrates). Further, perhaps women define rationality differently than men. The second implication leads to the focus of this essay.

The subject of this chapter is the power behind the notion of equal and different. In our business ethics literature (and discussions) we typically espouse the need to have equality to have a just society. However, the concept of equality is defined as treating women and men in the same fashion: applying the same standards and criteria to both genders. I am going to argue that this conceptualization of a just society is not just at all but reflects a masculine Band-Aid for the moral inadequacy of our social system. That is because women are *not* the same as men and therefore should not be considered the same in order to be equal to men. Freeman and Gilbert noted that

> most scholars take a view of "equality means treating everyone the same." The empirical nature of the field has meant that scholars then try to document whether or not men and women have been treated the same, or equally, or fairly. Of course we find that women are treated differently, and so we set forth to discover the reasons. But, some feminist theorists have questioned whether or not women and men should be treated the same. They have questioned whether or not there are real and relevant differences in the way the men and women experience the world. (1991:12)

At a recent Ruffin Lecture Series at the Darden Graduate School at the University of Virginia, I had the privilege of interacting with a number of well-known feminist theorists and business ethicists. The title of the series, as noted in this volume, was "Women's Studies and Ethics."

This interaction sowed the seeds for the thesis of this essay. During the course of the lectures, it became apparent that the masculinity of academe, as well as business, is well entrenched and will be difficult to overcome. The notion of women as being equal to men, yet different from them is one that renders significant power to begin to understand the incredible importance and implications of this task.

We have been besotted with this notion of equality. We have substantially institutionalized policies and procedures that demonstrate how correct we are in attempting to achieve this equality: Equal Opportunity Employment, Affirmative Action, and my personal favorite: Equal Rights Amendment. Consider Fagenson's (1990:271) discussion of biases in gender research: "Affirmative action laws and maternity laws can affect the way women are treated and viewed as organizational members. The notion that women have lower ascribed status in society than men (Schneer, 1985) can influence the way they are perceived and treated in their organizations."

These policies and procedures are structures designed to uphold gender bias in our society. This is so simply because their purpose is to create equality according to male standards. Women are considered to be subservient to these criteria. Perhaps the next social institution could be called the "Women Humane Society." Its purpose would be to ensure the humane treatment of the females in our society. Traditionally, only species of lesser importance need to be cared for in special ways—like the elderly, the handicapped, pets, and women. Thomas (1990:109) suggests this in his recent work on diversity in the workplace:

When we ask how we're doing on race relations, we inadvertently put our finger on what's wrong with the question and with the attitude that underlies affirmative action. So long as racial and gender equality is something we *grant* to minorities and women, there will be no racial and gender equality. What we must do is create an environment where no one is advantaged or disadvantaged, an environment where "we" is everyone. [Italics added]

The underlying premise has been that women should be treated equally: *just like men*. Why? Women are *not* just like men. In fact, I would suggest they do not want to be just like men. The notion that women can be equal to men, and yet different from them, seems foreign to our nature and most certainly to our existing systems of justice.

Gregory's (1990) discussion of three theoretical perspectives regarding differences of women from men serves to show how deeply rooted different as unequal is in our society. The person-centered view suggests that the position of women in our society (and in business) is a function of factors internal to women. Their biological and socialization experiences create traits and behaviors that limit women's success as managers. The organization-centered view, conversely, suggests that one's position in the organizational hierarchy determines traits and behaviors. Women traditionally occupy lower levels in the hierarchy and thus develop behaviors and traits in response to those positions.[1] The third perspective is the gender context view. This perspective suggests that the proportion of a certain gender in a given position, as well as the social status of that group, contributes to the traits and behaviors acceptable for that group. Women are the minority group (to men) in business and therefore of lower status.

Different as unequal is taken for granted. This is inconsistent with the perspective of women as the same as men, as well as with the perspective of women as equal to men. In most works (like Gregory's) difference is explicitly discussed as the reason (regardless of the specific theoretical perspective) for the inequality between women and men. Perceiving women as different yet equal requires a fundamentally different view of our society.

EQUALITY AND EQUITY FOR JUSTICE

I am discussing the inadequacies of our social system as designed by men. This is not to suggest that all men are bigots or sexists but rather that the system has sexist distinctions inherent in the structures that currently exist. Justice can mean equal, but more likely it means equitable. The distinction is a crucial one, since equity is typically determined by the contributions. Fairness becomes the result of contributing toward some set of criteria. Put another way, equity, not equality, should be the moral objective of our social system. Women should receive for what they contribute based on a universally agreed-upon set of standards—not male standards. If this were the case, glaring discrepancies in our society might disappear. For example, child care could become one of the most important contributions that could be made. Or, as in Atwood's *The Handmaid's Tale* (1988), childbearing. Why would this be true? Because *different* standards would apply. If this seems farfetched, envision a world in which children are extremely difficult to give birth to due to nuclear devastation or some other cataclysmic event.[2] Female capabilities would be in greater demand than male-oriented capabilities typified by doctors, lawyers, or Fortune 500 CEOs. Is this a rational argument? It follows the same path as the implicit argument for the equality of right brain (or intuitive information processing style) and left brain (or thinking information processing style) thinking. Are they different? Absolutely. Do we talk about them as equal? Absolutely. Do we really consider them equal? Absolutely not. Pick up any basic management textbook: the two types of thinking are introduced with careful verbiage regarding how they are equally valued and need to be integrated to create the best managerial skill. Elsewhere, in the same text, however, creative problem solving and creativity are introduced as crucial management skills. Of course, right-brain thinking is more creative than left-brain thinking. The real message is simply that right-brained individuals are more creative and therefore more valuable—certainly to businesses and likely to our society.

In her book *Women Managers: Travellers in a Male World,* Judi Marshall (1984) suggests that the suppression of women in business is due to their status as the subdominant group in society and in organizational hierarchies as a reflection of society. She suggests that the dominant majority (men) has two major objectives: (1) to maintain its power position and (2) to keep the subdominant group in its place by limiting the roles to which its members have access. The net result is that the subdominant group becomes preoccupied with survival and copes through adjustment or accommodation. Equity is an unrealistic goal when survival is the uppermost concern.

If the moral objective of our social systems was equity according to a set of standards that apply regardless of gender, there would be very different criteria for success in business. Qualities such as capability to nurture, comfort, build relationships, or network might come to the forefront. As it stands now, women are generally advised how to succeed according to the existing male standards. Consider the language used and the advice given to women in academic environments in a recent *Academic Leader* article entitled "Tenure-Track Women: A View from the Trenches":

> *Make Lemonade:* Avoid male colleagues who feel most threatened. Be visible outside of your department and in the community. Find out if there's any kind of mentor program for new faculty. Know your institution's rules inside and out. Make an effort to understand the unwritten rules too.

Some people would argue that the rules of the game are male; it would be a different game if female rules applied. However, this perpetuates the antagonistic spirit of "them versus us." It would be better to transcend gender as an issue and create new standards from scratch. Thomas (1990:113) notes: "Diversity and Equal Opportunity is a big step up. It presupposes that the white male culture has given way to one that respects difference and individuality." He goes on to suggest that the difficulty white males will have in giving up the driver's seat will be a barrier to this change. Perhaps if enough voices contribute to new views of our social systems the barrier will be overcome.

It is time for us to abandon this preoccupation with women as the same as men. Judgment standards should transcend gender in such a way that equality is obtained with differences intact. It is much like the equality of a pound of apples and a pound of pears. The two are equal quantities of different things. Would this really be so hard to translate to men and women in society? Some of the works in this volume suggest that it might not be all that difficult to create standards of justice that are independent of gender. Equality would not necessarily imply sameness, and equity would provide the foundation for just social structures for both men and women. We just have to let go of old, familiar ideas and methods and tolerate a little discomfort in the changes in order to achieve a better world.

11

Competition, Care, and Compassion: Toward a Nonchauvinist View of the Corporation

Robert C. Solomon

> *Many of them hadn't worked on Wall Street for more than a year, but they had acquired Wall Street personas. One of their favorite words was* professional. *Sitting stiffly, shaking firmly. Speaking crisply, and sipping a glass of ice water were professional. Laughing and scratching your armpits were not.*
>
> Michael Lewis, *Liar's Poker* (1989:28)

Something is happening in the modern corporation. Everyone knows it. The rules have changed. America is said to be losing its "competitive edge," major companies are going bankrupt, and life at the office has never seemed so insecure or under such pressure. Ruthlessness is rampant, even in the best corporations. At the time of this writing, IBM, the company that "never fires anybody," is about to lay off 17,000 *additional* people—after a major downsizing the year before. New York banking giants Chemical and Manufacturers Hanover merged a few years ago, with an initial sacrifice of at least 6,000 jobs. (A bank analyst at Warburg worried that the merger was "too friendly" and might lack the "toughness" to ruthlessly slash jobs [*Newsweek* 1991:37].) But the changes that follow a crisis are not necessarily negative, and there is hope that one positive shift in corporate thinking may well be the reconception of the very nature of the corporation. This essay pursues such a possibility and examines an idea whose time, perhaps, has come. It is the idea of the "caring corporation" (see e.g., Naisbett, 1988).

144

MACHO-MANAGEMENT: THE CHAUVINISM
OF THE MODERN CORPORATION

> *We can learn a good deal about the nature of business by comparing it*
> *with poker. No one expects poker to be played on the ethical principles*
> *preached in churches. It is right and proper to bluff a friend out of the*
> *rewards being dealt a good hand. . . . Poker has its special ethics, . . .*
> *different from the ethical ideals of civilized human relationships.*
>
> Alfred Carr, "Is Business Bluffing Ethical?"
> *Harvard Business Review* (Feb.–March 1968:145)

> *The drift of modern history seems to imply that the power of the human*
> *mind to learn principles of humane restraint and reform from modern*
> *wars is extremely limited. What people learn from wars seems to be this:*
> *the technique for making each increasingly efficient—that is, destructive*
> *and vicious.*
>
> Paul Fussell, *The Norton Book of Modern War* (1991:25)

Competition, we keep hearing, is the fuel of free enterprise. It is the
threat of competition that will keep the corporation efficient, the company honest, morale high, and everyone motivated. Management and
employees will be productive for fear for their jobs. Companies that fail
will disappear, and individuals in a company who are not fit will be fired.
Such is the law of the jungle or, perhaps more accurately, the battlefield:
"only the fit survive." The corporation, accordingly, is often structured as
a kind of military organization, built for battle, set and ready against any
and all competitors. The troops (employees and managers on the line)
are expected to be fit and to keep in shape. Campaigns are fought without mercy. Customers and consumers are not people or fellow citizens
but the site of battle, the terrain to be conquered. High-flying executives
are the generals. Their careers may be on the line, but they also rate
golden parachutes in case they fail. Managers are links in the chain of
command, and those who are weak must be eliminated (the golden
handshake, unlike the parachute, rarely breaks one's fall). Most employees are no more than cogs in the military machine, provided with just
enough salary and benefits to keep them in fighting spirit, but mere can-
non fodder when the battle gets going. It is a gruesome image, mani-
fested almost constantly in the military metaphors so often heard in and
around the corporation. In an only slightly more civilized spirit (and
usually in the less pressured context of affluent times), business seems to
be more of a game; the competition is a welcome "challenge" rather
than a fight for survival; and the corporation is viewed, in a more egalitarian way, as a "team." Accordingly, the virtues of team spirit, good
sportsmanship, and playing one's heart out are lauded above all others.
The only thing that counts is the company and its success against its
rivals. But the metaphor has shifted only slightly. Competition is still the
name of the game; belligerence toward the opposition is the mandatory

focus; the suspension of ordinary human relationships and subservience of the individual to the organization and the chain of command are the order of the day.

This is the picture of contemporary corporate chauvinism. Chauvinism is a form of belligerent competitiveness, coupled with prejudice and contempt. It is a stupid fidelity that manifests itself in such unprincipled and mindless directives as "just following orders" and "my company, right or wrong." But although chauvinism is defined in terms of its competitiveness, it is most evident in its immediate personal consequences: indifference, an uncaring, tough-minded attitude toward employees, a lack of compassion, and an eye on the bottom line. Of course, the word "chauvinism" now triggers an automatic association with "male chauvinism," which is not merely incidental. It has long been noticed by mothers, kindergarten teachers, and child psychologists—and it has been lately expounded in seemingly endless theory—that boys tend to be more competitive and girls more caring. But whatever one ultimately makes of the now much-discussed difference between the genders and their different voices, it remains historically unchallengeable that the corporation is almost entirely a modern male invention. The structure of the corporation, as well as its management and its metaphors, is based on the "old-boy" network and the hierarchical thinking of the old imperial and more recent military experience of the two world wars.

On an individual basis, what is central to such thinking is the mock-macho—"it's tough to survive" and "every man for himself"—imagery of the jungle or the battlefield. But it is really the corporation that counts, and however much individual self-interest and personal ambition there may be, it is essential (and one of the most basic if unspoken rules of the institution) that one speaks only of the interests and the success of the company. The language of that speech is wholly defined in terms of competition, the need for efficiency and effectiveness, the urgency of productivity and timeliness, and "results," which are virtually always reducible to a positive number in the quarterly report of profits. In the chauvinist corporation, the interests of individual employees come into play only in the context of motivation—how to get them to perform and not steal from the company via theory X, Y, or Z. The bottom line—not only profits (which, after all, are only a cardinal number) but ordinal *winning*, "beating the pants off" the competition—is everything. (The worst alternative, in similarly sexist parlance, is being caught unprepared, "with one's pants down.") To be sure, much goes on in the corporation that can be understood without reference to the competitive edge and the military metaphors that lend it weight, but most of these activities are secondary, at best mere "human interest" stories, suitable for the back pages of the annual report but hardly the stuff and substance of most organizations.

The concept of competition is used to assault, to terrify, and, of course, to sell products. In one recent but typical advertisement (for a telephone beeper), the shadows of a wolf and a rabbit are shown on a wall behind two executives (the executive who didn't buy the beeper is the rabbit). The concept of competition is also employed to excuse (or justify) lapses (or worse) in ethics. Twenty years ago, Alfred Carr (1968) made his name in business ethics circles when he published one of the two most often reviled and refuted articles in the field (the other being Milton Friedman's (1970) infamous and more sophisticated "Social Responsibility" essay). Carr argued at length that business is a lot like poker and, therefore, does not follow the rules of ordinary morality. But as the infuriated comments poured into the *Harvard Business Review*, it became apparent that the object of indignation was not Carr's game analogy but rather his choice of games. Poker is viewed as disreputable and primarily a vehicle for gambling. Had Carr chosen an equally competitive and more brutal sport such as football, he probably would have earned nearly unanimous enthusiasm (though he would have failed to create such a controversy—obviously his intent).

THE END OF COWBOY CAPITALISM:
THE LIMITS OF COMPETITION

> *A commercial banker was just an ordinary American businessman with ordinary American ambitions. He lent a few hundred million dollars each day. . . . He was only doing what he was told by someone higher up in an endless chain of command. A commercial banker wasn't anymore a troublemaker than Dagwood Bumstead.*
>
> Michael Lewis, *Liar's Poker* (1989:27)

> *I think a better strategy in business is to work hard, be honest, and be smarter than anyone else.*
>
> L. D. Barre (in response to Carr), *Harvard Business Review* (May–June 1968:164)

It is not entirely clear how much business really loves or thrives on competition, no matter what the rhetoric. How could Hertz be delighted when number two Avis rose in the market from one more other car company to become a true competitor, and could "Big Blue" have been thrilled by the rapid success of Apple and a half dozen other computer companies that now challenge IBM's one-time domination of the information market? (As of this writing, Apple and IBM have just signed an extensive cooperative agreement, a high-tech nonaggression pact.) The rise of foreign competition is even more spectacular in its hollowing of the competitive rhetoric. What passed for "competition" between American car makers in the 1950s and 1960s was, in retrospect, a friendly game of cards in the cozy living room of an exclusive club. None of the players welcomed the competition from Japan (they had long dismissed the growing market shares in Germany). But when Lee Iacocca pleaded for protectionism, of course, it was in order to "let us compete," and the anticompetitive message was nevertheless clear. A rather risky but obvious analogy to the American lack of enthusiasm for real competition is this: in 1994, the (by far) largest audience in the world gathered around television sets to watch the playoffs and finals of the most popular and competitive sport in the world. It was the World Cup in soccer, a game played with competitive enthusiasm by virtually every country in the world but the United States. It was not (what we presumptuously call) the World Series or the Superbowl. Our Big Three Sports, our three national pastimes, are almost exclusively our own. Except for foreign farm teams and a few novice leagues around the world, no one else plays much baseball or basketball or (what we call) football. And so when we in the United States call a competition the World Series and declare our teams world champions, there is a bit of irony if not hypocrisy in the embarrassing fact that nobody else is competing for the title (except, now, the Canadians). And yet, in at least one team sport where the competition is truly international, we prefer to remain at home. Do we Americans love the competitive spirit? Or do we prefer the comfort of established rivalries within a carefully protected arena? I say this not to be offensive but just to open our eyes. Competition is not the be-all and end-all of business, nor is it an attitude that we enthusiastically embrace, except within well-defined and hardly winner-take-all conditions.

Competition is variously said to be the backbone of business, the engine that makes it move, the mechanism that makes the great machine of capitalism go, the "magic" in the magic of the market. Corporations, in turn, are defined by their ability to compete and are characterized (in usually flattering terms) for their chauvinism. (In my book *The New World of Business,* I quoted a human resources spokesman for Pepsico: "Most of our guys are having fun. They are the kind of people who would rather be in the Marines than in the Army" [Solomon, 1994b:137].) Much of this talk, of course, is sheer demagoguery, an excuse for no-holds-barred strategy, otherwise unprincipled action, inexcusable behavior toward one's middle managers or employees, or a polemic against this or that government program. Much of it is deceptive self-congratulation, proclaimed by spokesmen for giant companies that have already won the field or, more likely, have accumulated such a monopoly that they themselves have ended the competition—and would like to keep it that way. Most of it, of course, is just one more macho metaphor, the self-gratifying male image of the lone Wild West champion or, in uniform, Audie "To Hell and Back" Murphy taking on all comers and "proving" himself against overwhelming odds. It is what Ed Freeman has recently called "cowboy capitalism," without, I hope, thereby meaning to question the integrity of those few remaining rough and underpaid ropers and herd tenders in Texas and elsewhere who have enough to cope with without having to live up to a cinematic myth as well.

But what is most obviously true about intercorporate competition, beneath the rhetoric and despite the current blood bath and battles in a number of core industries (banking, computers, telecommunications and automobiles, to name a few), is that it is all but over—at least in the fabulous form that has given rise to the language and mythology of corporate chauvinism. The Japanese success has inspired something more than empty cross-cultural emulation (and no small amount of racism). The new demands for business-government partnerships and industry-wide coordination and reorganization show a dynamic appreciation for the role of cooperation in business, and the increase in cooperative (as opposed to "unfriendly") mergers is an obvious sign that something other than competition is ruling the free market system. And serious productivity and morale problems make it quite clear that the future of the corporation cannot lie in the militaristic, tough-guy chauvinism of decades past. What will replace unfettered competition is not fettered competition but cooperation, and what will replace the military chauvinism inside the corporation is a new corporate culture of individuality and caring (Freeman and Leidtka, 1991).

This is not to say, of course, that competition has no place or that it is ultimately not very important for business. Anyone can think of industries that have grown lazy and inefficient because of lack of competition, especially in industries that are protected from competition by the government. (Or, alternatively, where the industry in question is actually run by the government.) The Canadian wine industry, for example, has been in operation for almost as long as its would-be competition in California, longer than in neighboring Washington State and much longer than in Texas, which began making wine only a few decades ago and put bottles on the shelves only in the past decade. Canada shares the geological good fortunes of these others, but—without offense to my northern neighbors—the wine it produces is almost undrinkable. (The reds *are* undrinkable.) The Canadian government protected the industry. It had a virtually captive clientele, and there was no reason to be self-critical or to experiment and improve. When the protection ended, the industry was on the brink of collapse, kept afloat only by chauvinism and already-ruined palates, until the new competition spurred the necessary incentives. We all know of dozens of similar examples, if we can remember the commodities in question before they disappeared from the market.

There can be no doubt about the value of competition, but it is neither the carrot nor the stick, though it does indeed hang over lazy and overly obstinate donkeys as a constant warning that nothing is guaranteed or assured, that there are no ultimate monopolies, and that business (your business) exists only because it succeeds in serving a purpose, in satisfying consumers. If it fails to meet these objectives, or someone else can meet them better or with more appeal, then the stick finds its mark and measures out its punishment. But, of course, competition isn't the only source of sanctions in the business world, nor should it be.

Companies that unknowingly manufacture deadly products but then refuse to take them off the market immediately—for example, the makers of flammable children's clothing in the 1970s—require a quicker hand than Adam Smith's "invisible" one. Too often the media don't always pay attention, and neither, accordingly, does the public. And all too often the segment of the population that is most vulnerable is the least informed.

Government regulation—itself not known for its speediness or its well-informed public support—is certainly not the best option. Ideally, the corrective to a business disaster is a company that cares, as laudably exemplified by Johnson and Johnson in its quick and caring response to the Tylenol poisonings in the early 1980s. But until industries and business in general exemplify widespread self-policing and are willing to prove that they care about more than the quarterly report and the stockholders (as exemplified by the chairman of Exxon after the oil spill in Prince Edward Sound), then competition and cooperation will have to be coupled with strict government regulation, more criminal indictments, and bankruptcy class action suits. The cumbersome if eventually effective sanctions of consumer sovereignty alone are not enough. But competition by itself is not a mechanism for fairness or safety, and it is by no means magic. What the free market system presupposes is not just the law of supply and demand but a cooperative and caring environment, the unspoken community, the compassion and "fellow-feeling" that Adam Smith presupposed.[1] The "invisible hand" is not a divine response to unbridled competition. It is a knowing (and not at all invisible) human solution to the problems of productivity and mutual caring and cooperation.

BEYOND CHAUVINISM: THE CARING CORPORATION

> *Corporations are places where both individual human beings and human communities engage in caring activities which are aimed at mutual support and unparalleled human achievement.*
>
> Freeman and Leidtka (1991:96)

The military metaphor of the corporation as a (predominantly male) hierarchical chain of command whose primary purpose is to beat the competition is, from an ethical point of view, even worse than the familiar legal characterization of the corporation as a legal fiction, an artificial person whose only reason for existence is to make money for and protect the owners or the stockholders. The latter has led to corporate irresponsibility and social unresponsiveness as well as to endless debates about the alleged social responsibilities of organizations defined solely in terms of their fiduciary obligations. The former leads to ruthlessness, hostility, bloodletting, and, often, mutual destructiveness.[2] But a very different image of the corporation is coming into view. It was anticipated (but without much insight) in the notion of a "corporate culture" that briefly floated in and out of the management-of-the-month mentality about ten years ago (prompting at least one corporate commander-in-chief to bring in a consultant anthropologist to "build me one of those corporate cultures"). The new (but, in fact, very old) view is that of the corporation as a community, a group of people working together for (more or less) shared goals and with an (again more or less) shared culture. What distinguishes this view of the corporation—which leaves quite open what sort of internal structure or culture it may be—is primarily the fact that it is first and foremost a group of people who stand with each other in a variety of personal and professional relationships.

The interests and individuality of each of those people are of paramount importance, not only as a means to an end (greater productivity, more efficiency, less internal friction, and less disruption of competitive aims) but as an (a qualified) end in itself. The meaning of the "individual," however, must be understood within the context of the community, the corporation. Of course, every person has his or her unique background and experiences, talents and ambitions, family and friends, sexual and social life, passions and hobbies, as well as quirks and idiosyncrasies. But most of these individual features are irrelevant, even in the most caring and communal corporation. (Exceptions must be made in times of personal trauma or crisis, but no one is suggesting that the communal corporation should become *in loco parentis*.) A corporation cannot be composed of individuals in this sense. The individuals who make up the corporation are in large part defined by the roles they play in the organization—"the individual-in-the-organization," and it is no denial of their individuality to insist on this. What is essential is that the individual-in-the-organization be treated and cared for as a full-fledged human being and not as a cog in a wheel, not as a mere means and not as a dispensable player whose place on the team is always open to competition and question.

People count, and not just because they happen to be (or not be) the best for the position. This is not just a question of a person "keeping his or her job"; it is a matter of personal integrity and self-identity, of keeping one's dignity and recognizing oneself (and being recognized by others) as a valued member of that community.

There is (or should be) a great deal of study and literature about the new nature of the corporation as a community and what that means. Harbingers of the new corporate mentality are already appearing in the popular press, in John Naisbett's *Reinventing the Corporation* (1988) and many mawkish and sermonistic manifestos on the importance of corporate caring. There is much to write about here; about the new forms of work and the alternatives to pyramidal corporate structure; about the proper relation between community and competitiveness; about the nature and limits of personal relationships within the corporation; about the motivational advantages of working together (a version, I suppose, of William Ouchi's (1981) Theory Z) rather than against one another, in order to earn a reward or avoid punishment (Theory X) or for the sake of the "nobility" of work itself and the prestige of the job (Theory Y).[3] But in this essay I will explore two of the core virtues of the corporation conceived as community. Those two core virtues are the so-called sentiments of care and compassion. Although their history in management theory can be measured mostly in a matter of months, their history in ethical theory and philosophy—not to mention religion—must be measured in millennia. But even there, their fate and fortunes vary considerably, from their predictable downgrading in times of war to their familiar celebration as essentially "feminine" and "motherly" virtues. There have been periods in philosophy in which these virtues have been seen to be at the very core of ethics—notably and significantly the period when Adam Smith was writing his *Inquiry into the Nature and Causes of the Wealth of Nations.* And there have been most unsentimental climates in which these and all such sentiments were dismissed with scorn and sarcasm— for example, Kant's drippingly ironic comment about "melting compassion" in his *Grounding of the Metaphysics of Morals* (Kant, 1964b:67). In the last few years, a very significant literature has been developing in which the male tendencies toward what I have been calling "chauvinism" and the more feminist (not necessarily "feminine") virtues of caring and compassion have been sharply distinguished along gender (if not sexual) lines.[4] I find much to admire and share in that literature, but I will have little to say about its more polemical "battle of the sexes" rhetoric.[5] Whether it is male or female, masculine or feminine or simply interweaving strands of ethics since the times of the ancient Greeks and Confucius, I am simply interested in distinguishing what one might call the ethics of care from the Darwinian ethics of raw competition that continues to be popular in the management literature. More philosophically, I also want to distinguish between care and compassion and to distinguish both from the more principled and rule-bound conceptions of ethics that are generally associated in philosophy with the name of Kant and that define so much of contemporary business ethics and the language of "social responsibility."[6] There is much more to do, of course, but I would like to at least make a beginning in this modest but important new direction.

It goes without saying that caring for someone is a good thing to do. But that indicates very little about the extent of one's commitment or even whether the "caring" translates into action. (Indeed, the ambiguity between "caring for" as a form of affection and "caring for" as an ongoing and possibly all-absorbing course of action is instructive in this regard.) So, too, having compassion for those in dire straits is a minimal requirement for someone to be a good person, but very little gets said thereby about what one is expected or should expect to do when so prompted. Indeed, the whole language of do-gooders and bleeding hearts is constructed around the supposition that, while it is all right and admirably human to feel such sentiments (and how many of the most tough-minded realists would willingly deny them), it is weak if not foolish to give in to them. Good managers care for their employees, to be sure, but when there is work to be done or a penalty to be paid, the minimally caring advice of *The One Minute Manager* is usually more than sufficient.

Beyond the platitudes, the status of care and compassion in contemporary moral philosophy and current management theory is anything but obvious. Care and compassion are all but excluded by most traditional ethical theories, relegated to the margins of moral discourse or simply assumed as elementary but not worth talking about. In management circles the idea of commitment to one's employees (and the expectation of loyalty in return) is bandied about as a mandatory bit of policy, but that commitment typically runs tragically thin when profits sour, the company's stock starts to sputter, or, worst of all, the company becomes an attractive target for a takeover artist. Indeed, the concept of caring in the corporation is even denied on conceptual grounds, on the old but tired basis that the corporation isn't a person and isn't the kind of thing that can care—and for the equally tiresome but more loathesome reason that caring (about people) is not part of a corporate job description. As for the first, I do not want to argue the case for corporate conscience or corporate agency here. I will simply refer to other arguments and insist more modestly that even if a corporation were a legal fiction or a military machine, it is enough to insist that the people in the corporation, individually and collectively, can and do care.[7] As for the second objection, I would simply argue that it is a pretty pathetic conception of a job description that is limited to stated responsibilities and does not also include those basic human attitudes and concerns that are essential to any collective enterprise.

Yet, care and compassion have more than once been moved to center stage by theorists who are antagonistic to the main modern tradition in ethics—notably Arthur Schopenhauer (1965) in his 1841 attack on Kant; Larry Blum (1982), Laurence Thomas (1989), and Annette Baier (1985) in recent attacks on the neo-Kantian tradition; and Nell Noddings (1984) in an attempt to suggest a substitute for the male-dominated, principle-mongering Western tradition in ethics. As I mentioned earlier, the first harbingers of the caring corporation have appeared in the popular business press, and, more significantly, the increasing success of executive women breaking through the glass ceiling and into top-management positions has prompted considerable speculation about a serious shift in values and attitudes in the corporation.

And yet, it remains unclear how the virtues of care and compassion will fit into ethics and moral philosophy, much less into the continuously pressurized context of the corporation. It is not even clear how care and compassion are to be understood. They are systematically excluded from Kantian and contractual accounts of morality and obligation, but neither are they obviously at home in the most prominent alternatives to those accounts. They have at best a dubious place in utilitarianism (and virtually none in the vulgar cost-benefit analysis that often passes for utilitarian thinking), and libertarians in particular seem to show little tendency to tolerate much less celebrate the more altruistic sentiments.[8] Care and compassion hardly seem adequate (even to their staunchest defenders) to ground an ethics by themselves, and, as "sentiments," they do not seem to be the right sort of thing to count as virtues, although what is now called "virtue ethics" would seem to be the most promising framework for understanding their importance.[9] Thus, in what follows I want to evaluate and defend the status of care and compassion as both ethical and corporate virtues, using as my historical fulcrum the work of the "father" of capitalism, Adam Smith. In particular, in this essay, I will return to Smith (and his friend and mentor, David Hume) and clarify what they called "sympathy" as a virtue, in the form of its two more often discussed versions today, care and compassion. The caring corporation is not just a hotbed of sentimentality and bleeding hearts, with no competitive sense whatever. Indeed, my argument is that a caring corporation cultivates the most basic strength of any organization, mutual dedication and a sense of security rather than defensive self-interest.

CARING, COMPASSION, AND THE SENSE OF JUSTICE

> *One is tempted to say that ethics has so far been guided by Logos, the masculine spirit, whereas the more natural and, perhaps, stronger approach would be through Eros, the feminine spirit.*
>
> Nell Noddings, *Caring* (1984)

I want to defend the sentiments of care and compassion as virtues, not just the capacity to have them but the actual employment of them—that is, as passions and not as mere "faculties" or "states of character." Being compassionate may be a virtue, but I want to suggest that what counts is actually having and expressing compassion, even in a single instance. Granted, one will not very likely have or express compassion unless he or she is already a compassionate person, but I want to shift the focus away from the usual emphasis on tendencies and traits of character to concrete actions and feelings. I do not want to thereby suggest that such sentiments are always good or good in themselves, without reference to the nature of the situation or the people involved. But what I do want to emphasize, against many of the most prominent prejudices of both the history of morals and management theory, is the importance of feelings, not as opposed to intelligent thought and action but as an essential part of them.[10]

Virtues are, first of all, feelings (and dispositions to have feelings) rather than any particular or type of action alone or abstention from action as such (e.g., courage, temperance, honesty). Aristotle had this right in his extensive treatment of the virtues, but it has often been lost sight of since, especially by some of those who are writing about the virtues and virtue ethics today. A notable exception, of course, is Adam Smith, the "father" of the free enterprise system, who deserves recognition as a latter-day virtue ethicist and also as a defender of the finer feelings. So, too, I do not think that anyone will disagree with me when I say that in the business world emotions in general are considered "unprofessional," and discussions of emotion, when these take place at all, are usually critical and condemning. (The exceptions, of course, are such passions as "team spirit" and admiration for the boss, not to mention "a hunger for competition" and "the killer instinct." But even here the display of emotion, rather than the manifestation of the motivational effects of emotion, is rarely welcome.) In recent years a number of new consulting groups have entered the corporate scene, addressing such issues as "the control of emotions" and "the role of emotions" in the corporation, but it is worth noting that such study groups are mainly composed of (and aimed at) women. It is also evident that their purpose and posture are largely defensive, trying to carve out a space for the sentiments in a world that systematically excludes them.

One place to locate the central importance of care and compassion is in the context of the central managerial virtue of justice. Aristotle, writing about the corporation he knew as the *polis,* listed justice as the basic virtue of good citizenship. In today's corporations, it is justice as "fairness" that holds the institution together, and it is the virtue of fairness that, above all, marks a good manager. But fairness is not, as many philosophers and managerial gurus would have it, the application of certain abstract and impersonal principles, although administrative equity is obviously not beside the point. Neither is it simply the respect for employee and other stakeholder rights, although this too, to be sure, is an essential part of the picture. But "rights" enter into the picture usually after harmony and community have broken down, when they appear as legitimate demands rather than as cooperative and mutually formulated solutions. What care and compassion do in the context of justice is that they provide just that mutual understanding and shared sentiment which makes for harmony and allows for cooperative and mutually formulated solutions. Justice, John Rawls tells us, is "the first virtue of social institutions, as truth is of systems of thought" (1971:3). But justice is, first of all, an attitude of caring, a sense of compassion for those in a less advantageous position, a relationship, and it is only secondarily a matter of rights or equality or even merit.[11] The free market, for all of its virtues, has little to say about fairness, not only because cheaters sometimes win and some good guys finish last but because the very nature of the market (and, in particular, the job market) reduces people to mere consumers or commodities, human dignity to market value, and personal worth to a salary. Fairness, on the other hand, is precisely that sense that one is respected as a person, being treated well because one is an essential member of the group, being recognized and paid for what one has accomplished or put up with because one has made a proper contribution. To reduce all of this to contractual obligations and rights or some abstract formula for distributive justice is not only demeaning, it is unworkable. People don't fit into formulas, and formulas for fairness are thereby self-defeating. The heart of justice is care and compassion, and without them there can be no justice, no matter how equitable matters may seem.[12]

Instead of insisting that any adequate sense of justice presupposes care and compassion, some recent authors oppose the (supposedly male) concept of justice to (female) caring and compassion.[13] But this is no Kierkegaardian "either/or," impersonal justice *or* personal concern. The kindly sentiments represented by care and compassion cannot by themselves explain the enormous range or the profound depth of the passions that constitute our sense of justice, including our often vehement and not at all kindly sense of *in*justice.[14] Sentiments alone cannot solve or account for the large policy issues that are (or should be) the ultimate concern of those theories of justice, but any sense of justice whatever begins with *caring*—about ourselves, our reputations, and our belongings; about those whom we love and live with, feel akin to, or are responsible for; about the way the world is and the fate of the sentient creatures in it. Without that care and concern, there can be no sense of justice. Why else would any of this *matter* to us—the distribution of goods in the world, fair and equal treatment, just rewards and the felt need to punish, even questions of life and death? Justice begins with and presupposes our emotional engagement in the world, not in philosophical detachment or in any merely hypothetical situation.

The Kantian turn in philosophy, now pursued with ever-increasing rigor by Rawls and his many students and colleagues, is largely responsible for the exile of the kindly sentiments and the "inclinations" in general from moral philosophy. "Melting passion" was Kant's devastatingly sarcastic phrase in his *Groundwork,* though he tried to cover up the more callous implications of his moral philosophy; and one can, without much difficulty, find kindly sentiments expressed and praised often enough. Rawls (1971) certainly doesn't dismiss the sentiments; in fact, he devotes a major section to them toward the back of his book. But he chooses to emphasize and to try to deduce the objectivity of his principles, which is why Rawls's book has had such influence in contemporary "analytic" philosophy, which loves a good argument but has little patience for nattering about personal feelings. But in the wake of this Kantian tradition, it is always worth remembering how closely Kant (Rawls too) claims to follow on the heels of his hero, Jean-Jacques Rousseau, one of the great defenders of the natural inclinations. Before Kant, and about the same time as Rousseau, a successful school of "moral sentiment theorists" emerged in Scotland (and elsewhere).

The leading and best-known proponents of moral sentiment theory were David Hume and Adam Smith. They defended the centrality of the "natural" sentiment of *sympathy* in morals, distinguishing between sympathy and justice, which Hume, in particular, declared not to be "natural" at all. Moral sentiment theory began with the view that the basis of morality and justice is to be found in our natural disposition to have certain other-directed emotions. This did not mean that morality is not, in part, a function of reason or, above all, a matter of "doing the right thing." Both Hume and Smith emerged as early champions of the importance of "utility." But it is clear that the right things don't usually get done for the wrong reasons, and we don't usually think of ourselves or of others as just or moral if the right thing gets done for the wrong reasons or if the wrong thing gets done for the right reasons. But surely among the right reasons are the sympathetic emotions. Contrary to much of the Kantian tradition, to be moral and to be just does not mean that one must act *on principle*. A good reason for helping another person in need is "I feel sorry for him." Indeed, one is hard put to think of any other reason that is so impervious to argument (which is not to say that it is indefeasible).

One can understand why so many philosophers and management "scientists" have been attracted to the logical precision of reason instead of the vicissitudes of emotion. Sentiment is surely not enough to construct wise policies, and what is often called "sentimentality" would seem to be the very opposite of wisdom. The former allows for considerable debate, precision, and hardheadedness, whereas the latter seems to encourage ad hominem arguments and some notoriously "soft" thinking. (These adjectives themselves are, of course, Exhibit B in the gender-hegemony prosecution.) For example, it is often suggested and sometimes claimed outright (e.g., by Noddings [1984]) that caring is always kindly, that it is "unconditional"—notably in motherhood.[15] Compassion is presented as a "sharing" of suffering, as if the only compassionate person were one who would suffer exactly the same as the original victim, and both care and compassion are presented as if they are always virtuous, always praiseworthy.[16] And again, care and compassion are contrasted with the sense of justice instead of analyzed as an essential part of justice. It is even suggested—for example, by many New Age feminist thinkers—that care and compassion are alone sufficient to provide a foundation for social order and decency, if not to save the planet.[17] I believe that such claims are bogus, if not nonsense, and in this essay I would like to defend qualified conceptions of care and compassion that will stand up to critical scrutiny and make managerial sense as well as be ethically edifying.

THE NATURE OF SYMPATHY: ADAM SMITH AND DAVID HUME

*How selfish soever man may be supposed, there are evidently some
principles in his nature, which interest him in the fortune of others, and
render their happiness necessary to him, though he derives nothing from it*

> *except the pleasure of seeing it. Of this kind is pity or compassion, the*
> *emotion which we feel for the misery of others. . . . The greatest ruffian, the*
> *most hardened violator of the laws of society, is not altogether without it.*
>
> Adam Smith, *Theory of the Moral Sentiments* (1759:I.I.i)

Traditionally, moral sentiment theory was concerned with a family of "natural" emotions, including benevolence, sympathy, compassion, and pity. (Care and caring, instructively, were not part of the standard list.) These emotions were often lumped together and not infrequently treated as identical (for example, by Hume). In the standard account of moral sentiment thinking, Francis Hutcheson's "moral sense" theory is usually included as a moral sentiment theory, despite the fact that Hutcheson explicitly denied any special moral role to the sentiments. Rousseau is usually not included as a moral sentiment theorist, although he was obviously one with them. With his Scottish colleagues he attacked the "selfishness" theories of Hobbes and Mandeville and argued for the naturalness of pity, an emotion closely akin to compassion in particular. But as developed by Hume and Smith, in particular, the exemplary moral sentiment was *sympathy*. This sentiment, I suggest, is an awkward amalgam of several emotional states and dispositions, including compassion and what we have come to call care.

There is considerable confusion about the meaning of "sympathy," however, both in the writings of the moral sentiment theorists and in our own conversations. In common parlance, "sympathy" means "feeling sorry for" someone, whereas for many philosophers (notably Hume) it is conflated with benevolence. (Smith tries to keep these distinct.) Feeling sorry for can be a sign of caring, but surely a minimal one, because we can feel sorry for strangers and even our enemies. Benevolence has much in common with the more activist concept of caring for, but benevolence has much greater scope than sympathy as such. We can feel benevolence in the abstract (without any particular object) and benevolence for those whose feelings are utterly malicious or indifferent to us (e.g., by being merciful to a condemned and still hateful wrongdoer, perhaps as an expression of our own largesse, but out of benevolence nevertheless). We often use "sympathy" or the verb "sympathize" to register agreement or approval, although neither of these qualifies as an adequate philosophical conception or a correct dictionary definition. Technically, sympathy (literally, "feeling with," like "com/passion") is the sharing of feeling, or, as a disposition, the ability to share the feelings of others. Or, if one wants to insist that the emotions can be individuated only according to the persons who have them and thus cannot be shared, one might say that sympathy is an "agreement of feelings" (Random House Dictionary, 1987), in the sense of "having the same [type of] emotion." One need not agree with in the sense of approve of the feeling in question, of course, any more than must always enjoy, like, or approve of one's own emotions. The feelings may agree, but we need not; sharing a feeling is one thing, but accepting or approving of the feeling is quite another. (In grade B movies, we might well share the offended hero's rather fascist sense of revenge while berating ourselves for having that feeling.)

Adam Smith uses the term in this technical way, as "agreement of emotion," but he does not thereby imply the agreement of any particular emotion or kind of emotion. Thus, there is a serious ambiguity between sympathy as a specific sentiment and sympathy as a disposition to share sentiments (*whatever* sentiments) with others. Sympathy so conceived is thus not actually a sentiment at all but rather a *vehicle* for understanding other people's sentiments, "a fellow-feeling with any passion whatever" (Smith, 1990:I.i.5). One can sympathize with any number of feelings in another person, not only the kindly and social moral sentiments but such unsocial sentiments as envy and hatred as well. Sympathy is not an actual sharing of sentiments (in the sense of "having the same feeling") but rather an act of imagination by which one can appreciate the feelings of another person by "putting oneself in his place," "a principle which interests him in the fortunes of others" (Smith, 1990:I.i.I.2). This provides him with a way of accounting for how it can be that people are not essentially selfish or self-interested but are essentially social creatures who can act on behalf of others whose feelings they do not (and logically cannot) actually share. But this raises the question whether sympathy can be the sort of motivating factor in our behavior that moral sentiment theory seeks to defend, in opposition to the equally natural (and often more powerful) sentiment of self-interest and in contrast to the similarly selfless but also passionless dictates of reason. ("The approbation of moral qualities most certainly is not deriv'd from reason, or any comparison of ideas; but proceeds entirely from a moral taste, and from certain sentiments of pleasure and disgust, which arise upon the contemplation and view of particular qualities or characters" (Smith, 1990:I.i.I.2). But sympathy, according to Smith's definition as "fellow-feeling," seems to be more concerned with comprehension than feeling as such, and comprehension is too close to the "comparison of ideas" to provide the "sentiments of pleasure and disgust" to play the role that sympathy is called to play in morals (Werhane, 1991:33–38). ("As we have no immediate experience of what other men feel, we can for no idea of the manner in which they are affected, but by conceiving what we ourselves should feel in the like situation [Smith, 1990:I.i.I.2].) Sympathy cannot mean merely "comprehension," but sympathy as shared feeling seems too strong for the role (Cropsey, 1957:12; quoted in Werhane, 1991). I thus want to argue that Smith is inconsistent. On the one hand, he wants a mechanism for "fellow-feeling" and on the other, a motive for morals. It is not at all clear that he can have both, and it is arguable whether either provides an adequate analysis of sympathy.

Hume's earlier theory of sympathy and justice, which greatly influenced Smith, is somewhat different from Smith's, and to make matters more difficult, it is clear that Hume changed his mind between the writing of his early masterpiece, *A Treatise of Human Nature,* and his later *Inquiry Concerning the Principles of Morals.* In the early work, Hume treats sympathy rather casually, commenting that it is usually a weak emotion compared with most of the motives of self-interest. In the later work, Hume defends sympathy as a universal sentiment that is sufficiently powerful to overcome self-interest in a great many cases. In the *Inquiry,* in particular, Hume takes sympathy to be a form of benevolence, a feeling for one's fellow citizens and a concern for their well-being. But for Hume, as for Smith, sympathy is too often countered and overwhelmed by selfishness and, for this reason, a sense of justice is required. But whereas Smith takes the sense of justice to be a somewhat natural revulsion at harming one's fellows, Hume takes justice to be an "artificial" virtue that is constructed by reason for our mutual well-being. It is an advantageous conventional "scheme" rather than a natural sentiment as such. Thus, for Hume sympathy is a genuine moral sentiment, and justice is not. Even so, Hume admitted that justice was so beneficial that it became inseparably associated with the moral sentiments, for what could be more basic to these sentiments than our sense of the general good for everyone, "a feeling for the happiness of mankind and a resentment of their misery" (1957:235). He writes,

> No virtue is more esteemed than justice, and no vice more detested than injustice; nor are there any qualities, which go farther to the fixing of character, either as amiable or odious. Now justice is a moral virtue, merely because it has that tendency to the good of mankind; and, indeed, is nothing but an artificial invention to that purpose.
>
> The whole scheme, however, of law and justice is advantageous to the society; and 'twas with a view to this advantage, that men, by their voluntary conventions, establish'd it. . . . Once established, it is *naturally* attended with a strong sentiment of morals. (Hume, 1978:577, 579)

Hume does not go so far as to say that justice itself is a matter of natural sentiment, but he insists that the moral sentiments in general and in particular sympathy for others are so essential to morals that there can be no ethics without them. Both Hume and Smith are dead set against the Hobbesian view that people are motivated only by their own selfish interests and advocate the importance of distinctive, natural "social passions." Indeed, the core of their argument is, in Smith's terms, that "nature, when it formed man for society, endowed him with an original desire to please, and an original aversion to offend his brethren" (Smith, 1990:III.2.6). Moreover, "nature endowed him not only with a desire for being approved of, but with a desire of being what ought to be approved of, or of being what he himself approves of in other men" (1990:III.2.7). It is not just sympathy but a whole complex of mutually perceiving and reciprocal passions that tie us together. Thus, it does not take too much tinkering with Scottish moral sentiment theory to incorporate justice along with sympathy under its auspices and take the whole as a welcome alternative to both the "man is essentially selfish" thesis and the overly intellectual "morality is rationality" view of Kant and most current justice theorists.

Both Hume and Smith sometimes talk about sympathy as if it were no more than a generalized sense of altruism, a concern for others with no thought of benefit to oneself. But altruism, like benevolence, doesn't involve sharing of feelings, as sympathy does, and Smith's phrase "fellow-feeling" too easily hides the distinction between "feeling for," "feeling with," and simple camaraderie, which is feeling oneself with but not necessarily feeling with the other. Altruism, however, might best be understood as the behavioral analog of benevolence, and sympathy is often used as a synonym for benevolence, a wishing well toward others, a sympathy *for* others. This is the way Hume often uses the term, and in the *Inquiry*, at least, he claims that this feeling "nature has made universal in the whole species." This is Hume's way of denying the Hobbesian portrait of humanity as essentially selfish, and it is a mistake, or at least it is unfair, I think, to attack Hume on the grounds that he is really an unreconstructed Hobbesian individualist who brings in "sympathy" only as a desperate measure to explain the noncoercive validity of morals.[18] What both Hume and Smith are concerned to point out, against Hobbes, is that we genuinely and "naturally" do *care* about other people and we are capable of feeling *with* others as well as for ourselves. But it is obvious that there is considerable room for misunderstanding about what Hume and Smith mean by "sympathy," and their various uses of the term seem inconsistent, or at best something of a grab bag of mixed kindly feelings and dispositions. Hume quite clearly changes his mind and his usage from the *Treatise* to the *Inquiry*, and Smith slips back and forth between the several vernacular uses of the term and the technical use ("sympathy" as a general disposition) that he sometimes insists upon. Hume equates sympathy and benevolence, whereas Smith insists on separating them, but Smith does so in order to defend his "fellow-feeling" interpretation, and Hume is too eager (at least in the *Treatise*) to downplay the actual motivational force of sympathy. By "sympathy" Smith seems to mean something very much like "compassion," whereas Hume wants it to mean something more like "care," but "compassion" and "care" here have rather emaciated meanings.

SYMPATHY, EMPATHY, BENEVOLENCE, AND COMPASSION

What is the relation between sympathy and benevolence? Both emotional virtues suffer from an excess of scope and vagueness that makes their relative terrains difficult to map and identify. MacIntyre notes that "the new conception of the virtue of benevolence . . . in the eighteenth century is assigned very much the scope which the Christian scheme of the virtues assigned to charity. But, unlike charity, benevolence as a virtue became a licence for almost any kind of manipulative intervention in the affairs of others." (MacIntyre, 1981:216). One might deny that benevolence too is an emotion; it is, perhaps, rather a motive or a broad category of desire. But what leads the moral sense theorists to so identify sympathy and benevolence is precisely the latter's motivational powers, whereas sympathy too readily remains nothing but a "feeling with" or "feeling for." Benevolence is indeed a much broader concept than sympathy, and though benevolence need not lead to action (it is a "wishing well" rather than a "making well" [bene-ficence]), it need have nothing to do with "feeling with" or even "feeling for." (One can want to help others on principle, for example, or because one cannot abide their noisy suffering.) In such cases, one may well "care," but not care primarily for the well-being of the other.

But this is just the problem with sympathy. It always seems to suggest more than it actually provides. It is one thing to say that one is upset and has kindly feelings toward a fellow creature in pain, that one in some sense "shares" the suffering. But feeling sorry for someone is not the same as wanting to help the person, and while benevolence typically leads to beneficence and helping behavior, "feeling sorry for" usually just stops at pity. One may be kindly or generous "out of pity," but though pity may motivate it readily remains a feeling unto itself—one of the reasons Nietzsche launched a relentless attack against it. "Feeling sorry for" isn't exactly sympathy either, even in the vernacular, for one can feel sorry for someone suffering without feeling anything at all, whereas we tend to think of sympathy, again in Smith's words, as something like a sharing of feeling. It is one thing to say that one shares feelings and something else—a much weaker claim—to say that one appreciates or "understands" the plight of another. Pity is even more problematic, for it includes within its structure an unmistakable sense of "looking down" at its object. And, even on a more benign account than Nietzsche's, pity cannot be conceived of as an unalloyed kindly sentiment, which sympathy is supposed to be.

"Sympathy" (like "compassion") literally means and is often meant to mean "shared feeling." But what is it to "share" a feeling—individuation problems aside (i.e., can one and the same feeling be shared by two people, or can each person have his and only his own feeling?) Insofar as sympathy involves actually *sharing* feelings, it is clear that the suffering one shares with the sufferer is, for the most part, pretty limp stuff and not nearly adequate to motivate ethical behavior. I may, in fact, feel slightly ill because you have just broken your leg in three places, but it would be absurd to compare my feelings to yours, much less to say that I am "sharing" your suffering. Indeed, it seems absurd to talk at all about "sharing" feelings in most such cases. I may feel upset to hear that you have just lost your grandfather, been called for a general audit by the IRS or been fired from your job because of a general downsizing. But the fact that I too have negative feelings (sadness, fear, indignation) *because* of you and even *for* you hardly adds up to a sufficiently equal measure of mutual emotion to call this "shared feelings." Of course, if indeed we share the situation, if it is *our* grandfather who died, *our* partnership that is to be audited, or *we both* who are to be fired, it is perfectly plausible to say that we share the appropriate feelings. But this would not be a matter of sympathy, for the whole idea behind moral sentiment theory is that I can and do feel for you on the basis of your suffering and not my own.

I may have a fairly mild sense of pathos caused by and in my concern about your rather awful suffering, and it makes little sense to compare the two, much less to talk about them as "shared." It is for this reason that Smith, in particular, suggests that a sense of justice is needed to supplement sympathy, which by itself is not nearly powerful enough to counter the inevitably self-serving motives of most people. Justice, for Smith, is an internalized sense of fair play, and it is justice, not sympathy, that provides the main pillar which supports the whole society. Justice, unlike sympathy, is a passion with a determined content, albeit a negative one; justice is the sense that one should not cause harm to one's neighbor (Smith, 1990:II.ii.2.1). Sympathy and justice, together with a sense of benevolence, provide Smith with a portrait of human nature in his *Theory of the Moral Sentiments* that is very different from the usual Hobbesian interpretations of his later work, *The Wealth of Nations*, in which the wheels of capitalism are (wrongly) said to be moved by individual greed alone. Sympathy is "fellow-feeling," feeling not so much *for* as *with* one's fellow citizens, *whatever* their particular passions happen to be. Our sense of justice moves us to avoid harming one another; and between the two, the Hobbesian picture of human life as "a war of all against all" and as "nasty, brutish and short" gets replaced by the much more flattering portrait of a society of citizens who care about, feel for, and naturally avoid harming one another.

Sympathy is often confused with "empathy," which is also defined as "identification with" another, "putting oneself in the other's shoes," and vicariously sharing his or her emotions. Certainly Smith uses the one term to mean the other, and Joseph Cropsey's explicit identification of the two (in TMS) is not at all inappropriate as an interpretation of *some* of Smith's text. "[Smith argues that] every human being has the power to feel the passions of those other beings who come under his observation. The man who observes joy of another will himself experience joy" (Cropsey, 1957:12). But empathy, too, has been characterized not so much as an emotion as a technique or a strategy for sharing and understanding emotions, an ability to "put oneself in the other's place," as well as the actual sharing of feelings that results from such identification, and Smith elsewhere denies that we can ever actually share the feelings of another (Smith, 1990:I.i.I.2). Moving from the eighteenth century to our own, however, we find that much the same debate and confusion continues, especially in the social sciences, where the validity of the "method" of empathy is much in dispute.[19] Recent studies of sympathy and empathy in

psychology by Wispe and Natoulos strongly suggest that the distinction
has become largely a stipulative matter. But we can take a strong hint
from etymology and the observation that sympathy means "feeling with,"
(1) "agreement in feelings" and (2) "sharing feelings, esp. sorrow or trouble" while empathy means "feeling into" and "identification with or vicari-
ous experiencing of the feelings or thoughts of another person."[20] Empathy, in other words, might better be thought of as shared feeling, whereas
sympathy is a more specific feeling, feeling sorry for, a kind of caring, but
caring at a distance, as an observer rather than a caretaker.

Alasdair MacIntyre has recently charged that sympathy is an emotion
that was largely invented by Hume.[21] MacIntyre is primarily concerned
with the tendency of the Enlightenment philosophers—Hume in particular—to project their own narrow English property-owning ideology as a
"universal" sense of morals, and he charges that Hume's presumed universal sentiment presupposed a very specific normative standard, "in fact
a highly conservative normative standard" (1981). MacIntyre denies
explicitly that sympathy could "supply the defects of an argument from
[long-term self-] interest and utility," and suggests that the invention of
an emotion called sympathy was Hume's attempt to "bridge the gap
between any set of reasons for action which could support unconditional
adherence to general and unconditional rules and any set of reasons for
action or judgment which could derive from our particular, fluctuating,
circumstance-governed desires, emotions and interests." MacIntyre adds
that "later on Adam Smith was to invoke sympathy for precisely the same
purpose. But the gap, of course, is logically unbridgeable, and 'sympathy' as used by Hume and Smith is the name of a philosophical fiction"
(1981:47). I think that this analysis is unfair to both Hume and Smith,
although it does betray a critical weakness in most prominent interpretations of these two great theorists, if not in their works themselves. The
tendency to split the passions into a "selfish" set of sentiments and an
"other-regarding" set such as sympathy and compassion raises deep
problems about how such internal warfare can ever produce a coherent
individual life, much less a coherent and harmonious society. But I
believe that the soul-wrenching individualism that MacIntyre and many
other commentators attribute to Hume and Smith is not the sole basis of
their theories, and the sentiment of sympathy—however ambiguously
defined—deserves recognition as a very real, indispensable, and probably "natural" ingredient in our moral sensibilities. Both Smith and Hume
were "classical liberals" (in other words, conservatives), and their individualism was always tempered by their sense of tradition and social unity.
Thus, I believe that both Hume and Smith were struggling to formulate
a more sociable sense of human nature, one in which mutual affection
and approval are more important than self-interest as such, one in which
shared emotions and feelings for others are more important than acquis-
itive desires. Their mistake, which they seemed to pick up from Shaftes-
bury and Hutcheson was to polarize the passions and characterize a few

of these as "moral" or "social" and others "selfish" or "asocial," when, in fact, almost all passions and sentiments of any complexity pour across these artificial boundaries like clouds over state lines. (cf. MacIntyre, 1988:268), Sympathy, in particular, is no simple sentiment and does indeed involve competitive and "self-interested" components as well as pure altruism and concern for the other. Accordingly, we should expect considerable strain in these theories, as Hume goes on to defend the British propertied classes and as Smith goes on to defend what has since been dubbed the "magic" of free market capitalism. But the central and undeniable truth of moral sentiment theory, I believe, is that we are essentially and "naturally" social creatures with fellow-feeling, care, and compassion for others and not only concerned with our own interests and ambitions in life.[22]

CARE AND CARING

Part of the IBM spirit was that no one was to have thoughts of being a boss. . . . One could be a leader; leadership was encouraged, but only in a one-to-one relationship, one man offering guidance to another.
William Rogers, *Think* (1969:84)

Care is perhaps the most general of all emotions. In a broad sense, to have any emotion already presupposes that one cares, that one is engaged, that one has interests, that one "takes something personally." Care thus embraces the hostile and vindictive emotions as well as the considerate and kindly sentiments. We should not forget, in our rush to sensitivity, that care (*die Sorge*) is introduced in Goethe's *Faust* as a burden, not a blessing, and it is because we care about someone or something that we become possessive, defensive, and vengeful as well as nurturing and supportive. Caring is not an unmixed benefit, and to think of care as only a kindly, nurturing affection is to get less than half the story. Caring can also hurt, and we can understand—though we do not forgive—the tough-minded executive who uses his facade of indifference to avoid the pain when he is forced to let go a trusted and faithful subordinate. But the point here is that caring is an essential feeling in any professional as well as personal relationship and an essential virtue in any person in a position of power or authority.

High-ranking military officers are typically told not to fraternize with their junior officers and enlisted men, precisely so they will not be personally affected if those men must be sent on a dangerous mission and perhaps be killed. This may or may not be good advice for the armed services, but it is dangerous nonsense in the corporation. Most managing does not consist of obeying and carrying out orders; it is establishing rapport, coping with emergencies, encouraging subordinates, reassuring superiors, performing various office rituals, comforting clients, and communicating between one office and another.[23] It consists, in other words, of relationships, however distant or comparatively impersonal. Indeed, the very notion of impersonality here is all too easily misunderstood, for there is all the difference between dealing with a particular human being (face-to-face or merely by memo) and just taking care of business, where "business" here refers to number crunching and paperwork. Managing is concerned first and foremost with people, and where those people are part of the same organization (or stakeholders therein), all such relationships are defined by caring. That need not mean that one has any particular affection for the particular individual; it would be a rare manager indeed who disliked no one, or it would be a rare organization. Care in the corporation is a sentiment that encompasses the individual-in-the-organization, and just because he or she is an individual-in-the-organization. But the strictly professional and the personal aspects of a person can never be kept wholly apart, and caring for the individual-in-the-organization therefore inevitably includes a certain concern for the personal. This can easily be abused or misunderstood. (Many cases of sexual harrassment are based upon such abuse or misunderstanding.) But the militaristic alternative—stiff formality and an almost fanatical insistence on avoiding the personal—tends to produce a paranoid work environment in which communication—not to mention frankness—is all but impossible. (One Fortune 500 company was run by a CEO who refused to meet the spouses of his executives, lest some personal impression affect his "purely professional" judgment of the managers' work.)

Care encompasses almost all emotions, insofar as one must care about the world in order to feel anything else about it. For our purposes, however, we can restrict our characterization of care to include just that set of "positive" feelings about another person (or any number of persons) such that one "wishes them well" and is moved to act (where possible) on their behalf. But note that being moved is not the same as acting, and we sometimes care for or about someone whose fate is quite out of our hands. One presumably cares very much what happens to the chief executives of one's company, but (apart from doing one's job or commiting sabotage) one can do little about their fate. So, too, "positive" feelings from a person are no guarantee of continued "niceness"; caring always sets up the possibility of ingratitude and betrayal, and though the limits of tolerance may sometimes be stretched remarkably far (notably between mentors and mentees and established good friends), that possibility is always there. Indeed, one might hypothesize that the more intensive the care and the more the limits of tolerance are stretched, the more violent the reaction should those limits be violated. There are no corporate vendettas, for instance, to match those between one-time colleagues turned bitter rivals. (Certain recent melodramas in the auto industry come to mind here.)

Of course, for some executives and managers, those limits might be reached by a simple act of disobedience or a particularly cantankerous morning meeting. For others, it may take a wholesale, humiliating act of rejection, the sort that Arthur Miller and Sam Shepherd (and, of course, Shakespeare) have portrayed. But however depressing some of the stories in Robert Jackall's *Moral Mazes,* life in most corporations is not a web of intrigue. Most managers genuinely care about their employees if they are not pressured not to do so. To care for is also to be prepared to fight for, and against the sweeter images of caring should be juxtaposed the not-so-sweet image of a hostility and defense against danger. Care breeds danger and sometimes violence. Zen and Stoic indifference promote peacefulness, but no one would say that they represent what is commonly called for as care. Nor is there much evidence, the Buddhist economics of the late E. M. Schumacher aside, that Zen attitudes are particularly successful in running large-scale organizations.

To care for someone is to be concerned about that person, but note that this is an expression that is interestingly ambiguous between an activity (which may or may not involve any particular emotions) and a set of feelings (which may or may not express themselves in any particular actions). As a special feeling of affectionate concern, with or without a sense of responsibility, care most often characterizes our emotional relationships with our friends and loved ones, but it is necessarily to generalize it as such to include other people with whom we are connected in professional as well as personal relationships. Mayeroff (1971) defined "to care for another person" as "to help him grow and actualize himself." It is clear that such a notion has much to recommend it in the context of the corporation, where the success and competence of a manager consists most of all in his or her success in nurturing and developing those who are subordinate and, inevitably, do much of the actual work, whatever it is. Of course, such caring has to be somewhat discriminate and well aimed, and while a good mentor may truly care for five, ten, or even twenty subordinates, when the number reaches a hundred or a few thousand, we have to admit that one loses that intimate sense of caring as personal concern and shifts into a more general sense of responsibility, which may be quite different. But a good manager's capacity for caring may expand almost indefinitely, and while caring is irreducibly personal, it may, in fact, be generalized as a remarkably expansive communal sentiment. (It is worth noting that Adam Smith refused to recognize love [as opposed to sympathy] as a virtue just because it is irretrievably particular and incapable of generalization.)

Even while celebrating care and putting it at the very heart of justice, I have insisted that we should not and ultimately cannot take caring to be an unqualified blessing, much less take it as another saintly ideal that few mortals can ever hope to achieve. But designating care as essentially "selfless" does just this, because virtually everything we care about does not abandon but rather *engages* the self. If caring means "selflessness," as is sometimes insisted, that would mean that virtually no one, and no one in business, ever really cares. But this false antagonism between self-inter-

est and caring is at the root of the problem, and many of the most spe-
cious (and most common) arguments against business ethics and the
social responsibility of corporations rests on this fraudulent dichotomy.
Caring about others is not necessarily putting their interests before one's
own, much less sacrificing oneself on their behalf—though admittedly
there may be rare occasions on which this is an option. Caring about
others might much better be conceived as taking their interests *as* one's
own; and, in fact, this is—in the typical corporate relationship—exactly
what is the case. The idealization of care as self-sacrifice violates the most
obvious facts of justice and human nature—that many if not most of our
interests and activities are communal interests and activities. So, too, the
idealization of care as a generalized, even global, concern for everyone
and everything (an uncritical "friends of the earth" mentality) without
regard to particular loyalties and obligations—including corporate loyalties and obligations—renders the idea of caring useless as a practical
virtue. Care so idealized as a global and nondiscriminatory affection thus
becomes just as much of a problem as the abstract and idealized rational
principles it was meant to replace.

COMPASSION

> *No man is devoid of a heart sensitive to the sufferings of others . . .*
> *whoever is devoid of the heart of compassion is not human.*
>
> Mencius, fourth century B.C.

Compassion is a more specific emotion than care, and so it may be much
easier to define, delimit, and examine as a critical ingredient in justice.
The most obvious specifying feature of compassion ("suffering with") is
that the object of one's concern is somehow in pain. One does not feel
compassion for a friend who has just been promoted or been given an
enormous bonus or raise (except, of course, in some very unusual set of
circumstances). One might well feel compassion for a colleague who is
about to be fired, but it would be inappropriate to feel compassion for a
friend who was about to be hired. (Again, one makes exceptions for the
unusual and ominous instance.) It is often suggested that (as the prefix to
the word might suggest) in compassion one *suffers with* the other, but one
need not actually feel his or her pain in any sense; indeed, compassion
suggests that one somehow stands safely "above" the misery of the other,
affording one the luxury of commiseration. A student who has just
flunked his exams does not feel compassion toward a fellow student who
has also flunked his exams. They just feel miserable together. It is the student who has passed her exams "with flying colors" who is in a position to
feel compassion for the other two, though the giddiness of her own success may make it difficult to do so. A manager who has just been passed
over for a promotion does not feel compassion toward a fellow manager

who has also been passed over. They can feel miserable together. It is the manager who got the promotion who is in a position to feel compassion for the other two, though one hopes accumulated maturity and some semblance of humility will make it easy to do so. Indeed, it is compassion, this ability to feel for those less fortunate than oneself, that comprises the cornerstone passion of our sense of justice. If one really felt that he or she deserved every advantage and others deserved their disadvantages, he or she would certainly be a sociopath (the fact that such positions sometimes succeed in American politics notwithstanding).

Compassion, on the other hand, is also an emotion with a much larger scope than care. One need not be intimately acquainted with a person or a creature in any sense in order to feel compassion for him, her, or it. One can feel compassion for millions of people at once, and one can feel compassion for complete strangers. (Yet, one cannot be completely ignorant of them either. I have often wondered about the fact that murder doesn't seem to mean anything or move us if we don't know anything about the person. For example, in Agatha Christie's novels, where the murder takes place in the first chapter, or in the play *Arsenic and Old Lace*, in which characters are dispatched whom we never (or only very briefly) meet, murder is much more of a puzzle to be solved than a tragedy to be lamented. I am not convinced that it is the fictional status of these characters that explains our lack of compassion for them.[24]) Compassion is a more specific and, accordingly, more complex emotion than caring. Indeed, it might be said not to be an emotion at all but rather a mode of having emotion—feeling with another person. Compassion is intimately linked with sympathy, understanding, pity, benevolence, fellow-feeling, and friendship. It is also associated with tenderness and kindness and, accordingly, identified with caring. Discussions of compassion, like sympathy, suffer from considerable confusion concerning the idea of "shared" emotion. But we don't need this strong sense of feeling with in order to make good, solid sense out of compassion. Despite the hardheaded (hard-hearted) rhetoric of tough management, compassion would seem to be a minimal requirement for a decent manager. Efficiency and effectiveness may be possible with a minimum of feeling, but loyalty and enthusiasm will not be readily forthcoming for a manager who does not display the requisite signs of sympathy for the hurt he or she has (perhaps quite rightfully) caused.

Compassion is, perhaps, not so much feeling with as feeling for someone who is suffering. This does not mean, as some of the early moral sentiment theorists seemed to argue, that we have to actually feel the same or share the suffering, albeit with somewhat diminished intensity. Hume, for example, suggests that sympathy and compassion are identified by such shared feelings, so that when a friend is suffering from a gouty toe or a migraine headache, for example, we feel at least a twinge of the same. If a friend is going through a nasty divorce, we relive (in shadow form) a similar experience of our own. But however such a picture may appeal to our sense of camaraderie, it is not an adequate portrait of compassion. One can have compassion for a friend in pain without having any semblance, no matter how faint, of his or her affliction. I am reminded of a friend in graduate school who, though fully compassionate with friends who had headaches, confessed that he had never had a headache and could not imagine what one would be like. (So too, I had a colleague who had never suffered from insomnia, and could not imagine it, until jet lag after a trip from the Far East temporarily treated him to an experience that most of us had enjoyed for decades.) One might suggest that this supposed feeling with is nothing more than an instance of the old saying, "misery loves company," but this would seem to confuse the (usually false) supposition that a friend in pain wants you to be in pain too with the Humean claim that your own compassion with a friend in pain means that you feel the pain as well. Indeed, one need feel nothing of the sort (though one will, of necessity, feel *something*, namely, compassion). To have compassion is to be concerned, to wish fervently that the suffering would cease and to want (perhaps desperately) to do what will bring this end about.

It makes good sense, but it can be deeply misleading, to say that compassion, pity, and sympathy are "feelings." They are indeed aspects of consciousness and not actions or activities, but they are also engagments in the world, instances of involving if not identifying oneself with the circumstances and sufferings of other beings. Compassion and its kin are above all else *motives:* they move us to act (whether or not it is evident what we should do). They are not simply self-enclosed sensations like a headache or a gouty toe that focus our attention within ourselves and distract us from the world. Compassion and its kindred emotions focus our attention on the world, on the person or creature who is suffering. Compassion, pity, and sympathy are feelings, but they are not "mere" feelings. Moreover, they are not, as John Rawls sometimes seems to say, dispositions to instantiate a theory or a principle of justice. This is, to put it politely, backward. One may be moved to accept a theory or a principle of justice on the basis of strong feelings of compassion that the principle or theory seems to address. The feeling of compassion may be elegantly articulate, as in some of the best socially conscious poetry and journalistic prose, but it can also be "dumb" and only felt. Indeed, I have no reservations about ascribing compassion to non-talking animals and very young children, although they may often be confused or have no way of knowing exactly what is going on (what the victim is suffering from). What I do not want to allow is for compassion (and related emotions) to either be dismissed as mere feelings or to be coopted by an overly intellectualistic account such that they become nothing more than applied abstract beliefs. To say that they are feelings makes them vulnerable to the first danger, but clearly saves them from the second. But so long as we keep in mind a healthy and intelligent picture of the passions, we should not feel tempted to minimize the significance of our feelings.

In his now well-known essay "Compassion," Lawrence Blum provides us with a very general but quite adequate sense of compassion as felt concern for another who is in some serious or grave condition. Compassion is not appropriate, for example, for a driver who merely suffers some inconvenience on the way to visit a friend. Compassion can be complex: one can still feel compassion for a blind man who has managed to get a rewarding job, marry well, and be happy, whereas pity, for instance, would be inappropriate. Blum analyzes compassion as an emotion ("or an emotional attitude") as a moral phenomenon with particular moral value. He too is anxious to provide an alternative to the currently overbearing "Kantian" interpretation of morality, and (a bit like Kant) he argues that the feeling of compassion is good in itself, a virtue even in the absence of beneficent action. "That compassion is often appropriate when there is a little or no scope for the subject's disposition to beneficence shows that compassion's sole significance does not lie in its role as motive to beneficence. . . . The compassionate person's expression of concern and shared sorrow can be valuable to the sufferer for its own sake, independently of its instrumental value in improving his condition" (Blum, 1980:515).[25] Blum also points out that compassion should not be thought of as a Kantian "inclination," for being compassionate is quite distinct from "doing what one is in the mood to do or feels like doing." Indeed, "compassionate acts often involve acting very much contrary to one's moods and inclinations. Compassion is fundamentally other-regarding rather than self-regarding: its affective status in no way detracts from this" (Blum, 1980:510). This is an extremely important point, first because it rightly rejects the tendency to treat all acts based on emotions (and the emotions themselves) as "self-interested" in an ethically damning sense, and second because it is important to recognize the moral significance of the moral sentiments independently of (though not entirely separated from) the actions to which they typically give rise. If a person frequently expressed compassion but *never* demonstrated willingness to help, we would eventually reject his or her claims to be compassionate; but it would be a serious misunderstanding of the virtue of the moral sentiments to insist that a person feels compassion *only* when he or she acts or volunteers to help. In his *Nicomachean Ethics*, Aristotle points out the independent virtue of *eunoia*—wishing another well but not "putting oneself out for it"; but, of course, this is not to be praised to the *exclusion* of helping others. The first virtue of our moral feelings is that we have them, that they represent a certain way of engaging with and being in the world. Their secondary virtue is that they sometimes prompt kindly and considerate actions and make the world more just, but the harsh, cynical critics of do-gooders are in one sense correct, that a world in which everyone acted on his or her compassionate impulses would very likely be almost as much a mess (certainly no more than that) as it is now.

It may seem odd or even masochistic to insist that pain in itself can be a virtue, but in compassion we can see how this may be so. An executive who is forced to fire someone, a military commander who has to order men to their deaths may well feel and ought to feel distress because, while doing their duties, they also feel compassion. At such times, it is good to feel bad, and to avoid the pain is, in some sense, immoral. Thus, when the executive pleads that "it's just a business decision" or the commander insists that "it's nothing personal," we can recognize in their detachment a kind of moral "bad faith." So much for the "wisdom" that says that "you shouldn't take it personally." Taking it personally is what converts a difficult or distasteful action into an acceptable one (which is not to say that any immoral act can be made moral if only one feels guilty or compassionate enough about it. The rapist who feels sorry for his victims is not much better than his purely hostile or cold-blooded colleague.) But it is in this sense, at least, that the so-called negative and painful emotions are essential to a sense of justice. One certainly has no such sense if he or she does not feel guilt as the result of being unjust or does not feel ashamed about betraying a trust. Thus, Aristotle, with some discomfort, insists that shame is one of the virtues, not because it is good to be ashamed but because it is wicked not to feel shame when one ought to. Painful emotions in such circumstances are good and desirable, and only an utterly amoral hedonist would deny their virtue.

One of the more disturbing features of the popular social philosophy of our time is a pervasive, confident contempt for do-gooders. Milton Friedman, for example, seems particularly enamored with this argument, so much so that one doubts that it is merely part and parcel of his faith in the free enterprise system.[26] So, too, in his "Cautionary Tales," Peter Drucker warns against corporate benevolence, though on grounds of incompetence rather than ideology (1974:320, 343ff). But what can possibly be wrong with a kind emotion and the actions that go along with it, whose aim is to help other people? The problem is that compassion, by itself, is often ill informed, even stupid, vaguely directed, and self-serving (though it pretends to be the opposite). It is true that compassion typically prompts kindly action. (It also inspires the search for ways of helping where none was evident before.) But compassion often prompts precipitous action or makes more difficult the sort of cold, professional behavior that may be necessary (e.g., in a medical emergency). Blum points out that compassion may make worse an already hopeless situation and may hurt its recipients by concentrating too much on their plight. It can be "misguided, grounded in a superficial understanding of the situation" (Blum, 1980:511). Indeed, we all can think of examples in which being too caught up in a tragedy makes us less rather than more capable of coping with the event and other examples in which "superficial understanding" of someone else's plight has led us to intrude where we were not welcome, intervene where we were not competent, interfere where we were not wanted. But this is not to give too much to the cynical critics. The limitations of compassion hardly undermine its virtue or the overall utility of compassionate actions. Blum rightly concludes that "because compassion involves an active and objective interest in another's welfare, it is characteristically a spur to deeper understanding than rationality alone could insure. A person who is compassionate by character is in principle committed to as rational and as intelligent a course of action as possible" (Blum, 1980:510). Compassion without intelligence is no virtue, but intelligence without compassion is not good management. Indeed, it might be argued that it is not management at all, whatever else it may be.

CONCLUSION: A NEW CONCEPTION OF BUSINESS?

Any conception of the caring corporation should expect and deserves to be greeted with smiles or scowls of skepticism. After all, haven't we all been raised to believe that business is business, and even if it isn't dog-eat-dog it is pretty rough stuff and no place for the kinder, gentler sentiments? But although the corporate world has its share of brutality (as does academia, I might add), the difference between the old images and the new are far more matters of perception than practice, and what I find odd is the extent to which the undeniably humane aspects of corporate life are ignored or denied while the more brutal features are highlighted and even celebrated. It takes no leap of faith to move from the actual cultures of most corporations to the recognition that these are cooperative communities, not military installations or mere legal fictions, and that mutual respect, caring, and compassion are what we all, in fact, expect and demand in our various jobs and positions. To be sure, it is unfortunate that so many managers and employees and even executives do not get that respect, do not care or show compassion as they should, in part because of the brutally competitive and chauvinist images in which they conceive of what they do. But once we start insisting that the ethics of business is not simply confined to business but begin by examining the very nature of the good life and living well in a business society, those conceptions are bound to change (Freeman and Leidtka, 1991; Solomon, 1992).

Notes

CHAPTER 2

1. The passages quoted in this chapter were published in Grusky and Miller, a popular introductory textbook of readings, pp. 7–36. The original source for the excerpts quoted is H. H. Gerth and C. W. Mills, *From Max Weber: Essays in Sociology* (New York: Oxford University Press, 1946), pp. 196–204, 214–216.

2. We are grateful to Ed Hartman and Andrea Larson for these observations.

3. This introduction to deconstruction is adapted from Martin (1990a). Readers unfamiliar with deconstruction might find useful as a general introduction Norris (1982). For a feminist perspective on deconstruction, see Weedon (1987).

4. This discussion of the public/private dichotomy is adapted from Martin (1990a).

5. Women entered MBA programs in significant numbers for the first time in the 1970s. When the children of women in this cohort enter their teenage years, gender inequality in salary may have decreased somewhat. However, the divergence of career paths of men and women may be so great by then that major changes will not have occurred.

CHAPTER 4

1. The first statistic comes from Shiva, 1988; the others come from Myers, 1984:42, 247.

2. The phrase "crimes of indifference" is George Kent's.

3. In discussing gender in terms of an opposition between male and female, I am transgressing against a common (though contested) practice of using masculine/feminine to refer to social and cultural differences (gender) and male/female to refer to biological differences (sex). I want to connect the many different dimensions of sexual opposition and difference and to suggest that all of these dimensions, including the biological, are at least to some extent negotiated meanings rather than fixed truths.

4. Ruddick's definition of a practice is a bit tightly drawn, very goal oriented, and even somewhat technical: "To engage in a practice is, by definition, to accept connections that constitute the practice" (41) Why couldn't practice be constituted more contingently, with more acknowledgment of layers and fissures? Ruddick claims that "[t]hinking itself is often a solitary activity; its cooperative forms are the dialogue or conversation, not the chorus" (15). Why not the cacophony?

5. I address the questions I am here setting aside in Ferguson, 1993.

CHAPTER 5

1. Of course, there may be mixtures of these. On the one hand, some marxist feminists may also be influenced by deconstructionism. The reverse holds. On the other hand, a marxist feminist need not also share deconstructionist views.

2. I wish to emphasize that when I speak of radical feminism in this chapter I am referring *only* to radical feminists whose theoretical commitments are derived from deconstructionism. In particular, I am referring to that form of radical feminism expressed in the chapters in this volume by Kathy Ferguson and by Marta B. Calás and Linda Smircich.

3. In particular, I have in mind the rather special metaphysical and epistemological tenets of radical feminism, which are linked with its deconstructionist views. I briefly discuss radical feminism's metaphysics and epistemology in the section "The Metaphysics of Postmodern Feminist Business Ethics."

4. Calás and Smircich admit as much when they say that "we do not claim that one can arrive at these impressions only through a feminist critique" (Calás and Smircich: 66).

5. This point remains correct even if, on the whole, business ethics tends to neglect other topics—for example, those of interest to women.

6. This way of viewing business ethics is suggested, though not stated, in Donaldson (1982).

7. On the face of it, an ethics focused on "letting difference be" is rather strange. Ferguson speaks of this central focus as an "ethical gesture" (Ferguson: 88). She does not call it a principle. But what is an "ethical gesture"?

8. It should be noted that Ferguson also cites William Connolly (1988), who in discussing an alternative ethics that might be attributed to Nietzsche, suggests that this ethics counsels us "to come to terms with difference and to seek ways to enable difference to be" (Ferguson: 91). However, Ferguson does not pick up on the notion of "enablement," which is used by Connolly (1988:161). She immediately goes on to speak of "active attention" and the like. In short, Ferguson does not seem to take any notice of this notion.

9. Calás and Smircich say that we are to "celebrate differences"—this sounds more active than passive. Still, it is unclear whether this involves creating differences or fostering them or what.

10. If radical feminists believe that letting difference be requires simply holding the hand of order in abeyance, they may be naive with regard to the relation of authority and autonomy. Indeed, it may be that intervention by authorities can help promote the differences and autonomy they seek rather than stifle it. Adina Schwartz (1984) has persuasively argued, I believe, that an acceptable view of autonomy may require such intervention. Ferguson herself raises the charge of political quietism (Ferguson: 91), but this is ambiguous. Ferguson's feminism might not be quietistic in that it seeks to stop domination, for example, but, nevertheless, still quietistic in that it proceeds with a negative program (i.e., a liberal one). In short, it may be quietistic when it comes to implementing positive programs to support differences or to support various members of the community.

11. I would add that this is an empirical criticism. How do radical feminists know that business ethics lacks effects? What if a few students of business ethics classes tried to change the way business is done—insisted on workers' rights? Would this constitute an effect of business ethics? Clearly, radical feminists are not looking for business ethics to bring this or that person to act more morally

within current business relationships but rather for persons to change the structure of current business relationships. Since this has not happened, current business ethics must not have had much effect. However, this raises the standard for the effectiveness of business ethics unjustifiably high. According to such a standard, few disciplines can be said to have an effect on the world about them.

12. Calás and Smircich distinguish between "Knowledge" and "knowledge," the former referring to the transcendent sense of "knowledge." Thus, they oppose what they call totalizing theories of "knowledge," ("justice," "beauty," and so on), which have ideas rooted in the modernist pursuit of transcendent reason and which claimed to be able to separate itself from historical time and place (Calás and Smircich: 73).

CHAPTER 7

1. I am using the expression "theoretical adequacy" in reference to theories sufficiently designed to accomplish normative or explanatory tasks that may arise in relation to them.

2. Ferguson (87) says "mothers are . . . beings whose work requires them to make efforts toward being peaceful." This is merely an attempt to give an example of how mothers as peacemakers might work in practice.

CHAPTER 10

1. On another level, note the underlying assumption that the organizational hierarchy is a network to be served by its employees. Freeman and Liedtka (1991) also point out this perversion of the role of corporate structures in our society. Rather than serve as tools to realize the dreams of people, organizational hierarchies have become entities of godlike proportions. It is not unlike the fictional episode of "Star Trek" in which people in the future worship the U.S. flag and chant the pledge of allegiance with religious fervor.

2. In fact, we are approaching such a world. The recent statistics on infertility suggest that larger and larger segments of the world population (especially in the United States) are unable to conceive children. The rapid increase in adoption rates coincides with this trend.

CHAPTER 11

1. Before *Wealth of Nations,* Smith published his *Theory of the Moral Sentiments* (1990), which in effect lays out the "natural" conditions for the artifice of the market. For an excellent discussion of these preconditions and the connection between Adam Smith's two theories, see Werhane (1991).

2. Paine (1989) distinguishes between "positive" and "negative" competition. Positive competition is fair-minded and promotes mutual excellence and well-being. Negative competition is mutually destructive. Adam Smith clearly had in mind the former, which is why he put relatively little emphasis on competition as such and much more on the laws of supply and demand, consumer sovereignty, and general prosperity. War and jungle metaphors give us only a picture of negative competition, as do all zero-sum games whose point is to "win at all costs."

3. These amazingly bland terms come from McGregor (1960) and Ouchi

(1981). The considerable fraud of the Puritan work ethic and the "nobility of work" has most recently been explored by Ciulla (1992).

4. Notably in Gilligan (1982), Calhoun (1988), and Noddings (1984). Lloyd (1984) has similarly argued for the gender origins of the notion of "reason."

5. The ground-breaking research by Gilligan (1982), for example, stands accused of being gender biased in its very conception—notably in her use of the abortion issue as a central example. It is hardly indicative of deep gender differences in ethics that women tend to be more personal and men tend to have a more abstract and less personal view of this controversial ethical dilemma. If instead Gilligan had utilized the example of care for elderly parents or, more to the point here, one's sense of personal and professional commitment in ethically loaded corporate situations, it is not at all evident that one would obtain anything like the gender-specific results of the abortion survey. Indeed, even the question of gender differences has been irreversibly biased by its classic formulation by Freud, who overgeneralized the difference between the male abstract conception of justice and women's characteristic compassion (in his essay on "Anatomical Differences"). But the extremely important point here would seem to be not about men versus women but about an overly restricted and inhuman conception of ethics that seriously neglects or demeans personal feelings in favor of abstract principles.

6. For example, what Goodpaster (1991:95f) calls "type 3 management." The Kantian view of responsibility also serves as a presupposition in Goodpaster (1982).

7. See, for example, French, who has argued extensively the position that I would endorse here.

8. "It was Midge Decter who declared that 'compassion' is a term she cannot abide. The pages of *The Public Interest* are full of articles by young technocrats who may well be able to abide the emotion but who insist that it would cost too much" (Birnbaum, 1988:557).

9. For example, Pincoffs, one of the most prominent defenders of virtue ethics, lists over 200 (1986:76–77). He develops a detailed hierarchy of five categories of "instrumental" and "non-instrumental" virtues and seven subcategories under "aesthetic," "meliorating," and "moral," but virtually none of them represents emotions or sentiments. Many virtuous traits, however, concern the control of the emotions (nonvengefulness, serenity, even-temperedness) or having pleasantly sociable passions, (e.g., cheerfulness) (1986:85).

10. I have argued this thesis at greater length in Solomon (1989b).

11. See Hoffman (1989) for an excellent recent discussion of the role of empathy in Rawls's "original position."

12. I have argued this thesis at length in Solomon, 1995. The literature I am opposing in this, beginning with John Rawls's monumental *Theory of Justice*, is voluminous, but what I reject in general (and in qualified terms with regard to Rawls's own multidimensional theory) is the emphasis on abstract theories and rational choice theory as opposed to concrete human feelings and relationships. A somewhat recent movement, also in revolt against the Rawlsian paradigm, is so-called communitarianism, notably in the work of Sandel (1982) and MacIntyre (1981, 1988), although MacIntyre rejects that label.

13. For instance, Noddings (1984) and Calhoun (1988).

14. I have argued this more fully in Chapter 6 of Solomon (1989b) and in Solomon (1989a).

15. Noddings (1984). Later on, however, Noddings promotes the much more controversial position that caring must also be "reciprocal." How caring can be both "unconditional" and "reciprocal" remains one of the central conflicts of her account. Here, I have no hesitation whatever in insisting that caring is always "conditional," although the conditions may be, in cases of extreme fidelity, almost invisible.

16. On the first, see some of Rand's (1964) rather outrageous objections to "altruism." On the second, see Mayeroff (1971).

17. For example, Griffin (1978), Lerner (1985), and Merchant (1980).

18. MacIntyre (1981:214–215), for example, dismisses Hume's use of "sympathy" on such grounds. Cf. Friedman (characteristically): "Smith regarded sympathy as a human characteristic, but one that was itself rare and required to be economised" (1977:16; quoted in Werhane (1991).

19. For example, in anthropology, see the now classic dispute (1975) between Margaret Mead and Marvin Harris and the more recent debate over Briggs's book on Eskimo emotions. See also Schweder and Levine (1984).

20. *The Random House Dictionary* (1987).

21. MacIntyre (1981:47), but see also MacIntyre (1988:291) and all of Chapter XVI.

22. I am indebted to Annette Baier for her work on Hume, and Patricia Werhane for letting me see the manuscript of her book on Adam Smith.

23. For a discussion of this idea, see Mintzberg, 1975.

24. For a good discussion of the mysterious effects of fictional characters on our feelings, see K. Walton, 1990.

25. An added benefit: Norma Feshbach, a child psychologist, claims to have shown that sympathy assures success, that fourth- and fifth-grade students who have been brought up to be compassionate and understanding tend to do better in school and in their relationships.

26. "Pure unadulterated socialism" is what Friedman (1970) calls the activities of corporate executives who (foolishly) indulge in generosity and good works.

Bibliography

Acker, J. (1990). "Hierarchies, Jobs, Bodies: A Theory of Gendered Organizations," *Gender and Society* 4:139–158.

Alvesson, M., and Berg, P. O. (1992). *Corporate Culture and Organizational Symbolism.* New York: Walter de Gruyter and Company.

Andersen, M. L. (1987). "Changing the Curriculum in Higher Education," *Signs* 12(2):222–254.

Andolsen, B. H., Gudorf, C. E., and Pellauer, M. D., eds. (1987). *Women's Consciousness, Women's Conscience.* San Francisco: Harper and Row.

Annas, J. (1977). "Mill and the Subjection of Women," *Philosophy* 52:179–194.

Aristotle (1985). *Nicomachean Ethics.* T. Irwin, trans. Indianapolis, Ind: Hackett.

Atwood, M. (1988). *The Handmaid's Tale.* New York: Harper and Row.

Baier, A. C. (1991). *A Progress of Sentiments: Reflections on Hume's Treatise.* Cambridge, Mass.: Harvard University Press.

_____. (1985). "What Do Women Want in a Moral Theory?" *Nous* 19(1):53–63.

Baker, A. J. (1982). "The Problem of Authority in Radical Movement Groups: A Case Study of Lesbian-Feminist Organization," *Journal of Applied Behavioral Science* 18:323–341.

Banks, O. (1986). *Faces of Feminism.* Oxford: Basil Blackwell.

Barnard, C. I. (1938). *The Functions of the Executive.* Cambridge, Mass.: Harvard University Press.

Barre, L. D. (1968). "Response to Carr," *Harvard Business Review* (May–June): 164.

Barrett, M. (1985). *Women's Oppression Today: Problems in Marxist Feminist Analysis.* London: Verso.

Barron, R. D., and Morris, G. M. (1976). "Sexual Divisions and the Dual Labor Market," in D. Barker and S. Allen, eds., *Dependence and Exploitation in Work and Marriage.* New York: Longmans, pp. 47–69.

Beauchamp, T. L. (1988). "Ethical Theory and Its Application to Business," in T. L. Beauchamp and N. E. Bowie, eds., *Ethical Theory in Business.* Englewood Cliffs, N.J.: Prentice Hall, pp. 1–55.

Beauchamp, T. L., and Bowie, N. E., eds. (1988). *Ethical Theory in Business.* Englewood Cliffs, N.J.: Prentice Hall.

Belenky, M. F., Clinchy, B. M., Goldberger, N. R., and Tarule, J. M. (1986). *Women's Ways of Knowing.* New York: Basic Books.

Benhabib, S. (1987). "The Generalized and the Concrete Other: The Kohlberg-Gilligan Controversy and Feminist Theory," in S. Benhabib and D. Cornell, eds., *Feminism as Critique.* Minneapolis: University of Minnesota Press, pp. 77–95.

Benhabib, S., and Cornell, D., eds. (1987). *Feminism as Critique.* Minneapolis: University of Minnesota Press.

Bentham, J. (1838). *Principles of the Civil Code—Works.* Vol. 1. Edinburgh and London: J. Bowring.

Bethel, J. (1984). "Sometimes the Word Is Weed," *Forest Management* June 1984:17–22.

Bielby, W. T., and Baron, J. N., (1986). "Men and Women at Work: Sex Segregation and Statistical Discrimination," *American Journal of Sociology* 91(4):759–799.

Billing, Y. D., and Alvesson, M. (1994). *Gender, Managers, and Organizations.* New York: Walter de Gruyter and Company.

Birnbaum, N. (1988). Editorial, *The Nation* April 23:557.

Bleier, R. (1984). *Science and Gender: A Critique of Biology and Its Theories on Women.* Elmsford, N.Y.: Pergamon Press.

Blum, L. A. (1982). "Kant's and Hegel's Moral Rationalism: A Feminist Perspective," *Canadian Journal of Philosophy* 12(2):287–302.

_____. (1980). "Compassion," in R. Rorty, ed., *Explaining Emotions.* Berkeley: University of California Press.

Bologh, R. W. (1990). *Love or Greatness: Max Weber and Masculine Thinking—A Feminist Inquiry.* Boston: Unwin Hyman, Inc.

Boralevi, L. C. (1987). "Utilitarianism and Feminism," in E. Kennedy and S. Mendus, eds., *Women in Western Political Philosophy.* New York: St. Martin's Press, pp. 159–178.

_____. (1838/1984). *Bentham and the Oppressed.* Berlin: Walter de Gruyter and Company.

Bremer, O. A., Logan, J. E., and Wokutch, R. E. (1987). "Ethics and Values in Management Thought," in K. Paul, ed., *Business Environment and Business Ethics.* Cambridge, Mass.: Ballinger.

Briggs, J. (1975). *Never in Anger.* Cambridge, Mass.: Harvard University Press.

Brooks, J. G. (1909). "The Conflict between Private Monopoly and Good Citizenship" (Barbara Weinstock Lecture). Boston: Houghton Mifflin.

Broverman, I., Vogel, S., Broverman, D., Clarkson, F., and Rosenkranz, P. (1972). "Sex Role Stereotypes: A Current Appraisal," *Journal of Social Issues* (28):59–78.

Brown, M. H. (1990). "Women's Centres: Relationships between Values and Action." *Journal of Management Studies* 27:619–635.

Brown, C., and Pechman, J. A., eds. (1987). *Gender in the Workplace.* Washington, D.C.: Brookings Institute.

Calás, M. (1993). "Deconstructing Charismatic Leadership: Re-reading Weber from the Darker Side," *Leadership Quarterly* 4(3/4):305–328.

_____. (1987). Organizational science/fiction: The postmodern in the management disciplines. Unpublished doctoral dissertation, University of Massachusetts, Amherst.

Calás, M., and Smircich, L. (1992). "Re-writing Gender into Organizational Theorizing: Directions from Feminist Perspectives, in M. I. Reed and M. D. Hughes, eds., *Rethinking Organization: New Directions in Organizational Research and Analysis.* London: Sage.

Calás, M., and Smircich, L. (1989). Using the F-word: Feminist theories and the social consequences of organizational research. Paper presented at the annual meeting of the Academy of Management, Washington, D.C.

Calhoun, C. (1988). "Justice, Care and Gender Bias," *Journal of Philosophy* 85:451–463.

Callaghan, W. (1990). Comprehensive exams, Department of Political Science, University of Hawaii, Question I, p. 10.

Carr, A. (1968). "Is Business Bluffing Ethical?" *Harvard Business Review* (May–June):164.

Chodorow, N. (1978). *The Reproduction of Mothering: Psychoanalysis and the Sociology of Gender.* Berkeley: University of California Press.

Chomsky, N. (1980). *Rules and Representations.* Oxford: Basil Blackwell.

Christian, P., ed. (1970). *Ethics in Business Conduct.* Detroit: Gale Research Company.

Ciulla, J. (1992). *Honest Work.* New York: Random House.

Clifford, J., and Marcus, F. E., eds. (1986). *Writing Culture: The Poetics and Politics of Ethnography.* Berkeley: University of California Press.

Collinson, D. L., Knights, D., and Collinson, M. (1990). *Managing to Discriminate.* New York: Routledge.

Connelly, W. (1988). *Political Theory and Modernity.* New York: Basil Blackwell.

_____. (1987). *Politics and Ambiguity.* Madison: University of Wisconsin Press.

Cook, A., and Kirk, G. (1983). *Greenham Women Everywhere.* Boston: South End Press.

Cropsey, J. (1957). *Polity and Economy.* Westport, Conn.: Greenwood Press.

Davidson, D. (1984). *Inquiries into Truth and Interpretation.* New York: University Press.

Deetz, S. A. (1992). *Democracy in an Age of Corporate Colonization.* Albany: State University of New York Press.

Derrida, J. (1982). "Choreographics," *Diacritics* 12:66–76.

_____. (1978). *Spurs.* Chicago: University of Chicago Press.

Derry, R., and Green, R. M. (1989). "Ethical Theory in Business Ethics: A Critical Assessment," *Journal of Business Ethics* 8:521–533.

Diamond, I., and Quinby, I. (1988). *Feminism and Foucault.* Boston: Northeastern University Press.

Dinnerstein, D. (1976). *The Mermaid and the Minotaur: Sexual Arrangements and Human Malaise.* New York: Harper and Row.

Donaldson, T. (1982). *Corporations and Morality.* Englewood Cliffs, N.J.: Prentice-Hall.

Drucker, P. (1974). *Management.* New York: Harper and Row.

Duddy, E. A. (1946). "The Moral Implications of Business as a Profession," *The Journal of Business* 18:63–73.

Eagleton, T. (1976). *Marxism and Literary Criticism.* Berkeley: University of California Press.

Epstein, S. R., Russell, G., and Silvern, L. (1988). "Structure and Ideology of Shelters for Battered Women," *American Journal of Community Psychology* 16:345–367.

Fagenson, E. A. (1990). "At the Heart of Women in Management Research: Theoretical and Methodological Approaches and Their Biases," *Journal of Business Ethics* 9:267–274.

Farrell, A. E. (1994). "A Social Experiment in Publishing: Ms. Magazine, 1972–1989," *Human Relations* 47:707–730.

Ferguson, K. E. (1993). *The Man Question: Visions of Subjectivity in Feminist Theory.* Berkeley: University of California Press.

_____. (1990). Personal communication at the Ruffin Lectures, University of Virginia, Charlottesville.

_____. (1984). *The Feminist Case Against Bureaucracy.* Philadelphia: Temple University Press.

Ferree, M. M., and Martin, P. Y. eds. (1995). *Feminist Organizations.* Philadelphia: Temple University Press.

Flax, J. (1990). *Thinking Fragments: Psychoanalysis, Feminism, and Postmodernism in the Contemporary West.* Berkeley: University of California Press.

_____. (1987). "Postmodernism and Gender Relations in Feminist Theory," *Signs* 12(4):621–643.

Follett, M. P. (1925). "How Must Business Management Develop in Order to Possess the Essentials of a Profession?" in H. C. Metcalf and L. Urwick, eds., *Dynamic Administration.* New York: Harper and Brothers, pp. 117–131.

Fortune 11(6): June 1935.

Fraser, N. (1988). "What's Critical about Critical Theory? The Case of Habermas and Gender," in S. Benhabib and D. Cornell, eds., *Feminism as Critique.* Minneapolis: University of Minnesota Press, pp. 31–55.

Fraser, N., and Nicholson, L. J. (1990). "Social Criticism without Philosophy: An Encounter between Feminism and Postmodernism," in L. J. Nicholson, ed., *Feminism/Postmodernism.* New York: Routledge, pp. 19–38.

Freeman, S. J. M. (1990). *Managing Lives: Corporate Women and Social Change.* Amherst: University of Massachusetts Press.

Freeman, R. E., and Gilbert, D. R. Jr. (1991). "Business, Ethics, and Society: A Critical Agenda." Paper presented at the annual meeting of the International Association for Business and Society, Sundance, Utah.

Freeman, R. E., and Leidtka, J. (1991). "Corporate Social Responsibility: A Critical Approach," *Business Horizons* 34(4):92–98.

French, P. (1991). "The Corporation as a Moral Person," in P. French, *The Spectrum of Responsibility.* New York: St. Martin's.

Freud, S. (1933/1965). *New Introductory Lectures on Psychoanalysis.* J. Strachey, trans. New York: Norton.

Friedman, M. (1977). "Adams Smith's Relevance for 1976," in *Selected Papers of the University of Chicago Graduate School of Business,* No. 50.

_____. (1970). *The New York Times,* September 13.

Frug, G. (1986). "The Ideology of Bureaucracy in American Law," *Harvard Law Review* 97:1276–1388.

Furman, F. K. (1990). Teaching Business Ethics: Questioning the Assumptions, Seeking New Directions *Journal of Business Ethics* 9:31–38.

Fussell., P. (1991). *The Norton Book of Modern War.* New York: Norton.

Geertz, C. (1988). *Works and Lives,* Stanford, Calif.: Stanford University Press.

Gerth, H. H., and C. W., Mills eds. and trans. (1946). *From Max Weber: Essays in Sociology,* New York: Oxford University Press.

Gilligan, C. (1987). "Moral Orientation and Moral Development," in E. F. Kittay and D. T. Meyers, eds., *Women and Moral Theory.* Totowa, N.J.: Rowman and Littlefield.

Gilligan, C. (1982). *In a Different Voice: Psychological Theory and Women's Development.* Cambridge Mass.: Harvard University Press.

Gilligan, C., Ward, J. V., and Taylor, J. M. (1988). *Mapping the Moral Domain,* Cambridge, Mass.: Harvard University Press.

Goodpaster, K. (1991). "Ethical Imperatives and Corporate Leadership," in R. E.

Freeman, ed., *Business Ethics: The State of the Art.* New York: Oxford University Press.

———. (1982). "Can a Corporation Have a Conscience?" *Harvard Business Review* January–February 1982.

Green, T. M. ed. (1957). *Kant Selections,* New York: Scribner's.

Gregory, A. (1990). "Are Women Different and Why Are Women Thought to Be Different? Theoretical and Methodological Perspectives," *Journal of Business Ethics* 9:257–266.

Griffin, S. (1978). *Woman and Nature.* New York: Harper and Row.

Grimshaw, J. (1986). *Philosophy and Feminist Thinking.* Minneapolis: University of Minnesota Press.

Grusky, O. and Miller, G. A., eds. (1981). *The Sociology of Organizations: Basic Studies.* New York: Free Press.

Hackman, J. R. (1984). "The Transition That Hasn't Happened," in J. R. Kimberly and R. E. Quinn, eds., *Managing Organizational Transitions.* Homewood, Ill.: Dow Jones-Irwin.

Hackman, J. R., Oldham, G., Janson, R., and Purdy, K. (1975). "A New Strategy for Job Enrichment," *California Management Review* 17(4):57–71.

Hagen, B. H. (1983). *Managing Conflict in All-Women Groups.* Binghamton, N.Y.: Haworth Press.

Harding, S. (1987). "Conclusion: Epistemological Questions," in S. Harding, ed., *Feminism and Methodology.* Bloomington, Ind.: Indiana University Press, pp. 181–190.

Harding, S. (1986). *The Science Question in Feminism.* Ithaca, N.Y.: Cornell University Press.

Harlan, A., and Weiss, C. (1982). "Sex Differences in Factors Affecting Managerial Career Advancement," in P. Wallace, ed., *Women in the Workplace.* Boston: Auburn House, pp. 59–100.

Harris, M. (1968). *The Rise of Anthropological Theory.* New York: Crowell.

Hartmann, H., and Reskin, B., eds. (1986). *Women's Work, Men's Work . . . Sex Segregation on the Job,* Washington, D.C.: National Academy Press.

Hassard, J., and Parker, M. (1993). *Postmodernism and Organizations.* Newbury Park, Calif: Sage.

Hearn, J., and Parkin, W. (1987). *'Sex' at 'Work': The Power and Paradox of Organization Sexuality.* New York: St. Martin's.

Heidegger, M. (1927/1977). *Basic Writings.* New York: Harper and Row.

Heilbrun, C. G. (1979). *Reinventing Womanhood.* New York: Norton.

Heisenberg, W. (1958). "The Representation of Nature in Contemporary Physics," *Daedalus* 87.

Held, V. (1987). "Feminism and Moral Theory," in E. F. Kittay and D. T. Meyers, eds., *Women and Moral Theory.* Totowa, N.J.: Rowman and Littlefield, pp. 111–128.

Helgesen, S. (1990). *The Female Advantage: Women's Ways of Leadership.* New York: Doubleday.

Hochschild, A. (1989). *The Second Shift: Working Parents and the Revolution at Home.* New York: Viking.

Hoffman, M. (1989). "Empathetic Emotions and Justice in Society," *Social Justice Research* 3:(4):283–311.

Hoffman, W. M., and Moore, J. M., eds. (1990). *Business Ethics: Readings and Cases in Corporate Morality.* New York: McGraw-Hill.

Hume, D. (1751/1957). *Inquiry Concerning the Principles of Morals.* Indianapolis, Ind.: Bobbs-Merrill.

_____. (1739/1978). *Treatise on Human Nature.* L. A. Selby-Bigge, ed. Oxford: Oxford University Press.

Irigaray, L. (1985). *This Sex Which Is Not One.* Ithaca, N.Y.: Cornell University Press.

Jackall, R. (1988). *Moral Mazes.* New York: Oxford University Press.

Joyce, G. (1990). "Training and Women: Some Thoughts from the Grassroots," *Journal of Business Ethics* 9:407–415.

Kant, I. (1784/1964a). *The Doctrine of Virtue,* M. Gregor, trans. Philadelphia: University of Pennsylvania Press.

Kant, I. (1785/1964b). *Grounding of the Metaphysic of Morals.* H. J. Paton, ed. New York: Torchbooks.

_____. (1785/1948). *Groundwork of the Metaphysics of Morals,* H. J. Paton, ed. London: Hutchinson.

_____. (1785/1981). *Grounding for the Metaphysics of Morals,* J. Ellington, trans. Indianapolis, Ind: Hackett.

Kant, I. (1763/1960). *Of the Distinction Between the Beautiful and the Sublime in the Interrelations of the Two Sexes.* Berkeley: University of California Press.

Kanter, R. M. (1972). *Commitment and Community.* Cambridge, Mass.: Harvard University Press.

Keller, E. F. (1985). *Reflections on Gender and Science.* New Haven, Conn.: Yale University Press.

Keohane, N. O. (1988). The public and the private as categories of human experience. Unpublished manuscript, Center for the Advanced Study of the Behavioral Sciences, Stanford, Calif.

Kittay, E. F., and Meyers, D. T. eds. (1987). *Women and Theory.* Totowa, N.J.: Rowman and Littlefield.

Koen, S. L. (1984). Feminist workplaces: Alternative models for the organization Unpublished dissertation, Union Graduate School, Ann Arbor, Mich.

Lehrer, S. (1987). *Origins of Protective Labor Legislation for Women, 1905–1925.* Albany: State University of New York Press.

Leidner, R. (1991). "Stretching the Boundaries of Liberalism: Democratic Innovation in a Feminist Organization," *Signs* 16(2): 263–289.

Lerner, G. (1985). *The Creation of Patriarchy.* New York: Oxford University Press.

Lewis, Michael. (1989). *Liar's Poker.* New York: Norton, 1989.

Lloyd, G. (1984). *The Man of Reason: 'Male' and 'Female' in Western Philosophy.* Minneapolis: University of Minnesota Press.

Lugones, M. (1987). "Playfulness, World-Traveling, and Loving Perception," *Hypatia* Summer: 3–19.

Lugones, M. C. and Spelman, E. V. (1987). "Competition, Compassion, and Community: Models for a Feminist Ethos," in V. Miner and H. Longino, eds., *Competition: A Feminist Taboo?* New York: Feminist Press of the City University of New York, pp. 234–247.

MacIntyre, A. (1988). *Whose Justice? Which Rationality?* Notre Dame, Ind.: University of Notre Dame Press.

_____. (1981). *After Virtue: A Study in Moral Theory.* Notre Dame, Ind.: University of Notre Dame Press.

MacKinnon, C. (1991). *Toward a Feminist Theory of the State.* Cambridge, Mass.: Harvard University Press.

_____. (1987). "Difference and Dominance: On Sex Discrimination," in C. MacKinnon, *Feminism Unmodified.* Cambridge, Mass.: Harvard University Press.

Malveaux, J. (1982). "Moving Forward, Standing Still: Women in White Collar Jobs," in P. Wallace, (ed.), *Women in the Workplace*. Boston: Auburn House, pp. 101–133.

Mansbridge, J. J. (1973). "Time, Emotion, and Inequality: Three Problems of Participatory Groups," *Journal of Applied Behavioral Science* 9:351–365.

Marshall, J. (1984). *Women Managers: Travelers in a Male World*. New York: Wiley.

Martin, J. (1990a). "Deconstructing Organizational Taboos: The Suppression of Gender Conflict in Organizations," *Organizational Science*. 1:1–21.

_____. (1990b). Rethinking Weber: A feminist search for alternatives to bureaucracy. Paper presented at the national meeting of the Academy of Management, San Francisco, August.

Martin, P. Y. (1990). *Rethinking Feminist Organizations, Gender and Society* 4:182–206.

Martzberg, H. (1973). *The Nature of Managerial Work*. New York: Harper and Row.

Mayeroff, M. (1971). *On Caring*. New York: Harper and Row.

McGregor, D. (1960). *The Human Side of Enterprise*. New York: McGraw-Hill.

Mendus, S. (1987). "Kant: 'An Honest but Narrow-Minded Bourgeois'?" in E. Kennedy and S. Mendus, eds., *Women in Western Political Philosophy*. New York: St. Martin's, pp. 21–43.

Merchant, C. (1980). *The Death of Nature*. San Francisco: Harper and Row.

Merriam Webster's New Collegiate Dictionary, 9th ed. (1988). Springfield Mass.: Merriam-Webster.

Miller, J. B. (1976). *Towards a New Psychology of Women*. Boston: Beacon Press.

Mill, J. S. ((1869) 1970). *The Subjection of Women*. Cambridge, Mass.: MIT Press.

_____. (1970). "Enfranchisement of Women," in J. S. Mill and Harriet Taylor Mill, *Essays on Sex Equality*. A, Rossi, ed. Chicago: University of Chicago Press, 123–242.

Mills, A. (1988). "Organization, Gender, and Culture," *Organization Studies* 9(3):351–369.

Miner, A. S. (1987). "Idiosyncratic Jobs in Formalized Organizations," *Administrative Science Quarterly* 32:327–351.

Mintzberg, H. (1975). "The Manager's Job: Folklore and Fact," *Harvard Business Review*, July–August.

Moi, T. (1985). *Sexual/Textual Politics*. New York: Methuen.

Morawski, J. G. (1988). "Impasse in Feminist Thought?" in M. M. Gergen, ed., *Feminist Thought and the Structure of Knowledge*. New York: New York University Press, pp. 182–194.

Morgen, S. (1986). "The Dynamics of Cooptation in a Feminist Health Clinic," *Social Science and Medicine* 23:201–210.

Mumby, D. K. (1988). *Communication and Power in Organizations: Discourse, Ideology, and Domination*. Norwood, N.J.: Ablex Publishing Corporation.

Mumby, D. K., and Putnam, L. L. (1992). "The Politics of Emotion: A Feminist Reading of Bounded Rationality," *Academy of Management Review* 17:465–485.

Murdoch, I. (1970). *The Sovereignty of Good*. London: Routledge.

Myers, N. (1984). *Gaia: An Atlas of Planet Management*. New York: Anchor Books.

Natsoulos, T. (1988). "Sympathy, Empathy and the Stream of Consciousness," *Journal for the Theory of Social Behavior* 18 (June).

Naisbitt, J. (1988). *Reinventing the Corporation*. New York: Random House. "A New Way to Work for Women," (1982) *Ms*. 10(2):30.

Nicholson, L. J. (1990). *Feminism/Postmodernism.* New York: Routledge.

———. (1986). *Gender and History.* New York: Columbia University Press.

Noddings, N. (1984). *Caring: A Feminine Approach to Ethics and Moral Education.* Berkeley: University of California Press.

Norris, C. (1982). *Deconstruction: Theory and Practice.* London: Routledge.

Oakeley, A. (1972). *Sex, Gender and Society.* London: Temple Smith.

Olsen, F. (1983). "The Family and the Market: A Study of Ideology and Legal Reform," *Harvard Law Review* 96:(7):1497–1578.

Ouchi, W. (1981). *Theory Z: How American Business Can Meet the Japanese Challenge.* Reading, Mass.: Addison-Wesley.

Paine, L. S. (1989). Ideals of competition and today's marketplace. Unpublished manuscript.

Paul, K. (1987). "Business Environment and Business Ethics in Management Thought, in K. Paul ed., *Business Environment and Business Ethics: The Social, Moral, and Political Dimensions of Management,* Cambridge, Mass.: Ballinger, pp. 1–17.

Perrow, C. (1986). *Complex Organizations.* New York: Random House.

Pettigrew, T. (1988). *Modern Racism: American Black-White Relations Since the 1960s.* Cambridge, Mass.: Harvard University Press.

Piercy, M. (1973). "Unlearning to Not Speak," in M. Piercy, *To Be of Use.* New York: Doubleday, 38.

Pincoffs, E. (1986). *Quandaries and Virtues: Against Reductivism in Ethics.* Lawrence: University Press of Kansas.

Popper, K. R. (1959). *The Logic of Scientific Discovery.* New York: Basic Books.

Powell, G. N. (1990). "One More Time: Do Female and Male Managers Differ?" *The Executive* 4 (3):68–75.

Powell, W. W., and DiMaggio, P. J., eds. (1991). *The New Institutionalism in Organizational Analysis.* Chicago: University of Chicago Press.

Pringle, J. K., and Henry, E. Y. (1993). Diversity in women's organisations: Maori and Pakeha. Paper presented at Fifth International Interdisciplinary Congress on Women, University of Costa Rica, San Jose.

Regan, T. (ed.) (1984). *Just Business.* New York: Random House.

Quine, W. V. (1960). *Word and Object.* Cambridge: Technology Press of the Massachusetts Institute of Technology.

Rand, A. (1964). *The Virtue of Selfishness: A New Concept of Egoism.* New York: American Library.

The Random House Dictionary of the English Language (1987). New York: Random House.

Rawls, J. (1971). *A Theory of Justice.* Cambridge, Mass.: Harvard University Press.

Reed, M. (1985). *Redirections in Organizational Analysis.* London: Tavistock.

Reinharz, S. (1985). "Feminist Distrust: Problems of Context in Sociological Work," in D. N. Berg and K. K. Smith, eds., *Exploring Clinical Methods for Social Research.* Newbury Park, Calif.: Sage, pp. 153–171.

Rhode, D. (1990). *Theoretical Perspectives on Social Difference.* New Haven, Conn.: Yale University Press.

Rich, A. (1986)

———. (1977). *On Lies, Secrets, and Silence.* New York: Norton.

———. (1976). *Of Women Born.* New York: Norton.

Rogers, W. (1969) *Think: A Biography of the Watsons and IBM.* New York: Stein and Day.

Rome, H. (1987). "Hand, Brain, and Heart: A Feminist Epistemology for the

Natural Sciences," in S. Harding and J. F. O'Barr, eds., *Sex and Scientific Inquiry*. Chicago: University of Chicago Press, pp. 265–282.

Rome, H. (1986). "Women's Work: Women's Knowledge," in J. Mitchell and A. Oakley, eds., *What Is Feminism? A Re-examination*. New York: Pantheon, pp. 161–183.

Rosenberg, H. (1958). *Aristocracy and Autocracy*. Boston: Beacon Press.

Rose, H. "Dreaming the Future," *Hypathia: A Journal of Feminist Philosophy* 3:119–137.

———. (1983). "Hand, Brain and Heart: Towards a Feminist Epistemology for the Sciences," *Signs* 9:73–90.

Rothschild, J., and Davies, C. (1944). "Organizations through the Lens of Gender: Introduction to the Special Issue," *Human Relations* 47(6).

Rothschild, J., and Russell, R. (1986). "Alternatives to Bureaucracy: Democratic Participation in the Economy," *Annual Review of Sociology* 12:307–328.

Rothschild-Witt, J. (1979). "The Collectivist Organization: An Alternative to Rational-Bureaucratic Models," *American Sociological Review* 44:509–527.

Ruddick, S. (1989). *Maternal Thinking*. Boston: Beacon Press.

Russell. (1988).

Sandel, M. (1982). *Liberalism and the Limits of Justice*. New York: Cambridge University Press.

Schlafly, P. (1977). *The Power of the Positive Woman*. New Rochelle, N.Y.: Arlington House Press.

Schneer, J. A. (1985). The impact of gender context on behavior in small groups. Dissertation, City University of New York. Ann Arbor: University of Michigan Dissertation Information Service.

Schopenhauer, A. [1841] (1965). *The Basis of Morality*, E. F. J. Payne, trans. Indianapolis, Ind.: Bobbs-Merrill.

Schuster, M., and Van Dyne, S., eds. (1985). *Women's Place in the Academy: Transforming the Liberal Arts Curriculum*. Totowa, N.J.: Rowman and Allanheld.

Schwartz, A. (1984). "Autonomy in the Workplace," in T. Regan, ed., *Just Business*. New York: Random House.

Schweder, R., and Levine R., eds. (1984). *Culture Theory*. New York: Cambridge University Press.

Scott, J. W. (1988). "Deconstructing Equality-vs.-Difference: Or, the Uses of Poststructuralist Theory for Feminism," *Feminist Studies* 14 (1):33–50.

———. (1986). "Gender: A Useful Category of Historical Analysis," *American Historical Review* 91:1053–1075.

Scott, W. R. (1995). *Institutions and Organizations*. Thousand Oaks, Calif.: Sage.

Sealander, J., and Smith, D. (1986). "The Rise and Fall of Feminist Organizations in the 1970s: Dayton as a Case Study," *Feminist Studies* 12:321–341.

Shapiro, M. (1985). "Metaphor in the Philosophy of the Social Sciences," *Cultural Critique* 2:195.

Shiva, V. (1988). *Staying Alive*. New Delhi, India: Kali for Women.

Showalter, E., ed. (1989). *The New Feminist Criticism: Essays on Women, Literature, and Theory*. New York: Pantheon.

Silko, L. M. (1977). *Ceremony*. New York: Penguin.

Simon, H. A. (1947). *Administrative Behavior*. New York: Free Press.

Smircich, L., Calás, M. B., and Keele, R. (1988). Questioning the ethics and values of organizational science from feminist perspectives. Grant proposal to the Ethics and Values Project of the National Science Foundation.

Smith, A. (1759/1990). *Theory of the Moral Sentiments*. London: George Bell.

_____. (1776/1976). *An Inquiry into the Nature and Causes of the Wealth of Nations.* Chicago: University of Chicago Press.

Smith, P., and Midlarsky, E. (1985). "Empirically Derived Conceptions of Femaleness and Maleness: A Current View. *Sex Roles* 12:313–328.

Solomon, R. C. (1995). *A Passion for Justice.* Totowa, N.J.: Rowman and Littlefield.

_____. (1994a). "Business and the Humanities: An Aristotelian Approach to Business Ethics," in T. Donaldson and R. E. Freeman, eds., *Business as a Humanity.* New York: Oxford University Press, pp. 45–75.

_____. (1994b). *The New World of Business.* Totowa, N.J.: Rowman and Littlefield.

_____. (1992). *Ethics and Excellence.* New York: Oxford University Press.

_____. (1989a). "The Emotions of Justice," *Social Justice Research* 3(4):345–374.

_____. (1989b). "The Virtue of Love," in P. French, ed., *Ethics: Character and Virtue,* Midwest Studies in Philosophy, Vol. 13. Reprinted in K. Higgins and R. Solomon, eds., *The Philosophy of (Erotic) Love.* Lawrence: Kansas University Press, 1991.

Sophia, Z. (1984). "Exterminating Fetuses: Abortion, Disarmament, and the Sexo-Semiotics of Extraterrestrialism," *Diacritics* 14:(2):47–59.

Spelman, E. V. (1988). *Inessential Woman: Problems of Exclusion in Feminist Thought.* Boston: Beacon Press.

Spence, J., and Sawin, L. (1985). "Images of Masculinity and Femininity: A Reconceptualization," in V. O'Leary, R. Unger, and B. Wallston, eds., *Women, Gender and Social Psychology.* Hillsdale, N. J.: Erlbaum, pp. 35–66.

Spivak, G. C. (1987). *In Other Worlds.* New York: Methuen.

_____. (1983). "Displacement and the Discourse of Woman," in M. Krupnick, ed., *Displacement: Derrida and After.* Bloomington, Ind.: Indiana University Press.

Stacey, J., and Thorne, B. (1985). "The Missing Feminist Revolution in Sociology," *Social Problems* 32:301–316.

Staudt, K., ed. (1990). *Women, International Development and Politics: The Bureaucratic Mire.* Philadelphia: Temple University Press.

Strober, M. (1982). "The MBA: Same Passport to Success for Women and Men?" in P. Wallace, ed., *Women in the Workplace.* Boston: Auburn House, pp. 25–55.

Szalai, S. (1972). *The Use of Time: Daily Activities of Urban and Suburban Populations in Twelve Countries.* New York: Mouton.

Tannen, D. (1990). *You Just Don't Understand.* New York: Morrow.

Taylor, F. W. (1911). *Principles of Scientific Management.* New York: Norton.

Thomas, L. (1989). *On Being Moral.* Philadelphia: Temple University Press.

Thomas, R. R., Jr. (1990). "From Affirmative Action to Affirming Diversity," *Harvard Business Review* 68:107–117.

Time, Special Edition (1990). "Women: The Road Ahead" 136(19):Fall.

Tronto, J. (1987). "Beyond Gender Difference to a Theory of Care. *Signs* 12(4):644–683.

Vecchio, R. P. (1988). *Organizational Behavior.* Chicago: Dryden.

Velasquez, M. G., ed. (1988). *Business Ethics.* Englewood Cliffs, N. J.: Prentice Hall.

Walker, M. U. (1989). "Moral Understandings: Alternative 'Epistemology' for a Feminist Ethics," *Hypatia* 4(2):15–28.

Walton, K. (1990). *Mimesis as Make-Believe.* Cambridge, Mass.: Harvard University Press.

Walton, R. E. (1975). "The Diffusion of New Work Structures: Explaining Why Success Didn't Take. *Organizational Dynamics* Winter: 3–22.

"Was Headquarters Responsible? Women Beat Up at Control Data, Korea," (1982). *Multinational Monitor* 3(10):16.

Weber, M. (1946). "Bureaucracy," in H. H. Gerth and C. W. Mills, eds. and trans. *From Max Weber: Essays in Sociology.* New York: Oxford University Press, pp. 196–244.

Weber, M. ([1946] 1981). "Bureaucracy," in O. Grusky and G. A. Miller, eds., *The Sociology of Organizations: Basic Studies.* New York: Free Press, pp. 7–36.

Werhane, P. (1991). *Adam Smith and His Legacy for Modern Capitalism.* New York: Oxford University Press.

Weedon, C. (1987). *Feminist Practice and Poststructuralist Theory.* New York: Basil Blackwell.

White, S. K. (1986). "Foucault's Challenge to Critical Theory," *American Political Science Review* 80(2):419–431.

Wispé, L. (1986). "The Distinction Between Sympathy and Empathy," *Journal of Personality and Social Psychology* 50:314–21.

Wittgenstein, L. (1953). *Philosophical Investigations.* Oxford: Basil Blackwell.

Williams, J. (1989). "Deconstructing Gender," *Michigan Law Review* 87:797–845.

Zuboff, S. (1988). *In the Age of the Smart Machine.* New York: Basic Books.

Index